THIS
WOMAN'S
WORK

THIS WOMAN'S WORK: ESSAYS ON MUSIC

Edited by Sinéad Gleeson and Kim Gordon

hachette BOOKS

New York

Hachette Books
Hachette Book Group
1290 Avenue of the Americas
New York, NY 10104
HachetteBooks.com
Twitter.com/HachetteBooks
Instagram.com/HachetteBooks

First Hardcover Edition: May 2022

Published by Hachette Books, an imprint of Perseus Books, LLC, a subsidiary of Hachette Book Group, Inc. The Hachette Books name and logo is a trademark of the Hachette Book Group.

The Hachette Speakers Bureau provides a wide range of authors for speaking events. To find out more, go to www.hachettespeakersbureau.com or call (866) 376-6591.

The publisher is not responsible for websites (or their content) that are not owned by the publisher.

Library of Congress Cataloging-in-Publication Data has been applied for.

ISBNs: 9780306829000 (hardcover); 9780306829024 (ebook)

Library of Congress Control Number: 2022930247

Printed in the United States of America

LSC-C

Printing 1, 2022

For my parents, Maura and Joe,
and growing up in a house full of music.

Contents

Introduction

I'm in Linda's closet at Foxfire Apartments. The light is off. We're trying to be as quiet as possible, making sure we can still hear her parents watching television next door while we get ourselves better situated. Even in the dark, I know the contours of this small space so well. This isn't the first time we've done this together, though that doesn't stop us from sweating and breathing heavily, the air humid with the palpable fear of getting caught. We're both fully clothed in denim and fluorescents. I can just about make out her hot-pink top and green lace hairbow as she lies down on her back. I set up the Fisher-Price tape recorder in the corner on top of her jellies shoeboxes. She's pretty, so she's spoiled, and, unlike me, who has only one baby pink pair of jellies that I love to wear with white tights, Linda has them in all the colors of the rainbow. I press down hard on the plastic record button, denting one of those stupid boxes, then I lie on top of Linda and we moan. We fill one side of a 60-minute Memorex cassette with our moaning. Later, at home, in my 1980s bedroom with a pastel-colored rainbow canopy bed and matching rainbow curtains, I play along to the tape with my chord organ, pressing hard on the big circular buttons with my left hand to match the drones of our moans, while my right hand is lost in melody.

In her conversation with Kim Gordon, musician Yoshimi recounts doing her first home recordings on cassette using the equally intimate and unarmored sound of her peeing layered

1

to the point of sensory overload. Her tale takes me right back to Linda's closet where I fully inhabit my body across time and space, reliving every detail I thought I'd forgotten. I, too, was an impulsive only child who was introduced to the magical possibilities of music through an uncle. I have a searing memory of dancing to an 8-track copy of AC/DC's "You Shook Me All Night Long" in my uncle T's sparse bedroom in West Virginia in front of my astonished grandparents, though like Fatima Bhutto's father when she dances to "Papa Don't Preach" by Madonna, they know I don't fully comprehend the meaning of the words at such a young age, so aren't upset by my precocious moves.

Like any reader, I don't share the same background with any of the sixteen female contributors to this book, yet every essay in this vivid collection evokes a powerful memory from my own timeline. Perhaps this speaks of music's ability to connect us to the recurring highs and lows of human life: birth, love, heartbreak, romance, pain, sex, aging, loss, illness, loneliness, and, ultimately, death. Indeed, music becomes "placeholders in life," as described by Yiyun Li in her touching essay about "Auld Lang Syne." Music dissolves differences and brings us back to life's eternals, whether we like it or not. "Myths about the human heart that I thought I'd debunked revealed themselves to be persistent," says Jenn Pelly in her poignant piece about Lucinda Williams. Yes, music is a great leveler, time and again. Often it can confound us, not simply giving us the logical answers we seek, but invoking more questions, thereby continually evading the obvious; an endless mystery much like we are to ourselves. Yiyun Li finds herself moved by Communist songs of her youth when she sings them in the car as an older woman, even if she recognizes them as propaganda, just as Fatima Bhutto feels "a combination of bruised longing and joy" when she hears her home country's cricket anthem. We can't help but surrender to what moves us in the sound even if it seems contradictory or irrational; in fact, our experience of music is full of contradictions.

This Woman's Work asks probing questions that strike at the heart of such contradictions—notably, the writers even question their own prose, wondering if it's doing justice to the music they're writing about. Has it encapsulated music's soul? They acknowledge that music somehow remains intangible. We can try to explain and to rationalize it, but we're seduced back by the song. Music catches you. You can't explain it, you have to experience it, and these essays are more scores than explanations, pieces that honor the music and are rooted in autobiography to get closer to it; rich articulations of experience. Through highly personal, lucidly detailed memories, the writers' essays become songs themselves, fluid and sensuous. While on one level I feel compelled to seek out all of the music mentioned throughout the book, a playlist of new discoveries and old favorites that I'll undoubtedly hear in a fresh way, it's the writer's attempts to articulate the inarticulable and their search to echo the unfathomable sound in their texts that stirs me emotionally. There's no better way to understand music and its emotional character in our lives, than to *be* song, though the mystery of the music continues to allude us. I'm reminded of Sinéad Gleeson's essay about the pioneering composer, Wendy Carlos, whose music she found refuge in during the pandemic; the feeling of isolation inherent to her sound mirroring the isolation of living through lockdown. Gleeson experiments with playing a Moog to try to better understand how Carlos is generating this incredibly moving music, but, despite coming to grips with the technical mechanics of the instrument, the music remains unsolvable.

I realize my friend Linda is a bit like Maggie Nelson's "Brilliant Friend" Lhasa, someone who I idolized that probably meant much more to me than I meant to her. We've all had that friend who we feel will always be a bit cooler than us, yet our adoration unlocks and reveals something about ourselves in our desire to embody life as they seem to embody it. We emulate, but must follow our own paths, and there's something preciously vulnerable about making a fool of ourselves when in the presence of someone who we're a fan of, as Anne Enright illuminates in her essay centered on Laurie Anderson. We all start out as fans and the essays in this book illustrate that fandom endures—all the essays are from the perspective of a fan in one way or another. I'm so seduced by Lhasa, swept up in Nelson's prose about leaky New York lofts, strutting stylishly down high school halls, soundtracks with tea and plants, a pink nightgown and a nude photo. I imagine myself as the third in their friendship, grateful to watch it blossom and die, even as I cry. I really do cry as Nelson describes watching old videos of Lhasa to see if she can identify Lhasa's awareness of her illness before she died. Had she been "blinded by life" as she intended? Is it the song speaking or Lhasa? Who was she? Who am I?

Zakia Sewell mines old cassettes of her mother singing, "a ghost, immortalized on tape," searching not only to better understand her mother, who, though still alive, feels absent due to mental illness, but to better understand her own identity as well. She has the revelation that the voices that haunt her mother are the "echoes of ancient traumas, reverberating through the family line," and Sewell is able to commune with her mother and her distant ancestors through the music they've left behind; the music is the source of the illumination and connection she's unable to establish in a direct relationship with her mother. I think of my own mother, of all mothers and difficult family relationships, and Sewell reminds me to forgive. And to honor the dead. It's through the grace and generosity of a piano teacher, Valentina, that Ottessa Moshfegh realizes her divine calling is not playing music but, rather, being a writer, recognizing she had initially turned to music like her mother to "battle through the muck and mire." Music embeds our emotions in the body.

Gleeson's description of Wendy Carlos feels like a mapping of lockdown emotion: "Carlos can switch from sinister to melancholic in a sound wave, and the score suited the dystopia, my torpor, the sense that the world once familiar, would never be the same again. Similarly, Leslie Jamison has a revelation during the pandemic that music need not be a harbinger of hurtful emotions, "the true pulse of music is the sound of it, the way it moves through your body. Dancing with my daughter during the pandemic, I discovered just how liberating it can be to move beyond the words and live in the sound instead—to seek out music as a source of pleasure rather than simply an expression of pain, or a stage for dark interior unraveling."

In her "essay in eight mixes," Jamison punctuates her memories with mixtapes, most particularly her relationships with men, whether her brothers or lovers, though it's her first mixtape, given to her by her aunt Kelda that is the most enduring. When replaying Ani DiFranco's "Galileo" not as the young girl who first heard it, but as an older single mother, she realizes "perhaps the soul getting it right wasn't about finding a soulmate, but the pleasure of the song itself..." I find myself almost singing Jamison's words as I would a song, and in turn, it begins to inspire my own work. I think, Scar Fuel would be such a terrific band name, that's Jamison's mishearing "funeral" in a song. I'm a huge sucker for mishearing song lyrics, it's why I generally prefer not to include printed lyrics with my own albums; there's something very special about this mishearing and how it supplants what's being sung. Cabaret Voltaire's "Nag Nag Nag" will always be "Live Live Die" to me, and I like it that way. Are we always projecting our own lives onto song? Does this in some way cause the mishearing? The writer and the reader are swept away by the music, moving beyond lyrics into the sound of the body. Jamison's essay extends the quality of song form and brings it in tune with the body, a feature of many of the essays throughout this book; itself a body of music. Simone White writes to reconcile rap music's vocabulary with the physical feeling it produces in her body. I feel physically fired up and called to action when reading Liz Pelly's history of the pioneering

Sis Cunningham, Rachel Kushner's inspired history of fearless Wanda Jackson and Megan Jasper's life transformation working for Sub Pop Records. That feeling of pushing forward through song even in the most difficult circumstances. The rhythm and flow of Margo Jefferson's "Diaphoresis" reflects the "suave rapture" of jazz and Ella Fitzgerald's singing cut with Greek myth. The ecstasy of psychedelic sex giving way to ecstatic poetry in Juliana Huxtable's "praise poem" about Linda Sharrock is a synesthetic form; the barriers she's breaking in her own life are mirrored in the music and just as Linda moves beyond words, Huxtable moves beyond form, allowing the text to extend freely like the music.

Jenn Pelly quotes Lucinda Williams's father Miller's definition of poetry as "the use of language to communicate more than the words seem to say" in passages where "the reader or listener feels like a co-creator," and, of Lucinda, that she is "like all the greats, her songs create a mirror, into which we look and feel seen." This perfectly describes my feelings reading *This Woman's Work*. A symbiotic relationship develops between these writers, the music and the reader, much like the performer–audience relationship. It presents an open channel that feels alive. Just as Yoshimi seeks to commune with the "notes in-between notes," so does this prose reach to the heart of music. A *body* of music that compels repeated readings, the text alive and forever changing. With every new reading, new memories emerge for me. This time it's not AC/DC in my uncle's bedroom, but rather it's me dancing to "Thriller" by Michael Jackson with my friend Lisa. I still have two photos of us. I was jealous her arms curved more perfectly when she raised them over her head. This was the same apartment block that was eventually burned down by the landlords for insurance money—my grandparents woke to smoke and flames, desperately fleeing the building with anything they could grab only to find the landlord and his family in the parking lot with all of their belongings neatly packed away.

A lot of cassette recordings made of me and by me were lost in that fire, including the ones of me and Linda moaning. What memories will *This Woman's Work* inspire in you? Fall under its spell. This is music returning to music.

Heather Leigh

Fan Girl

Anne Enright

It is always interesting to watch—the Fame Thing. Or perhaps I should call it the Fan Thing, because I don't mean the mysterious lives of the Famous: their skin regimes or breakfast routines, their ordinary days with extraordinary moments of money or unreality mixed in (moments in which cause and effect are upended and the rules do not apply, when they do not eat or need or love or shit but just *are*, when fingers are clicked and things appear, when there is no friction, only fame). No, I mean the weak-kneed, wet-eyed, *Oh my god you are so famous* thing that we all do sometimes. Or we observe, sometimes. Indeed, I have, on occasion, been shoved aside so that someone can get closer to the object of their fame hunger, which looks more like a fame crisis, or fame famishment; their focus is so locked, their need so great. What do they want? I wonder.

As they make contact and start to glow, it is the Me-ness of the fan's facial expression that is most striking. The *Here I am, yes, it is Me, just as you always expected*. Some fans blush or look excruciated, and that too can be concerning. Very rarely, one will turn to wither you with their Fan Contempt (the wives of famous men get this a lot, apparently). If you are incidentally adjacent to the truly famous, a fan might swivel as though to say, Who are you? or, Who do you think you are? or, Who the actual *fuck* are you?

*

In fact, the flooding of the brain caused by meeting a celebrity makes your frontal lobe fritz out. You become not just excited but also impulsive, not just impulsive but also disinhibited. It is a bit like being drunk and a bit like being demented. Language centers fail. That is why the fan is rude to the point of assault, that is why (and it has only happened to me a few times in life) the fan opens their mouth to speak and says, *Haasfyhhy lgnny phillibat yer*. You cannot make a sentence.

There it is. You are standing in front of your own personal icon and the stuff spilling out from between your teeth is rubbish. Grammar falls apart. Content is lost. Words are deleted or weirdly distorted. It all merges into a single gloop of word-sentence-blurt. This is not delight, it is a short circuit. And afterward you say, *What just happened? I can't remember a thing*.

Yes, I am speaking of the time when I met Laurie Anderson in the small auditorium of the Irish Arts Center on 51st Street in New York or, if "met" is the wrong word, let me try "accosted" instead; the time I was two feet away from Laurie Anderson and then one foot away, which was certainly close enough to see the flicker of terror in her eye. Or not terror. Of course not! It was just a quick peripheral scan; her brain checking the exits were clear while her eyes kept me right there in plain view. I don't think her eyeballs twitched. Perhaps it was my smile that alarmed her. I am a middle-aged Irish woman who certainly could do with a bit of dental whitening, and I was smiling my face off a foot away from Laurie Anderson, while trying to make word speak mouth out of noticing her actual dimples DIMPLES!!! yes on her face-sides, both of them, oh my, one on the left and one on what??!?

And afterward I said to myself, *I don't even remember what I said*.

A fan can only be left with regret after such an encounter, the way you regret a dream when it is done. You can't get back in there to fix its beautiful disaster, you will never say anything better now than *fiffloopidiggllyblop*.

So, for my own satisfaction, this is what I did not say to Laurie Anderson.

The summer I left college in Dublin, I traveled as a roadie to the Avignon Theater Festival with a couple of one-woman shows, one of which was a piece called *The Diamond Body*, based on a short story by Aidan Mathews and starring Olwen Fouéré—who is herself a bit of an icon, for her gift for making an audience think that everything has, very slowly, started to float a few inches above the floor. *The Diamond Body* was the story of Stephanos, an "hermaphrodite," who ran a gay nightclub on a Greek island and was killed by locals outraged by his (in the story) female breasts. It is told by the lover who lost him, and ends with an account of the surgery the narrator gets in order to share Stephanos's fate. The lights fade with Olwen unbuttoning to show her naked torso to the audience, her body in an almost religiously sacrificial pose. This gesture was made with great tenderness and sorrow.

The piece was conceived as a musical collaboration with Roger Doyle. His electronic score was dense with the night-sound of crickets, there was a dance number set in the club, a lyric set on the beach. Olwen spoke through a vocoder, an electronic synthesizer which split her voice into different registers, turning her spoken monologue into a kind of sung chorus, and this was one reason why the story felt ancient as well as new.

It premiered in 1984, ten years after Kraftwerk used a vocoder for their chunky electronica hymn *Autobahn*, and just three years after Anderson took the technique to the top of the British pop charts with "O Superman," her ethereal challenge to the authority of the machine. Two years later, on this alarming French excursion, I was just the roadie. I did not know where Doyle got the technology, which was the source of some pride and much fussing with leads, jacks and dials. He was working close to the beginning of electronic music in Ireland. *I know it wasn't New York, Laurie! but it was very far from trad.*

11

"O Superman" was given its start by John Peel, who had what is now called the bandwidth for maverick wonders like Anderson. When he aired the track in 1981 she was happily planted in the communal downtown New York Art scene, which was then impoverished and small: "six people in a loft" as she described it. Her Canal Street studio, which she still owns, was above a methadone clinic, with patients coming up the stairs and snow coming down through the roof. There was "plenty of sex and drugs" and "it was fun" she said in a *New York Times* interview, though history does not relate whether she partook, or just enjoyed the fact that sex and drugs were all around. Philip Glass, also part of the scene, said, "People didn't have careers then, they had work. We didn't know what a career was. We were artists. It didn't occur to us that you would make a living at it someday."

Anderson grew up in Chicago, where she had been a high-school cheerleader and was voted "girl most likely to succeed." She came to New York to get away from all that. For her first performance art piece, in 1974, she filled a violin with water and played it anyway—the decision she had made, at sixteen, to abandon a career as an orchestral violinist still weighed on her, perhaps. Later, she invented an electric "self-playing" violin which she plied on a street corner while wearing skates encased in a block of ice. She told a story to passers-by about the day her grandmother died, when she walked out onto a frozen lake and found some ducks with their feet trapped. When the ice around her own feet melted, the piece was done. Anderson was busy enacting her freedom. She was not prepared for the success of "O Superman," which is to say she was not able to physically print the required number of records back on Canal Street, so she had to strike a deal with Warner Records to do the job for her. Mentally, we can hope that she was neither prepared nor unprepared. She was wherever she was, because that is the place where Anderson lives. "I never believed that one," she said of the British fans who screamed outside her limousine. "Even at the time…It's really bizarre and manufactured." (You might ask what is being manufactured here—adoration? Capitalism?)

According to one commentator, Anderson was not successful in Europe until she got her spiky haircut, when she became the androgynous cyberpunk we know today. Indeed, we were all cutting our hair and wearing boys' suits, in those days. At least I certainly was. In Avignon, however, it was too hot for suits, so I dressed as a girl throughout. *The Diamond Body* played in a stifling basement down by the river, with no natural light and many mosquitoes, and the person who shared the dressing room with Olwen was a French performer who described herself as "trans-sexuelle."

She was very austerely beautiful, with a Kim Novak chignon and manners more melancholy and formal than you might expect, even in France. We saw her down by the municipal pool, bickering with her beautiful mother, and her breasts were an education. I had never seen implants before—I am not sure you could get them in Ireland at that time, for whatever reason. And, also, we were all topless. It was France, it was a dream of sophisticated nakedness that was very dream-like and inevitable, and lovely too.

It seems to me strange that a play about transitioning, written nearly thirty years ago now feels so contemporary (pronouns aside) when the theme felt so ancient to us then. The fabulous, futuristic vocoder, meanwhile, is now retro as a Sony Walkman, and common as any other slightly esoteric piece of kit. Operating Theater was simultaneously behind and ahead of the times, a temporal loop and swoop that feels entirely Laurie Anderson. Though it should be said that Anderson does not adopt a gender, so much as let the idea of gender go. And even the details I recall— the heat, the darkness, the insects, the way the character died onstage with her torso bared—these tender and slightly fetishized effects would have no place in a Laurie Anderson piece, because her work treats the body as though it were a suit of clothes.

But I wanted to say, when I was grinning like a goon in front of her on 51st Street: *You would have liked it, Laurie,* The Diamond Body *was a good show.* I also wanted to tell her that when I became a television producer, just a few years later, I put the video of "O Superman" out on my first broadcast, which was also the first time it played on Irish TV. *I know Ireland is a bit small, Laurie.*

A few years later I suggested a line from *Strange Angels* as the epigraph to my first novel, a book which, like the album, was about both angels and television sets, among other things. But someone at the publishers made a little face and that tiny implication, whatever it was, spread through my love of Anderson's work quietly afterward for many years. The epigraph was set aside, and with that dropped stitch the entire jumper of my love for Laurie started to unravel. Unbelievable, when I think of it, but there were years when I listened to her in a wan sort of way, wishing that I was allowed to like this as much as I liked it, feeling slightly out of fashion. I was not a true fan. If I were a true fan, I would have held all that close. You offer your liking to the world and the world goes "meh." Some people survive this and some people cannot survive this and I am one of the latter.

It was the nineties by then and the electronic moment had shifted and spread. Anderson herself was less musically productive. She made four albums in the busy 1980s and only three after that, devoting more time to performance and film. In 1992 she met Lou Reed, and he brought her out every night. "Every night. At first it was hard for me. I was more interested in working. But then I began to really love it." Meanwhile, Techno had been born again in Detroit; in Britain, they started to rave; while others moved toward opera—Roger Doyle's latest lockdown piece *iGirl* was recently broadcast on Irish radio with lyrics by playwright Marina Carr.

Which splitting and normalizing makes you realize that, in the early world of electronic music, Anderson held the lyrical and the cerebral together in a way that was all her own. She was part of the same crystallization that produced artists like Brian Eno, Philip Glass, John Zorn, and Talking Heads, all of whom were interested in the intersection of human and machine. Most of these artists were male. Most of them, like Anderson, were interested in simplicity and in the absence of affect. They tried for a kind of electronic dreaming; they wanted distance and disliked sentiment. Anderson did not write about falling in love, she wrote about falling, though there is love in the music, too. Or there are stories in the music, and that is why it continues to ring true.

Anderson is a storyteller. The tales she spins are distilled and redistilled until they feel as though they happened to someone else, or to no one. She repeats herself all the time: she gave up the idea of being a professional violinist so she could learn German and physics, but many decades later she still does not know German or physics. She survived a plane crash in which other people died. (*Where, Laurie? Which plane?*) When she was eight, she pushed her twin brothers' stroller onto that same frozen lake, and had to dive in to save them when it broke through the ice. She wrote to John Kennedy in high school and he sent her roses. She loved her dog and the dog died. These tiny fables about identity, death, fame, and love are carefully curated, polished, and retold. The more you tell the story, she reminds us, the less you remember the original event.

When Anderson was twelve, she broke her back and had to spend a long time in the hospital, where she was surrounded by the sounds of children dying or in distress. She set these sounds aside for many years, and only spoke about how annoying the doctors were when they said she would never walk again. "As I've got older I've realized how much my memories of childhood are just stories I came up with to explain, or cope with, what was going on," she said.

So there is, in her free-floating lyrics, a refusal of pain. Does this mean that we have only two options, death or fiction? Actually there is one more. Her stories are funny. Each one has the shape of a joke, with no punchline. More than that, her Special Performing Laurie Voice makes every single sentence funny, for reasons that are not clear. Anderson can be witty in a single word, though it takes two to really hit home. *"Hi Mom."* The doubleness is frozen into the delivery; she is both still and mutable, like a flame.

"I didn't love my mother—I really didn't—but I did admire her. Her mother didn't love her either. Sometimes it just comes down the line." What is the difference between love and attachment? Where some musicians, like Glass, are trying for perfection, Anderson is trying for freedom, and these are not the same things.

In 2013, I read her account of the death of her husband Lou Reed, which was published in *Rolling Stone*, and it was astonishing: "I have never seen an expression as full of wonder as Lou's as he died." She was holding in her arms the person she loved most, and his passing seemed to leave her grateful. "I had gotten to walk with him to the end of the world. Life—so beautiful, painful and dazzling—does not get better than that. And death? I believe that the purpose of death is the release of love."

With that telling, which made me weep, I was freed, in my own tiny way, from the business of loving or not loving, having or not having, admiring or not admiring, publicly or privately, the work of Laurie Anderson. Which is a little grandiose of me, I know. But I can't tell you how difficult I find the music conversation—the one where people gather into tribes, swap favorites, judge, include, exclude, bond, claim status or coolness or an identity because of their choices. Music undoes me. It does not tell me who I am. It is something I listen to on my own.

"When I was sixteen," Anderson said. "I didn't work at having a consistent personality. I knew you were supposed to but that seemed crazy to me, to be just one person all the time." In a recent book of photographs about New Yorkers, she is described thus: "When Laurie was a little girl she wanted to be '70 different things' when she grew up. She worked as an art teacher, a critic, an illustrator, invented some instruments, made records, wrote books, performed, was an artist-in-residence at NASA, produced movies and was on TV. She collaborated on recordings with Lou Reed, who she married in 2008."[1]

In the photograph, Laurie poses in the apartment she shared with Reed in the West Village. It looks nice. The windows behind her are large and hold a nighttime view of skyscraper lights. I search this picture the way a fan might. I eat it up. I weigh her choices in decor, and feel how personal they might be. I am the fan as intruder, the scary fan. Look! The frames on the windows are intense, dull gray, the couch is also a Dickensian gray, one that contains a lurking amount of green, the walls are dark green and, in the corner of the frame, there is the swag of a huge tapestry curtain in dark reds and gold. Anderson has placed some objects around her, for the lens. On a side table are two or three cacti in small terra-cotta pots. By her feet is a strange slab of resin or fiberglass, balanced on a small industrial trolley, which looks—very faintly—like a melted book. This is probably by some famous artist—all Laurie's friends are famous, and they all ignore their fame: David Bowie, Carrie Fisher, Julian Schnabel. *She has friends!* A small buddha sits on a windowsill. Behind her on the wall is a black and white photograph of a naked human back with something like a train track placed along the spine. This may be Anderson's own naked back (she is famously up there, on her own wall) or it may belong to someone else. Anderson is on the couch with Will, her dog, who has a dressy-looking tag on his collar. Placed on the arm of the couch is a fluffy toy—a gopher, or a beaver, or a chipmunk; some prairie thing, with prominent front teeth. Of course Laurie Anderson has a silly fluffy toy sitting up on the arm of the couch. She is silly the way Buddhists sometimes are. Other celebrities are merely silly: she is a world view.

In the surprisingly small auditorium of the Irish Arts Center on 51st Street in New York, Anderson was performing one of a series of the "Picnics" curated by Paul Muldoon. It was 2016. She tucked her wired-up violin under her chin, took it out again to talk a little more. Then she put it back, struck down with the bow, and filled the room with genius. She was so good. A woman talking to the audience, on her own.

And afterward there she was. Tiny. Beanie. Dimples. And because I had also been on that stage just the week before, I stood up and hurtled her way. Because I only have this one life (currently) and there she was. It had been so long since we had each cropped our hair. Too long. But let's not think about that now.

"Hi," I said. *Well you don't know me. Yes it is me. Here I am. You know you were expecting me, and now I have arrived.*

No, of course I did not say that. I said *fiffloopidiggllyblop.*

---

[1] Sally Davies, 2021. *New Yorkers*, East Sussex: Guild of Master Craftsman Publications Ltd.

Songs of Exile

Fatima Bhutto

I am not in my country and since I have been away from it, I feel absent from the world. Not quite in it, not quite outside. There is no food that sits exactly the way I want it to on my tongue, the sounds are all misshapen, the humor of every new place tonally strange, the clothes beautiful but not mine, ill-fitting and uncomfortable. I have trained myself well over the years not to remember how things are, what my country feels like to me, but when I hear certain songs, certain music, I am sure that in all the archipelagos of grief, there is a large swath of land reserved for lost homelands. I was born in exile, away from my country, and grew up outside it. But even as a child, never having stepped foot on Pakistani soil, I ached for it. The aching is more acute now, after a life lived somewhere between the borders of where you belong and the world outside it. Bob Marley said the one good thing about music was that when it hits you, you feel no pain.

I think of several cases where Bob is very wrong.

I am in Damascus, Syria, where I grew up, a child of my father's exile from his homeland. Like his eyes and his hands, I inherit my father's homesickness for a country I have never been to myself. He eats chilies at every meal; pickled mango and lemon sent in oily jars from home. He covers a table in his study with an *ajrak*, a traditionally block-printed Sindhi fabric, in

19

maroon and black. He searches 1980s Damascus for newspapers carrying headlines from home, listening to the BBC World Service every evening, the bells chiming loudly in our small apartment. When the newspapers yield a story, he cuts the box of news out of the paper and clips it into a folder, careful not to lose any of the precious words.

But I really know we are homesick because of two songs.

The first is "Sitting On the Dock of the Bay," sung by Otis Redding. My father has it on a cassette and it plays in the car as we drive around the ancient city of caliphs and kings. Damascus has not been touched then; it is insulated, protected. No one has harmed it yet, no one has laid their hands or filthy weapons on this city of sweet jasmines. In the summer, the air is thick with the perfume of the delicate white flowers. And we two strangers drive through the city listening to Otis Redding sing of leaving his home in Georgia. My father loves the song. Why, I ask him? Because it's about a man far from his home, he says. I know we are far from our home. I am a small child when General Zia-ul-Haq, a CIA-backed dictator, is in power in Pakistan and he casts a sinister pall over my family's exile. I know we are not in our country because of the dictatorship. I know my father's sorrow throbs, I know it burns and blazes with a fury that increases every day. I understand why my father is quiet when the song plays, why he never fast forwards it or skips past the whistling near the end.

There is another song but this one we listen to at home. "Ho Jamalo," a Sindhi folk song beloved and revered by our people. My father listens to it in the car sometimes, but mainly when he is sitting and reading in his study. I know it does something different to him than "Sitting On the Dock of the Bay." Even as the song plays and the pulse of his sorrow quickens and slows, "Ho Jamalo" fortifies him. It gives him happiness.

One legend says that in 1889, Jamal, a young man from Sukkur, had been sentenced to death by hanging on the orders of John Jacob, an officer of the British East India Company and acting commissioner of Sindh. The company men were pillaging their way across Sindh, cutting down all those who resisted their occupation and robbery of native land. The legend says that Jacob had Jamal jailed at the same time that a new steel bridge had been built across the Indus River. The bridge was so alien, so large and imposing, that no existing train drivers were willing to cross it, so the British trained death row prisoners to move their machines across the bridge. Jamal was offered a commutation of his sentence if he crossed the bridge and, ever daring, he does it. "Ho Jamalo" is sung as he returns home, called out by his wife, celebrating her husband's victorious return.

Other legends say the folksong has nothing to do with the British. Sindhis are not especially famous for fighting back invaders, least of all the Brits (a nearby town is christened Jacobabad in John Jacob's honor), and this other legend claims that Jamal earned his famous folk song for fending off a neighboring tribe. Regardless, it's a song Sindhis play wherever they are in the world. They sing "Ho Jamalo" at weddings, at parties, whenever their heart aches.

This is the absurdity of the whole thing. When I am away from my country, even the pop anthem for a cricket league comes at me hard, a combination of bruised longing and joy. Not all music is written by poets.

In the dark night of dictatorship, lasting from 1977 to 1988, Pakistan's military junta were afraid of everything. General Zia-ul-Haq and his men were so panicked by peaceful protestors that they sent combat helicopters to disperse crowds in Nawabshah. The junta subjected newspapers to twice-daily censor checks but the broadsheets were not afraid, and rather than run watered-down news stories, they took to printing blank pages. The junta were so terrified of journalists that they publicly flogged them, inspired by Saudi Arabia, hoping to draw big crowds in stadiums where whipping and torture might become spectator sports. But Pakistan is not Saudi Arabia. People didn't have an appetite for public cruelty.

The dictatorship banned the party flag of the Pakistan People's Party, whose democratically elected government they had overthrown, arrested thousands of political workers and handed down a minimum of twenty-five lashes for anyone caught taking part in political organizing, agitation, or gatherings. All political activities were banned. Lawyers, journalists, artists, protestors, and defiant women were incarcerated by the tens of thousands. Under General Zia it became a crime to think, to protest, to speak, to be.

Women were policed with sinister vigilance—newsreaders who did not cover their hair were taken off air, adultery and fornication were made crimes punishable by stoning to death, effectively criminalizing rape victims. If you were raped and married, you had just committed adultery. If you were raped and single, you were guilty of fornication. Though courts seeking to please the military government handed down twenty-three death-by-stoning sentences to women, none were carried out. Instead, the jails swelled. In 1979, Pakistan housed a total of seventy women in all of her jails. By 1988, there were six thousand. The majority of the prisoners were poor, illiterate women. The Hudood Ordinances meant that while a rape victim was imprisoned, rapists always went free because you can't prove a man is a rapist with a medical test. Zia's laws only acknowledged rape if four adult Muslim men of impeccable, upstanding character happened to witness the exact moment of rape. This addendum was meaningless; why would four men of great character hang around to watch a rape?

There was no end to the brutalization of Pakistani society. Thieves were to have their hands amputated by law, but in this poor country not one man could be found willing to carry out an amputation. No executioner would do it. Fine, martial law administrators were not deterred; they went to butchers. But not a butcher in all of Pakistan would agree to take a thief's—any thieves'—hands. Everything was a crime then, everyone a criminal. "Only in Russia is poetry so important," Osip Mandelstam once said, "it gets people killed." Not only in Russia, but here too. In the long night of the most oppressive dictatorship in Pakistan's history, secrets were canceled, poets were banished, singers who defied martial law were ruined, taken off stage and television. But they sang. When there were no more lyrics, they sang the banned verses of poetry.

We were lucky to have music in exile. It carried us over the swells and tides of loneliness. When my father was happy, the music changed—it was Elvis, smirking about teddy bears, fever and escaping jail, the Beatles singing about the Soviet Union, Ray Charles on the piano. I listened to Madonna and wore cut-off lace gloves. I noticed as my father watched me learning the words to "Papa Don't Preach," but he wasn't worried. I didn't know what any of the words meant. We watched Michael Jackson's "Thriller" over and over again, screaming. No fan of Arabic music, my father relented only once that I remember—giving "Abu Yousef," a Damascene pop song, his rare mark of approval. I have tried for years since to find the song, but we listened to music back then on bootleg cassettes, copied by friends, or else on CDs burned by kindly shopkeepers. You had to play your music carefully in those days, delicately, lifting CDs with just the ridges of your fingers so that you wouldn't scratch them. Rewind a cassette too carelessly and its tape could spool out, knotted and in a jumble. Worse yet, the tape could break and no hack could piece it back together. There were no iTunes accounts, no Spotify, none of that in 1980s Damascus. I've looked for "Abu Yousef" on YouTube and SoundCloud but it has vanished, lost in the past.

When my brother was born and would shimmy to the sound of anything, my father curated music for him too. "Kiss" was at the top of their song list, not the Prince original, but the more sanitary Tom Jones cover; my brother would run from the opposite end of the flat if he heard Jones's deep baritone, like a pigeon called home. My father lived, like all exiles, in the promise of return. *Someday soon. Maybe a year, or a few months, in the new year, by spring. We'll be home by spring.*

Faiz Ahmed Faiz wrote anthems of resistance that have crossed the borders beyond Pakistan. His poetry is scrawled on placards by students in Delhi and chanted by protestors in Kashmir. In his own country, Faiz was jailed and eventually banished by General Zia. Living in Beirut in exile, Faiz wrote poems for the Palestinians. The junta forbade public readings of his poetry, whether about tyrants or Palestinian persecution, and all of Faiz's verses became crimes. *We will see, certainly we will see, the day that has been promised to us,* Faiz wrote in the poem known as "Hum Dekhenge," We Will See. *When tall mountains of tyranny will blow away like wisps of cotton, and beneath our feet, the feet of the oppressed, the earth will tremble.*

A dictatorship that was terrified of everything, of everyone, met its opposite in a population that was scared of nothing and nobody. Students fought Zia's martial law, women, lawyers, actors, artists, writers, comedians—no one collaborated with the state. Everyone resisted. Madame Noor Jehan, Pakistani cinema's most famous and prolific playback singer, was known as Malika-e-Tarannum or the Queen of Melody. She acted and sang in films in both India, before Partition, and Pakistan, after. In 1965 as Pakistan and India prepared for war—their second in less than twenty years—Noor Jehan rang up Radio Pakistan to tell them she wanted to sing for the nation. No one at the station believed it was really her, Madame Noor Jehan, idol, actress and singer on the line.

"Is this funny to you?" a Radio Pakistan director asked her, "There are bombs and shells flying around here." She eventually drove to the station, with a curfew pass, to prove that her offer was genuine. Though everyone was fleeing, Noor Jehan, who often performed in a tightly wrapped sari, stood in the empty studios and sang her songs of war. For this, she was compared to Umm Kulthum, the Egyptian legend who sang rousing numbers for Egypt before battle and defeat. Her music was so emotional, so precious to Egyptians, President Gamal Abdel Nasser timed his radio addresses to air after her concerts.

But though she sang for soldiers, Noor Jehan wasn't afraid of them. One of her most famous numbers, "Mujhse Pehli si Mohabbat," was taken from a Faiz poem, "My Beloved, Do Not Expect that Old Love From Me."* Faiz was so entranced by her rendition that he said the poem no longer belonged to him, it was Madame Noor Jehan's now. During the dictatorship, when Faiz was being held by the junta on sedition charges, Noor Jehan was warned against singing the ghazal at a concert. "If Faiz is a traitor, then I am one too," the diva declared. She not only sang the song but began the concert with it.

But the most famous story of how music marshaled itself against the country's most notorious dictatorship comes not from Madame Noor Jehan, but another songstress, Iqbal Bano. Two years after the poet's death, his family organized an evening dedicated to his memory. Artists and musicians refused their normal fees to come and pay homage to the great Faiz and hundreds of people squeezed into a packed hall at Lahore's Alhamra Arts Council. Political workers came in large numbers that night and, finding no seats, crowded into the staircases and sat on the steps to listen to Faiz's poetry.

---

* I read somewhere that Faiz wrote the poem not for an old lover, but after reading *The Communist Manifesto* for the first time.

Bano took to the stage and, wearing a black sari, began to sing the poem Faiz wrote in 1979, two years after Zia's coup, "Hum Dekhenge." There is no video recording of the performance but an audio technician secretly recorded Bano. According to Faiz's grandson, his uncle had the foresight to smuggle the recording out of the country and to a friend in Dubai who had it copied, ready for distribution so Pakistanis everywhere could hear Faiz's anthem against dictatorship. It is chilling to hear, preserved on YouTube, with no images, just a photo of Iqbal Bano as the background. Her voice is warm and clear, interrupted by shouts and chants of *Inquilab Zindabad*, or "Long Live Revolution," as she sings beautifully for eleven minutes. Every verse about the fall of tyrants is met with waves of applause. *All crowns will be tossed*, Bano sings, *all thrones will fall. We will see, we will watch.*

What is it about song that threatens dictators so much? Why did Chile's General Augusto Pinochet order the folk singer Víctor Jara not only killed but also tortured, his fingers broken for the music he wrote? Pinochet had Jara arrested the very day after his coup d'état, imprisoning him in Chile Stadium with hundreds of other activists and dissidents. After the soldiers broke his hands, they laughed and asked Jara to play the guitar. But dictators and their men are so simple, so unaware of the forces that they fight. Jara kept writing his music. On the day they killed him, he wrote "Estadio Chile," a song that was smuggled out of the torture camp. *How hard it is to sing when I must sing of horror*, Jara's lyrics read.

Fela Kuti was imprisoned by Nigeria's various military henchmen no less than two hundred times. It wasn't just his music that was in direct opposition to dictatorship, but his life. Kuti declared his commune and recording studio, the Kalakuta Republic, independent from military rule. After he released *Zombie*, an album against the junta, a thousand Nigerian soldiers stormed the Kalakuta Republic. The soldiers beat and injured Kuti's mother and the Republic was set on fire. Kuti moved to a new home which he decorated with a coffin, placed high up on the roof. When General Olusegun Obasanjo was nearing the end of his reign, Kuti delivered the coffin to the door of the barracks where the dictator lived and wrote a song to say goodbye, "Coffin for Head of State." *Dem steal all the money, dem kill many students, dem burn many houses, dem burn my house too.* Very few will remember the names of the men who jailed him, but no one will forget Fela Kuti. This, I suppose, is the threat.

Musicians helped end apartheid by boycotting South Africa, refusing invites to perform—the Beatles were among those who said no—and by singing protest songs. Peter Gabriel wrote "Biko" in honor of the freedom fighter Steve Biko, and Miriam Makeba and Hugh Masekela brought the horror of white South Africa to the world. More recently, it was a young musician from Mansoura, Ramy Essam, who sang to the crowds in Tahrir Square. His song, "Irhal," or "Leave," became an anthem of the Egyptian Spring. Essam took the chants reverberating around the square and sang them, accompanied by his guitar. Everyone already knew the words: *All of us, with one hand, have one demand: leave.* It was, he later said, "the magnificent, wonderful, beautiful magic of what's called revolution" that drew him to sing in Tahrir Square. For his role, creating music out of people's political demands, Essam was picked up and tortured in the hallowed halls of the Egyptian Museum. He was forced to flee his country and now lives in exile.

There are exceptions to the catalog of musicians who lent their voices to the cause of justice; some sang for tyrants rather than against them, and some grossly misidentified what causes to get behind (Bono wearing Aung San Suu Kyi's face in music videos and concerts comes to mind). But this is the danger and power of lyric: music is for the masses of people who feel alone in a jarring, uncertain world. A writer can waffle on about speaking to a generation or a group of underrepresented beings, but a musician sings for everyone. *No te conoce nadie*, the poet Federico García Lorca wrote. *No. Pero yo te canto*. No one knows you, no. But I sing to you.

There is liberty in musical dissonance. And where there is liberty, there will be mutiny. Tyrants hate music because no matter their force and their power, they will never, not ever, be able to control what is beautiful.

After the concert in Lahore had ended, General Zia's goons raided the homes of the organizers, Faiz's family, but they were too late. The cassette of Iqbal Bano's performance had already left the country. Faiz was no longer in the world, they couldn't punish him, but for her defiance, Bano was banned from singing in public. She was not allowed to appear on stage or on television. The junta did everything they could to end her career and in doing so made her, and the poem, eternal.

And us, we spent many more days in exile, waiting and hoping for return. My father told me stories about my country, making promises of homecomings. I didn't want to leave Damascus. But that's because I didn't know what awaited us back home, Papa said. He told me again and again how the air in Karachi smelled of salt and honey, how the palm trees shaded you from the burning sun and how the ancient banyan roots covered the earth. How you could race horses and camels on the beach and be swept out into the Arabian Sea on boats captained by honest fishermen for an evening meal. When the seasons changed and our location remained the same, we listened to our standard songs: "Guantanamera," the most famous song of exile there is; Motown; "My Girl;" Harry Belafonte was somewhere between happy and longing, so we danced to his music—but mostly we listened and waited to be called back to where we belonged. "Day-o," Belafonte cries out, as though singing only to us. Papa and I were always ready, dancing on our toes, filling our lungs with air to sing back in response: "Daylight come and we want to go home."

The Highway
Jenn Pelly

Lucinda Williams spent the 1970s and 80s in the small clubs and street corners at the fringes of American music, fitting nowhere—too country for rock, too rock for country, a woman on a self-determined mission insisting that the world catch up with her. A poet's daughter who grew up between Louisiana and Mexico and Chile and a dozen Southern towns, who was thrown out of high school for refusing to pledge allegiance to the flag, Williams was—to quote one of her early tunes—"born to roam." She spent decades empty-handed in music and unlucky in love. Across the board, she was "nobody's girl."

She traveled on, writing sweet odes to fellow misfits—people broke and broken-hearted with no money, no gigs, at the edge of the bar, on the wrong track. She never grew too hardened to admit, "I just wanted to see you so bad." She was never too coy to stare an uncaring lover dead in the eye and seethe an outlaw's threat: "It's my heart and there's a price you've got to pay." The cracked incandescence of her voice—warbling, like Hank Williams, into the red of its very limits; reaching through the depths of its poetry—cast its bittersweet ache into reality and relief.

Her first collection of original material was the 1980 feminist string-band album *Happy Woman Blues*, for the Folkways label. Eight years later, when she was thirty-five, she followed it with the ripping and eloquent bar-room rock of her critical break-through, *Lucinda Williams*, for Rough Trade Records—the London countercultural outpost that thought of itself as a Marxist label, saw the marketplace as a false creation, and was besotted by Lucinda's rejected Sony demo. "It took a European punk label to get me, which tells you a lot," Lucinda once said. In a dry Louisiana drawl, hers are songs of yearning, betrayal, and death; odes to lost friends and abandoned love; about self-annihilating poets and restless women saving tips, changing the locks, pawning possessions to split town. They form mini-manifestos for female life.

At the center of *Happy Woman Blues*, Williams addressed a woman, not unlike herself, the rambling would-be cowgirl "Maria." Sometimes I imagine Lucinda is singing to the Maria of Joan Didion's 1970 novel *Play It As It Lays*—another vagabond for whom the highway "has always been your lover," she sings—misunderstood, rootless, ever in motion. In the opening sentences of her book, Didion wonders about a sinister Shakespearean villain and his demons: "What makes Iago evil?" Didion writes. "Some people ask. I never ask." Lucinda always seems to ask. Staring into the void, her lyrics do not spare questions. "My dad used to talk about a big dark well and we're all standing on the edge looking in," Williams recalled in the 2011 book *Right by Her Roots*. "And he said some of us fall in and the rest of us don't. But we're all kind of standing on the edge, you know, and at any given moment… I guess I'm always questioning," said Lucinda, "what makes someone lose that strength."

Lucinda's father was the poet Miller Williams, who secured his first job teaching English at the University of Arkansas thanks to his friend and Lucinda's hero, Flannery O'Connor. (As a child, Williams chased peacocks in O'Connor's front yard, and she would never let go of her dream of setting a Great Southern Novel to record.) The elder Williams once defined poetry as "the use of language to communicate more than the words seem to say" in passages where "the reader or listener feels like a co-creator," and his daughter's writing proves it. Like all the greats, her songs create a mirror, into which we look and feel seen. What artist has not related, at some point, to Lucinda's deadpan declaration, on 1980's shimmering "Sharp Cutting Wings (Song to a Poet)," *"I wish I had a ship to sail the waters / I wish I had about a hundred dollars"*? The grain of her bruised twang and lucidity of her articulation extends a hand to anyone who's been there. And I have always had a particular fondness for an unassuming *Happy Woman Blues* cut called "Hard Road," in which Lucinda empathizes with her down-and-out buddy, Bill, whose "heart's on fire" while his "head is reelin'." "Let me buy you a beer or something," Lucinda offers to her pal, who she cares for so much that she tells him, "I got your picture up on my wall," before sweetly proclaiming, "I love you, Bill, as I would my brother." It's like Carole King's "You've Got a Friend" during last call at an emptied Texas bar. Platonic friendships of any kind, but especially those between men and women, are rarely articulated so tenderly, or plainly, in song or anywhere.

We can enter into her lines of inquiry. Lucinda was always wondering how things could really be as they are, why someone had to die, how life possibly went so astray. In her blue-skied tribute to the late Blaze Foley, dead in a shoot-out in 1998: "Why'd you ever let it go that far?" In the most devastating elegy to a weekend-long fling I've ever heard, in 2003: "Did you only want me for those three days?" In 1980, to a bohemian woman wanderer: "Maria, is loneliness a virtue? Are the songs we sing worth a broken heart?"

Twenty-three years on from *Happy Woman Blues*, Williams was still looking for answers. By age fifty, she had finally achieved conventional success. She was five years removed from her prize-winning 1998 Southern travelogue *Car Wheels on a Gravel*

Road—the album where the world at large had, at last, caught up. In the wake of its zeitgeist-crashing commercial triumph—topping the *Village Voice*'s critics poll and winning a Grammy for Best Contemporary Folk Album—Lucinda kept searching.

She opened her seventh album, 2003's *World Without Tears*, with the wearied country-blues ballad "Fruits of My Labor." *Car Wheels* and *Lucinda Williams* are her definitive albums, but "Fruits of My Labor" seems to absorb the weight of them, becoming her definitive song: a postscript of sorts to her *Car Wheels* era and all of the decades that built to it. Even as Lucinda's scratched languor evokes her hero, Neil Young, she subverts one of his best known songs. Forces other than love can break your heart: work can too.

Lucinda situates herself in a room of her own, a personal desolation row, addressing a distant lover with six charged words: *Baby see how I been living*—every delicately cracking note of her voice says it's been hard, even before Lucinda presents the skewed elegant image of *"velvet curtains on the windows"* and sings out their purpose: *"Keep the bright and unforgiving / Light from shining through."* Is she hiding? Does she keep out the light to avoid how messy things have become? Is it simply easier to write in a room with no view, when the sun and world aren't beckoning you out? She remembers, in a subtle rush, everything—*"when we slept together,"* *"the blue behind your eyelids"*—remembrance being the ultimate currency and chaos source in a brutal breakup song. *What makes our dreams so complicated?* she seems to ask. *After decades in pursuit of one—what about eyes?*

She sings "Fruits of My Labor" from the crossroads of love lost and knowledge gained. But the theme at those coordinates is the work itself. Like her early inspiration, Joni Mitchell—who once sang of her "struggle for higher achievement" and never-ending quest for "love that sticks around," and who Lucinda told me definitely influenced this song—she was singing from the precise moment at which heartbreak gives way to revelation. She wants a relationship to work out, but life has become too complicated.

And so she takes what she can: uses the mess, the "dirt," to respond in kind, with a gesture that is uncomplicated: flowers. She luxuriates in naming them—lavender, lotus blossoms, and literal fruits, like tangerines, persimmons, "and sugar cane, grapes and honeydew melon, enough fit for a queen." Maybe she wants to focus on living things in the wake of this connection that died. Maybe she wants to focus on things that grow because she is trying to. Maybe she wants to acknowledge small beautiful things, for fear she was all too busy to notice before. "Fruits of My Labor" is Lucinda at her most sensory and alive.

The steel pedal and harmonica and brushed drums of "Fruits of My Labor" all play through a squint; every line brushes dust off the moment as it is touched by the glare of light coming in. "I've been trying to enjoy all the fruits of my life," Lucinda sings. "I've been crying for you boy, but truth is my savior."

Suspended between "try" and "enjoy" is a lifetime. There is the weight, sacrifice, demands, and promise of an existence guided by the artist's eye. There is the joy and frustration, success and failure, lust and solitude of being a woman with a calling. There is romantic disarray and the self-contained satisfaction of the devoted writer's life. All of the independent-minded genius and desire Lucinda sang in the eighties and nineties is tangled up here—"give me what I deserve 'cause it's my right," she insisted on "Passionate Kisses"; "I want to know you're there, but I want to be alone," on "Side of the Road"; "you took my joy, I want it back," on "Joy"—in these carefully calibrated notes. Art-making, ambition, heartbreak, freedom, and becoming are inextricable "Fruits of My Labor." A life flashes through it. Behind these velvet curtains. In the dark. Searching for another song.

"I was writing about a guy I had been with, and still wanted to be with and everything—I was thinking about him when I wrote it," Lucinda told me, when I called her up one spring afternoon to talk about "Fruits of My Labor." "You were with someone at a certain point in your life, and then maybe that person went away for a while, and then all of these things happened, and now you're in a different place, emotionally and mentally...the idea of 'Fruits of My Labor' popped into my head. Sometimes we forget to enjoy the things we worked for. Everybody talks about having a dream of doing a certain thing, a career or whatever, but then people get so busy that they can't stop long enough to enjoy it."

The first time I heard "Fruits of My Labor" it was not Lucinda singing. In a dark Brooklyn rock club on a November night, I was watching the singer-songwriter Katie Crutchfield, a.k.a. Waxahatchee—one of at least two dozen times I've seen her perform this decade. With a voice more sweet than bitter and utterly its own, Crutchfield was on the brink of recording her career-best album, *Saint Cloud*, during which a photo of Lucinda would hang in the studio. That night, her vocals seemed bigger than ever: she was obviously tapped in and growing, bracing in itself to witness. Still, when she sat at her keyboard and intoned those first lines—*Baby see how I been living*, then an electric prism of yellow and violet and *tangerines* and *persimmons* and *sugar cane*, which I can only call sublime—I was not prepared. The air felt charged with the kind of acute presence the caliber of which I mostly associate with cemeteries and bodies of water.

I was twenty-nine, and I am not sure that "Fruits of My Labor" would have made tremendous sense to me at any other time. The song was defenseless. In a catalog of such rigor and weight—songs delineating the particular comforts a man loses in death, songs that trace a lover's words in her veins like blood, songs with Dylan-esque poetry collages traversing rock history, serpent handlers, angels, the ineffable—here was a lovesick song about flowers. Not only about flowers, but about the work of writing a preternaturally perceptive song about flowers—"traced your scent through the gloom 'til I found these purple flowers," she explains—and also about how the work was tiring, and it was

OK to say it was tiring. It felt like Lucinda pulled the veil back on the whole artistic process—despondency, isolation, inspiration, transforming. Every word she sang glowed like lights of many colors in an otherwise pitch-black night.

I was at a point in my ever-emerging adulthood where I was finding that achieving in your work does not necessarily make life easier. I was finding that it does not automatically exorcize the void, nor make clouds disappear, that the eradication of a problem, many times, creates room for new and potentially more stubborn ones, buried away by the subconscious. Myths about the human heart that I thought I'd debunked revealed themselves to be persistent. Intellectualizing could clear me only so far. "It's a myth that if you do what you love, you'll be happy all the time," Lucinda told me. "I have a problem with melancholia...being kind of down. Sometimes I wonder what it's like to not feel that way: What does complete happiness feel like? Where's the joy that I thought was going to come with all this?" I am not sure that Lucinda Williams fans are particularly well-equipped to know. But "Fruits of My Labor" helps.

"A lot of this song is about fame and success in that way," Lucinda told me, "Because that's one of those things that...you can't reach out and touch it, but it's there, and it changes you and changes everything around you and how people see you. And you don't have to be real famous for that to happen—just a little touch of it. It goes along with the, 'You achieved this, why aren't you happy?' thing. Fame would be one of those things you've *achieved*. And it does make it hard from a romantic point of view, trying to bring someone into your life when you're going through all that stuff. So that's what I was trying to say."

In 1980, on *Happy Woman Blues*, Lucinda sang, "Gonna get in my Mercury and drive around the world / When I reach that mountain top, I'll stand with flags unfurled." But as Emerson said: From the mountain you see the mountain. And on "Fruits of My Labor," she had reached no destination: "Got in my Mercury and drove out West, pedal to the metal and my luck to the test," still betting miles to begin again.

At that point, I asked Lucinda, *What were the fruits?*
    "More free time?" she asked, the question in her voice.

"Fruits of My Labor" is a requiem, a road song, an escape hatch, a poem. I also hear it as a labor song. Lucinda always had a labor consciousness. Coming from a family lineage of radical progressives and union organizers, citing the intellectuals of the folk revival as formative influences—as a teenager she even distributed "Boycott Grapes" leaflets at the grocery store in solidarity with Filipino–American farm workers on strike—she was primed to identify creative work, correctly, as labor.

The possibility of locating joy in work, the socialist artisan William Morris once said, lies in three "hopes": "hope of product" (songs), "hope of pleasure in the work itself" (writing, recording, performing), and "hope of rest." Without rest, Morris seems to say, one cannot hope to be anything but disillusioned by the promise of fulfilling work.

How to square the necessity of rest with restlessness? How to make sense of this equation in a world that still refuses, too often, to take the work of women seriously? That treats our high standards as neurotic perfectionism—as was too often the case for Lucinda in the press at the height of her fame—or as overbearing? That asks us, historically and constantly, to work harder? (Lucinda: "That's true all the time with everything.") I think of the implications, of stress and how it wreaks havoc on us, caring about music so much that the thing that saves you becomes what wears you down. I hear "Fruits of My Labor" as evidence of negotiating these lines from 1979 to 2003: a testament to how hard Lucinda worked.

I hear it, too, as an anthem for an era of reckoning with the mythology of "doing what you love." As a person who was sold this promise young—I was a teenager when "Fruits of My Labor" was released in 2003, as a generation was being told to work hard, do what we love, then swallowed by vortexes of joblessness and debt—the song has been an antidote to exhaustion and chronic overwork. As the labor journalist Sarah Jaffe writes, "work won't love you back." It is a peculiar dichotomy to have music, my ultimate obsession, at the heart of such a cold fact—music being what has always made the world feel most alive to me, even when I felt like I lost control over my life, and I have usually felt like I lost control because of work, work around music. I know it's capitalism, not music, that can make me feel like I'm drowning. When I am lost in the waves of all of this, I often pull up "Fruits of My Labor."

It is not a song I can ever remember listening to with another person. "Fruits of My Labor" is a song I most often turn to when I'm at sea in my desk chair with a blank page and the curtains drawn to trick myself into believing I'm writing at dawn. It's a reminder that I'm not the only person who has sat alone with my thoughts and wondered how life got so very confusing, wondered if I can be satisfied, wondered if I can regain the plot, wondered if I can work through my doubts and come out with some beauty.

There is power in how "Fruits of My Labor" does feel resolved. In the face of the endlessness of the work, it is a complete thought: an invitation, in its slowness and ease, to put the pen down, if only for a moment.

Lucinda said "Fruits of My Labor" is about how hard she is on herself. She sang the names of literal fruit because it felt good to sing them. It felt good to eclipse with the light of open vowel sounds and brilliant flashes of color, to hold onto flowing slant rhymes and clarity. "Lemon trees don't make a sound / 'Til branches bend / And fruit falls to the ground"—but you'll notice them now.

Sometimes I listen to "Fruits of My Labor" and imagine Lucinda in her Mercury headed West, "pedal to the metal," as she sings, and her "luck to the test," crossing the country alone. I think of another monumental alt-country song from 2003, by Gillian Welch, who was known, in her earliest sets, to cover Lucinda's "Crescent City." Gillian's own "Look at Miss Ohio" finds its titular pageant queen taking control of her destiny, fleeing a doomed would-be marriage: "Gonna drive to Atlanta," Welch sings, "and live out this fantasy." I imagine Miss Ohio and Lucinda passing each other on their respective journeys toward opposite coasts, starting over, becoming someone else, ever-searching for joy in song and rest.

Praise Poem for Linda

Juliana Huxtable

The winter of 2017 into 2018 was a particularly tumultuous and transformative season in my life. I had, for the first time, broken away from serial monogamy and set out on a road of psychic exploration, musical immersion, travel, and sexual independence. Music and literature were my primary lovers. I was firmly in the "psychedelic era" of my life and, in this period, learned certain things about myself.

Most of these realizations came through music. My basement room, which I loved dearly, nestled my unruly spirit through albums that I cohabited with. I did everything with music, played my flesh as an instrument, commanding an array of sensibilities in recitals for a string of lovers that passed through my room, inviting them to join me with their instruments. I tripped and danced and fucked and dressed and spun elation in my conversation intoxicated by what came to me through speakers and headphones.

I now know, because of this period of my life, which could be called *Journey in Satchidananda*, that there was distinct and fervent musical experimentation that took place between the years 1967 and 1973 that warmed and ignited my curious winter. Music emanating from a matrix of noise, chaos and synesthetic incantation came to me in the form of gifts from friends, lovers, and deep digs online desperate to find yet another instance of

41

the musical sublime that, only after the fact, I would realize *again* came to be in this playful epoch.

One lover, who I'll reduce to the initial J, I met out, would see him at shows that I played and shows I attended. He met me at precisely the moment my psyche opened itself into an orifice, receiving and secreting as an expansion of the corporeal and mucal into new terrains...a force I had yet to fully understand, yet one that was crafting the way I played, moving me into a cacophonous register, an offspring of chaos. I was being booked for "noise shows" and at no point found issue with the designation. J was a noise musician himself, unable to shake his nervous habit of abjuration; the last show he played was always already a silly pastime he had outgrown or grown enough shame to let go of. Our dates were musical...from a punk show to a roomy basement dance-floor afterparty, chewing mushroom bits sporadically, hoping to ingest enough mycelial energy for guidance. The music elaborated my elements into complex polymers. One night, as we came back to my place and descended soiled stairs into my basement cauldron, illuminated by a decoupage of lights refracting color and texture, he asked to put an album on.

"Sure, what is it?"

"Just listen, I think you'll like it."

For the next thirty or so minutes I felt something that registered vaguely as being spoken to...being seen by something like, but clearly not, language, free from words save the occasional muttered name. It was an album by Sonny and Linda Sharrock. It broke me open while I opened for J, gesticulating in response to the calls of Linda's vocals and Sonny's expressionist guitar. I was struck by a sense of the uncanny and the sublime merging, a strange and altogether unprecedented experience for me. Where Freud found difficulty in reconciling the uncanny and the sublime, insofar as the sublime had to incorporate the terrifying; must, as elaborated in Kant's *Analytic of the Sublime*, arrest the subject's faculties of comprehension and make quite clear that the sublime moment is beyond them, I found no such issues in my experience of listening to the sounds the album contains.

My romance with J didn't last so long, as tends to be the case with New York affairs. But Linda stuck with me. In the sexual act with J, the anarchic sounds moving through me could not be confused with the carefree happenstance that brought me to swelling orgasm. Her voice, an ecstatic, troubled counterpoint to Sonny's riffs, seemed to have already invited me in, dared me recognize what it was that made me feel at home in sonic chaos figured in momentary compositions as sound. I chuckled on learning after orgasm that the album was titled *Black Woman*.

In many ways I am convinced Linda's renderings *found me*, folded me into her call, and my response has been in the works since.

I am encouraged to think of the many ways one can approach the analysis of music—the formal structures of the music itself, its lyrical and vocal content, the social and cultural conditions of its genesis. This, my textual undertaking, is first and foremost a praise poem. It seeks not to mend, but to nurture the breaks— from language, from musical structure, from decipherability—that Linda and her artistic contemporaries harness in their sonics.

The itinerant nature of these breaks is difficult to trace, and music criticism, which has suffered increasingly in the digital age, has struggled or has flatly refused to do so. For many years, music traveled in ways that the written word simply could not. It flooded radio waves and emerged phenomenally on records, tapes, CDs, and MP3s. Until very recently, one could argue that the dissemination of music outpaced the ability of printed text to freely describe, contextualize or otherwise supplement the experience of listening to it with more information. Music journalism thrived (in quantity) not only as a product of this latency (the gap meant time for reflection, that music could *do* and text could *reply*), but also because, before the digital era, access to music (at least in commodity form) was controlled by distributors and labels, who orchestrated much of the (major and mainstream) press tied to releases, leaving independent publishers to the later commentary. The world of independent music both relied on independent magazines, journals and later websites and suffered limited circulation outside of urban metropolises. Even as a child of Napster and LimeWire, I needed a *lead*, a *tip* to an initial artist, song or genre, that I could then search the magazines, blogs, and various sites for and find other points of entry into the increasingly large world of music available. Kodwo Eshun, writing about writing about music in 1998 Britain, laments:

> Since the 80s, the mainstream British music press has turned to Black Music only as a rest and a refuge from the rigorous complexities of white guitar rock. Since in this laughable reversal a lyric always means more than a sound, while only guitars can embody the zeitgeist, the Rhythmachine is locked in a retarded innocence.

Here the tension between "guitar music" and "dance music" is a site of Manichean differentiation, rhythm denoting the domain of "Black Music" that resists critical interrogation or appraisal. Eshun seeks to write about dance music as the Black musical form contemporary to the times his essay emerges from and speaks to. I am interested in expanding his assertions about music writing, as music *thinking*, beyond the limitations of rhythm to other forms of Black music and in particular the sonics of Linda Sharrock. When Eshun asserts that "All today's journalism is nothing more than a giant inertia engine to put the brakes on breaks, a moronizer placing all thought on permanent pause [...] Too much speculation kills 'dance music,' by 'intellectualizing' it to death," I can't help but think of the critical failure to account for the interesting fact that "the voice innovators within jazz during the 60s and early 70s were all women [...] the most captivating were Linda Sharrock, Jeanne Lee, Annette Peacock and Patty Waters."[1] I would add as a foremother to the innovators of this particular epoch Abbey Lincoln who, in *Triptych*, on Max Roach's *We Insist!*, set in motion a noise that Linda would carry to its fullest blast over the course of her career. Much of the critical writing about jazz of the late sixties and early seventies exploited the tension between European and Black musical forms to wax infatuated over the formal qualities of the music, particularly those that could be understood within the theoretical topography of classical music. Many pioneers of what would come to be known as free jazz, like Cecil Taylor or John Coltrane, are canonized for their marked and virtuosic departure from the formality of their trained abilities. I'm interested more in the failure of critical writing to accommodate for music like that produced by Linda than in undermining the existent engagement with the free jazz greats, and wonder if there is always an *inertia machine* manufacturing an inability or resistance to reflect in writing Linda and Sonny's voyages in sound:

> The fuel this inertia engine runs on is fossil fuel: the live show, the proper album, the Real Song, the Real Voice, the mature, the musical, the pure, the true, the proper, the intelligent, breaking America: all notions that stink of the past, that maintain a hierarchy of the senses, that petrify music into a solid state in which everyone knows where they stand, and what real music really is.
>
> And this is why nothing is more fun than spoiling this terminally stupid sublime, this insistence that Great Music speaks for itself.[2]

While great music may speak for itself, those to whom the music speaks are neither immediately evident nor necessarily likely to find the music, and it is to these hypothetical listeners that, at least in part, music writing addresses itself. I was one of these listeners, identified as such in the reading and subsequent listening. A desire to write in service of music was kindled in me and some of the difficulty I've encountered in preparing this essay arises from the fact that it is the fulfillment of dreams, many reignited by Linda's gift.

Deferred dreams unearthed themselves as closeted "could be"s, and I felt a distinct nostalgia for the time when music thinking and writing merged most productively, during the "blog era." This writing was found on various websites, beginning with the early free web—Angelfire and GeoCities—and extended into music blog aggregators like elbo.ws and hype.m(machine). These entities, alive in memory, partition both a moment in time and a relationship to music and its reflection in writing that I had somehow abandoned or felt had been eclipsed in the sprightly and celebrated emergence of a new form of medium; the transition from desktop media to what we now understand as (mobile) "social media."

Writing that engages music as its object (subject?) of critical inquiry, as the beloved of textual elation, has gone through many transformations in recent history. Struggling like all published writing to compete with a mobile-social-media attention economy and overcrowded marketplace, it has culminated in what some might identify as a crisis for writers and writing, where (now largely digital) music magazines abandon writing in part or altogether, to produce more "dynamic" content for revenue streams. I would have hoped that something like music blog culture could take up the task of unearthing music lost to the canon of music writing, but we seem to be at a strange impasse.

By the time I came to being an *engaged* fan, one immersed in the reading and writing about and for music, blogs represented not only a means of extended, communally generated "album notes," but also a means of instantly sharing music itself in the form of files or videos. Sensuous experiences danced with the written word. An exegetical engagement tethered to the sonic event at the point of encounter. This is my praise poem in long form blog post.

Since my first *choice* in the matter of what music I listened to, my obvious desire for Linda's voice was clear. The cold, echoey talk-singing of post-punk-cum-electro vocalists populated my early hard drives, skipping in synths cross-fading though the nomadic and divinely famished runs of Kirk Franklin's women soloists. The fury-laden bellows of gospel's unsung provocateurs, loosened at the moment when a praise song became *praisecore*, multiplying the rhythm structures and densifying the time stamps in violent clamor. Black women led the call to thrash, to jump, to destroy the polite decorum of the surveilled body and come undone before the divine. I cried running for miles connected to the pearlescent indigo MP3 player that rendered into flesh the inflections of Rihanna.

Voices like Linda's voice arrested me. The feminine third-person plural pronoun made its inaugural proclamation in music… *their* voices, or at least what I understood as their voices, offered an inexplicably novel form of audio play…The song belonged to her; She, alone, authored it.

Though I'm sure the issue is a bit more complicated, this was the view of music I would come to understand as naïve; that the voice, and the role it played in the historicity of music, owed its conditions to the virtuoso player, the mastermind producer. That the condition was the composition, the voice the mere articulation of a budding beauty yet to be fully delivered.

Serial and never fully unique in nature, I was told the voice(s) was (were) interchangeable. As if her voice's addition to the composition was merely textural; lacking the threshold degree of instrumentality or musicality. I believed I had forgotten, but was never given the opportunity to know the names of the sirens who "went uncredited for their contributions to tracks that turned into number one gold for their producers"[3]; their affective powers were sacrifices for profit and later exegesis.

Linda is no uncredited ghost singer. She was essential to the musical project that she and Sonny built in the three albums they made together; she is memorialized in the title of one of their most well-known songs. I am an ardent fan of Linda and

Sonny, both of whom I am convinced have not been given their proper dues. The dynamism of their work is to deploy and fold the codification of Black musical expression in genre, market, and lyrical class back into the rupture out of which came to be the Black anti-self; outside of language and forever bedfellow of the ineffable. It is a speaking-to—shaping noise into something that cannot be understood as figuration—and yet is music. The unaccountabilities within English (and other despotic tongues) grow into abscesses which Linda joyfully pops, her *din* the virus disallowing a flat return to surface.

After I first heard *Black Woman* in bed with J, I listened to the album incessantly. The music took elements of blues, gospel, "folk" schools like calypso, rock, and jazz and abstracted them into noise that shape-shifted through vignettes, each given a title and guided by Linda's voice. The references are never clear, nor are they ever announced in language. The procession of titles on the album reads like the table of contents in a modernist chapbook:

Black Woman
Peanut
Bialero
Blind Willy
Portrait of Linda in Three Colors, All Black

Black Woman opens with Linda crooning like a church soloist crying mid-spiritual, catalyzing a collective yolk-breaking into rolling, pathetic ecstasy. The rumbling sadness swings low with the syncopated drums and arpeggiating key flits, all elevated by Sonny's curving vibrato guitar, which at times carries the sea-facing lightness of calypso. Linda is leading a melancholic procession up a knee-deep stream at a steep incline, falling, returning again, and sing-crying to narrate and proceed. Linda's larynx sculpts silhouettes of Baptist women rocking, swaying, eyes closed, awaiting delivery in vociferous struggle. She uses not a single word throughout the song, and for nearly the entire duration of the album.

Linda was born in in Philadelphia in 1947. She was raised in a Black church and sang in the choir. Her musical interests expanded to include folk and jazz music, which she would later incorporate into a decidedly avant-garde sensibility. She moved to New York after art school, where she immersed herself in the burgeoning experimental jazz scenes. By the mid 1960s, she was performing with Pharoah Sanders's band and by 1966 had married the jazz guitarist Sonny Sharrock. While working with Sanders in 1969 she also met and performed with Herbie Mann, who would produce a later album made by the Sharrock duo. Linda's musical interests were catalyzed in her masterful performance on *Black Woman*, which was recorded in New York that same year.

The terrifyingly alien nature of the music and its shadow play of black psychosocial motif is where the uncanny and sublime meet. The weft of Afro-Caribbean and Afro-Latino diasporic musical tropes amplify the noise of Linda's vocals. My encounter with the album is also the encounter that French philosopher and poet Édouard Glissant apprehends in *Caribbean Discourse:*

> From the outset...the spoken imposes on the slave its particular syntax...the word is first and foremost sound. Noise is essential to speech. Din is discourse.
> ...meaning and pitch went together for the uprooted individual, in the unrelenting silence of the world of slavery. It was the intensity of the sound that dictated meaning: the pitch of the sound conferred significance. Ideas were bracketed.[4]

Black diasporic experience, from its genesis, is one in which language is violently disinherited as the pretext for the world in which sound itself—*din*—emerges as the currency of signification.

49

The imposition of new languages from the European core also first appear as noise. It is in this context that Blackness is inseparable from noise. In her screaming and screeching, Linda insists on an intrinsic value in the outcry... carrying the fetishized tropes of Black rhythm and tonality to its most extreme, she says without language an expression that is unique to a Black experience, in which there is no "mother tongue." If, as Fanon suggests, to speak "means above all assuming a culture and bearing the weight of a civilization," Linda's refusal to do so marks even lyrical language as unfit for the task of an album that seeks to elucidate the notion of "Black Woman."[5] The weight which she would bear in speaking, or singing, in lyric is one she would carry in vain, a burden with no payoff. There is no linguistic redemption after the break has occurred, so it is to noise, the echoes and possibilities therein, that Linda returns. Like much of the malignant writing on Linda's vocal contributions to the record, her noise is taken as nonsense, as Glissant writes in *Caribbean Discourse*:

> No one could translate the meaning of what seemed to be nothing but a shout. It was taken to be nothing but the call of a wild animal. This is how the dispossessed man organized his speech by weaving it into the apparently meaningless texture of extreme noise.

In this *extreme noise* is an emittance of complexity from a place of disconnection. The utterance of no language and yet meaning is carried. The overseer lingers in the speech act as there always exists "the possibility of being watched in language." For the inheritors of a language given to them as forceful misrecognition "not only is language something spoken, it is something to be watched over in speaking."

Betrayal is an immanent risk. The disciplinary structure of language which announces its presence at many encounters—class, gender, race, national border—is a cancer endemic to any attempt at the command or disavowal of a language built to monitor, scrutinize and direct expression and labor. This betrayal, or its risk, is a terror from which the only escape is a different register altogether. What this seems to produce in the filiation of language and cultural production is, more often than not, what Glissant calls a *forced poetics*, "any collective desire for expression that, when it manifests itself, is negated at the same time because of the *deficiency* that stifles it, not at the level of desire, which never ceases, but at the level of expression, which is never realized." It also speaks to the conspiratorial success of vocalist Abbey Lincoln on *We Insist!: Max Roach's Freedom Suite*, the true break into free expression. Or what Glissant counter-defines as *free or natural poetics*, "collective yearning for expression that is not opposed to itself either at the level of what it wishes to express or at the level of the language that it puts into practice," comes in the form of language-less eight-minute and ten-second dramaturgy. *Triptych (Prayer, Protest, Peace)*, the composition by Roach I am describing here, is abolition in sound elevated to music by its flirtation with jazz forms.

The critical mistreatment of the women about whom I write, scorning their gestural use of *extreme noise*, sits comfortably with formulations of noise in white criticism and scholarship that take it as an interruption to systems of meaning. White American and European countercultures, linked to notions of the avant garde, see noise as a return to some form of "unintelligibility," not unlike the redemptively othered African figures of cubist modernism; noise is where things become unorganized, where language cannot signify. Strangely enough, a more recent piece on Linda's music describes how she "howls, gasps and whinnies over Sonny's serrated cubist blues."

At work in what I'm proposing here is a communicative noise, a noise that emanates from encounters in which speech is both foreign (unintelligible) and sovereign...where noise, which frames the outbursts that reconcile or recompense audibly for the multiple denials that frame the strictured life of the dispossessed. Noise becomes an opportunity to literally break, but break as a form of recognition.

Linda Sharrock's medium is quintessentially vocal noise, adding to a rich legacy of Black women vocalists uncredited and yet antecedent to other women whose adjacency to the white bourgeoisie credited them as pioneers of certain avant-garde vocal styles.

Noise is not a break from, but a rupture *of*—an insistent drive. Unclear, but nonetheless bound within recognizably Black textures, it advances music as an opportunity to retrieve noise from the myopically white traditions that rendered it something like exterior, anterior, or primordial—based on its role in relation to Eurocentric formulations of sound, speech, musicality, and written language.

What is novel about Fanon's weight of a civilization, *for my purposes*, is not necessarily the imposition of a colonial language, a language that imposes itself and its cultural assumptions onto the racialized subject, but that, in the case of the African diaspora writ large, there is no other tongue to return to. Igbo doesn't linger as a force that English reckons with and battles. What lingers is an absence—the "din" that Glissant articulates in the first encounter with the European seafaring class. It is from this din that Linda works the originality, the ineffable lucidity of jazz, both as a masterful eruption of unmistakably Black expression, but also as an illuminating force in the tradition of noise, atonality, and sonic abstraction.

I once attended a magnificent lecture by Coco Fusco in which she, through the exposition of cultural artifacts from the subaltern world, upended the proprietary claims Western modernism had to the twentieth-century emergence of abstraction and minimalism in painting and sculpture. The notion of abstraction as a diverse, culturally specific practice has lingered with me since. In the tradition of noise, as music and as performative counterpoint to what one might formally understand as musicality, Linda is articulating the very real specificity of noise—of speechless cry, of freakish fanatical scream—to her mother tongue. In doing so she offers modes of thinking, dramatizing the instrumentality of the voice itself as an expression of the conditions from which she—from which free jazz—from which the gestural chaos of her counterparts like Ornette Coleman arose.

What is often understood, even in the realm of "noise music," is that "noise" largely denotes sound that is recognizable as neither vocal nor musical in the traditional sense. There is a droll cruelty in the analysis of voice in relation to experimental sound and music. In the canonisation of jazz, particularly what is understood as free jazz, the sonic innovation of vocalists, especially women, is always a secondary consideration to the appraisal of musicality. Claims that Linda's voice undermines the very listenability of the album, that she is simply a different version of Yoko Ono or Patty Waters, or that her contribution to the record is simply as part of the group, listing her with the pianist and drummer, abound. Much of the praise the album received yields little mention of Linda.

Her legacy seems to have been lost in the encoding, the reification of the vocal/instrumental or vocalist/instrumentalist dichotomy in which what she offers the musical composition is a *technical* potentiality waiting to be activated by the virtuosic genius of the instrumentalist, who, in this case, was also her husband.

I have no interest in reading the voice as somehow in closer orbit to an original earth-mother music, in granting cert to the idea that the pianist is somehow advancing the dialectic of man and machine; "technology" firmly inhabiting the ambit of men, and women, the Black woman, vocalist, Linda herself as embodiment of something "natural"—whether in the recording booth at BYG Studios in Paris or in the music of West Africa that lingers in traces, reformulated after the break. The instrumentality of the voice is rendered docile when it gestures lyrically and vulgar when it breaks from that structure. As Abbey Lincoln, the vocalist for Freedom Suite, said of her *Triptych* recording, "I got rid of a taboo and screamed in everybody's face."[6]

I believe the music that evolved into and out of the free jazz movement was trepidatious with regards to its use of language. But language and voice are not inseparable after all. It is worth noting that "soul music," which found its genesis in the 1950s and fully elaborated into a form at the advent of the sixties, was coeval with the emergency of this strain of jazz. Soul music was understood, rendered culturally intelligible via the legibility of Black lyrical performance.

If what we understand as "soul" emerges in this music and initiates a filiation between voice and "soul" to such a degree that this quality, this *soulfulness*, is inexorably part of the connotation of Black vocal permanence, we have to unsettle this dynamic so that what Abbey and Linda perform is understood outside of this oversaturation.

The celebrated and fetishized "authenticity" of Black musical expression is, in light of this betrayal of language, of the *extreme noise* of the tongueless mother's tongue, a fundamentally failed relationship to language. The mother tongue of no mother (tongue). Of a mother whose tongue was taken out in punishment doled out in response to her insistence on speaking... of making herself visible in her own language.

The mother tongue of no mother tongue, working its desires, its expressive needs put through a language it understands but that will never understand or fully see it. It is as the inheritors of such a condition—the children of this tongueless mother—that noise—din—arises as something like an inescapably resonant expression of the condition.

Linda, in her abstract caterwauls, is speaking to me, calling out in the dirty talk of transatlantic ghosts. I came with Linda, rode the warping waves of her cries that make Donna Summer's moans on "Love to Love You" seem polite, afraid to detach themselves fully from the scrutiny of words…to go "where shriek turns speech turns song—remote from the impossible comfort of origin."[7]

If, as American cultural theorist Fred Moten suggests, freedom-seeking jazz deploys "an erotics of the cut, submerged in the broken, breaking space-time of an improvisation. Blurred, dying life; liberatory, improvisatory, damaged love; freedom drive," then it is the voice, perhaps, that is most fit to dramatized these erotics. Its refusal of script and its subsequent evolution into the sonic texture of Glissant's encounter is central to the power of the music I'm writing of here. Linda brilliantly does "with the voice what John Coltrane, Albert Ayler and Pharoah Sanders did with the saxophone: pushing beyond their natural range to find ecstatic new forms of expression."[8] Yet it is also, sadly, this pushing beyond the natural range that conditions the inability to account for or appraise such performances, what they engender.

Not directly recognizable as human, emitting from the boundary between musical (harmonic, melodic, rhythmic) sounds and sounds more broadly. British philosopher Ray Brassier, thinking through noise, asserts that it "exacerbates the rift between knowing and feeling by splitting experience, forcing conception against sensation."

But for whom does noise serve this function? Like most totalizing theories of noise, this may be true for some, but is not particularly useful when speaking of the producers of free jazz or their audiences, presuming they are at least in part Black. This perceived rift between conception and sensation is the space from which much appraisal of Linda's music and that of her contemporaries emerges.

Jazz enthusiasts and critics alike rapaciously map the terrain of the music's history and its typology. Knowledge of jazz is wielded with scientific precision and anthropological enthusiasm.

The pioneers of free jazz, for me, made music that moved lucidly between music and noise, exploding the latter's possibilities as "a surplus of structure and complexity, as an ongoing super-imposition of incompossibles."[9] The nature of jazz as a seminally Black form is carried to some its most ecstatic, complex, and sublime performances in the music made by Linda and Sonny, led by the brilliant bursts, breaks, and breakdowns of Linda's interventions.

American poet and political activist Amiri Baraka was getting at an important point in his essay "Apple Cores #5: The Burton Greene Affair" that perhaps says more (in reversal) about the writing of jazz than it does necessarily about the playing of jazz. This contemplative and indirect criticism of Greene ends with the setting of the following scene:

> In the beautiful writhe of the black spirit-energy sound, the whole cellar was possessed and animated. Things flew through the air.
>
> Burton Greene, at one point, began to bang aimlessly at the keyboard. He was writhing, too, pushed by forces he could not use or properly assimilate. He kept running his fingers compulsively through his hair.
>
> But the sound he made would not do, was not where the other sound was. He beat the piano, began to slam it open and shut, slapping the front and side and top of the box. The sound would not do, would not be what the other sound was. He sat again and doodled; he slumped his head. He ran his fingers desultorily across the keys. Pharoah and Marion still surged; they still went on screaming us into spirit.
>
> Burton Greene got up again. A sudden burst like at an offending organism, he struck out again at the piano …he beat and slammed and pummeled it. (The wood.) He hit it with his fist.

Finally he sprawled on the floor, under the piano, shadow knocking on the piano bottom, on his elbows he tapped, tapped furiously then subsided to a soft flap, bap bap, then to silence, he slumped to quiet his head under his arm and the shadow of the piano.

Pharoah and Marion were still blowing. The beautiful sound went on and on.

After *Black Woman*, Linda went on to make two more albums with Sonny. Like so many Black American artists who struggled to support their experimentation in the States, the pair traveled to Paris where they recorded *Monkey-Pockie-Boo*, what many consider their most "difficult" album, on the BYG Actuel label. It saw Linda pushing her voice into increasingly more novel terrain, still playing with gospel, folk, blues, and Latin and Caribbean diasporic motifs, with both Linda and Sonny disavowing musicality for long swaths, putting what they expressed and how they expressed it to the test. Their final collaboration *Paradise* was produced by Turkish tape composer İlhan Mimaroğlu and expanded the ingestive drive that animated much of their music, absorbing disco, funk, and their genre siblings into their uncanny sublime. In the decades since, Linda has gone on to play with a number of musicians, rightfully assuming a central role in directing the music. I love everything Linda makes, but she is at her most exquisite when her voice explodes in form, shape, and texture. I write endlessly about what Linda does in her music, but I will keep *Black Woman* as the central text for this praise poem. In 2009, Linda suffered a stroke, which severely affected her mobility and left her partially aphasic. She disappeared for three years before returning, perhaps all the more dynamic in the wake of her aphasia. Linda continues to expand a body of work that provokes so much in those who listen to its vocal undoing. In many ways, I understood a bit more about my own complicated relationship to language, voice, sound (and I say that as a writer). Perhaps this is the first of many praise poems that I will forever be indebted to Linda for inspiring.

---

[1] Sam Shalabi, 2016. "Why You Should Know Mystical Jazz Singer Patty Waters," *Le Guess Who? Treasure Guide*. October 13, 2016, p. 6.

[2] Kodwo Eshun, 1998. "Operating System for the Redesign of Sonic Reality," *More Brilliant Than the Sun*, 00[-006]. London: Quartet Books.

[3] Krystal Rodriguez, 2019. "Ghost Voices: The Women of House Music," *TIDAL* magazine, March 18, 2019.

https://tidal.com/magazine/article/women-of-house-music/1-54410

[4] Édouard Glissant, 1991. *Caribbean Discourse*. Virginia: University of Virginia Press.

[5] Frantz Fanon, 2008. "The Black Man and Language," *Black Skin White Masks*, pp. 1–2. Translated by Richard Philcox. New York: Grove Press.

[6] Fred Moten, 2003. *In the Break*, p. 23. Minneapolis: University of Minnesota Press.

[7] Ibid, p. 22.

[8] Stewart Smith, 2017. "The Strange World of…Linda Sharrock," *The Quietus*, November 8, 2017.

[9] Ray Brassier, 2009. "Against an Aesthetics of Noise," *nY # 2*, October 5, 2009.

Music on the Internet Has No Context

Kim Gordon

The first time I met Yoshimi was in Tokyo, where Sonic Youth were playing for the first time. It was in a classic small club, very crowded and hot, during our Day Dream Nation tour in 1998. Yoshimi was wearing a pair of days-of-the-week underwear on her head—I forget which day. I was jet-lagged, tired, and nervous about playing. The club was murky but suddenly exploded with Boredoms who were also on the bill. They blew our minds. She was a blast of force as the drummer to Eye, the singer, who was all over the audience. Eye's small size made him seem like a flash of energy flying into the audience, his screams like an electrical experiment. Yoshimi's drums pummeled as she jumped up and down, bringing extra power to each hit with her movements. The guitars swirled in the heavy air and mingled with our bodies, melting our minds. As a listener it was a disorienting feeling; rather like being on the ceiling instead of the floor, or a non-orientation. The walls faded into the background and the architecture was replaced with dissonance and chaos. It made me think of New York No Wave and how free and unconventional it was in song structure. I always wondered what the connection was—how did they know, or was it as simple as meeting kindred spirits? There is so much valor in the playing of free/experimental music.

When Julie Cafritz and I asked Yoshimi to play with us in our dup Free Kitten (later Mark Ibold joined on bass), the language barrier seemed minimal. Yoshimi understood more English than she could speak but we spent a lot of time laughing so hard we cried, bonding over shopping and our daily hunt for perfect tuna-fish tea sandwiches. Free Kitten's first tour of Japan really made us into a band. The playing melded us together. The music we intuited and produced together made us aware of our outsiderness, all of us having played in groups with men, making eccentric music. Finally, through this book project, I'm finally able to ask Yoshimi things I'd always wondered about, pulling back the curtain with the help of a translator. I couldn't quite remember how we first asked her to play with us in Free Kitten, so that's where I started...

Yoshimi Yokota was born in 1968 in Okayama. It was a time in Japan with immense student uprising and protests. If you look her up on Wikipedia it doesn't list her full name, only Yoshimi P-We. She is best known as the main drummer of the beloved, inspirational experimental rock band Boredoms, started by Yamataka Eye in 1986. She first played with Eye in UFO or Die. Yoshimi also has an all-girl band OOIOO, as well as many other musical projects including the improv groups Saicobab, Saicobaba and an avant-garde clothes line, Emeraldthirteen. She has two children.

A few years after meeting her, Julie Cafritz (Pussy Galore, STP) and I asked her to join our irreverent duo Free Kitten, that we started on a whim to counteract the overindulgent white male free improv scene at CBGB Sunday afternoon matinees. It was all in good fun!

Yoshimi: I think it was in 1992. Through John Zorn, Boredoms got to do their first U.S. tour opening up for Sonic Youth. A lot of things happened on our first U.S. tour, but after touring about five cities on the east coast with Sonic Youth, Boredoms went in to record our fourth album *Wow 2*, which was produced by John. We recorded at Martin Bisi's studio for about four days, and then I remember going to perform our last show of the U.S. tour in 1992 at Roseland in NYC with Sonic Youth, which also happened to be the first time the Jon Spencer Blues Explosion performed live.

During this time, I was staying at friends' houses in NYC. My friend Tomoyo always took care of me when we were in New York, and I stayed at her place for a while. One day, Kim, Thurston, and Julia suddenly showed up at Tomoyo's front door and said: "Yoshimi! Get your drumsticks and trumpet, and get in a taxi with us now!" So we headed over to a studio, and when we got there, they had me listen to "Oh Bondage! Up Yours!" by X-Ray Spex. They told me, "Learn this song now, we're gonna start recording right away!"

This was the first time I'd heard the song, so I listened to it a bunch of times, then covered the sax part with my trumpet, and kinda did my own take on the drum part [*laughs*]. I remember covering the song in my own way right after listening it. I saw Kim and Julie both playing guitar, and thought to myself, *There's no bass?* All three of us sang on the song, and they told me, "Yoshimi you gotta scream," so I screamed as loud as I could! Julie and Kim told me they'd started a band called Kitten and that they wanted me to join as the drummer, and I was like "Yeah sure!" so the band came together quickly like that.

I couldn't speak English very well, so it was a really thrilling and fun experience for me. It made me realize that even if you don't exchange words that much, as long as you do what's in front of you and have fun with it and if you're being yourself, then you can communicate that way. Everything came together quickly even without us speaking much about it, and it was a really easy process.

Back then, I had misheard the pronunciation of the word "kitten" as "kitchen." There were some people from another band called Kitten who complained that we had the same name, so I remember that our band name was changed to Free Kitten right after I joined. Until I saw the band name Free Kitten on our picture disk vinyl for "Oh Bondage! Up Yours!," I had thought that our band name was Free Kitchen [*laughs*].

There's another thing I remember telling Kim back then. I told her: "In Japan, when people reach the age of twenty, they participate in a coming-of-age ceremony called *seijinshiki*, where women wear traditional kimonos called *furisode* and men wear *haori-hakama*. I didn't go to the ceremony, but I dressed up in a *furisode* like it was cosplay, and took this photograph. I'm giving you this photo as a gift from Japan." I was staying at Tomoyo's house back then, and she used to work as a BDSM dominatrix. So when I was staying at her place, she let me wear her bondage costume, and I had my picture taken just for fun. I told Kim, "Hey, I took this cosplay photo. Don't show these photos to anyone, they're gifts just for you!" Kim was like, "Thanks!" but now that I think about it, she might have had a slightly evil smile on her face, like she had thought of an idea...

Our cover of "Oh Bondage! Up Yours!" was released on Sympathy for the Record Industry, which was a label that only released 7" singles. The B-side featured a live recording of a song that Free Kitten performed in Japan. I knew that Kim had put one over on me when I saw the actual picture disk with me in a bondage outfit on the "Oh Bondage! Up Yours!" side and me in a *furisode* on the other side with the song "1, 2, 3" which was recorded live at Shelter Club in Tokyo. So I saw myself wearing these costumes on the record and spinning on the turntable, and there was no way for me to stop people from seeing the record...but my mom saw the side with me wearing a kimono, and she was like "What a pretty photo!," as if it were one of those souvenir dinner plates that people get with their photos printed on them. So I kind of freaked out when this record was released, but now looking back on it, I'm so thankful for the experience.

Kim: I'm sorry Yoshimi, I totally forgot about this, that was very naughty of us, we thought you were good with it. To me you're a very unconventional person within Japanese culture, which from the outside seems to place a great value on conformity. Can you talk a bit about what your parents were like—were they unconventional as well? And how you were you trained as musician—if you were? How did you come to make such experimental music but also with so much spirituality? In Japan you are a huge icon and yet completely uncommercial. I see you as my musical sister: playing with men, but not thinking about it too much, forming your own group OOIOO with all women, making an avant-garde clothes line...I'm asking all these questions because I have never found an in-depth interview with you in an English publication...

Yoshimi: My mother is the youngest of three siblings and has two older brothers. Her family owned a store that sold traditional Japanese and Western clothing. My mother's father died in a car accident when she was still in junior high. She loved animals and music, and all the neighborhood cats loved her, so she was called the "cat girl." Her family had a pet goat, and she even witnessed it giving birth to a baby goat. So she grew up milking goats, dancing to traditional Japanese dance, playing piano, and studying for music school. She's a very cheerful, limber, cute mom, and was introduced to my father through her mother.

My father is the eldest of three siblings. He sang in a male chorus group when he was a student, and loved singing and baseball. He is a kind man, and he worked as an executive at a company owned by his father, a wholesaler of Japanese and Western clothing, bedding and fabrics. My parents had an arranged marriage which was popular in Japan during the Shōwa era, but they also felt they were destined to meet each other, and they love each other very much. My mother apparently wanted to have lots of children, but I didn't have any sisters or brothers, and grew up as an only child.

My mother taught piano, so I'm not sure if it was my own choice, but I took piano lessons for a while. Actually, at first, I wasn't taking conventional piano lessons, it was a class called *"cho-on"* which was taught by nuns at a church. In *cho-on* classes, a nun would play an improvised melody, which I would notate onto paper, and I would have to pronounce the notes "C, D, E, F, G, A" in German, rather than the typical "do-re-mi-fa." I started taking these lessons from the age of three, and my mom said I could start taking actual piano lessons after I completed the *cho-on* classes, which I took at a local church.

Apparently I have perfect pitch, but never really understood what that was; I was actually a little embarrassed about having this ability, since it is bound by the limitations of Western music theory. In the classes, I would have to answer correctly which note was C, but when you think about it, we don't even know who came up with the concept of the C note. I was more interested in the notes in between do-re-mi-fa-so-la-ti-do, and I would hum melodies using those in-between notes, because it felt good when those notes reverberated in my skull. Since I loved the in-between notes so much, the piano felt limiting to me. I started taking piano lessons when I was in the first grade. My mom decided not to teach me herself since it might lead to arguments, so she hired a piano teacher that she thought would be a good fit for me.

But I didn't have fun taking piano lessons. I couldn't find any songs that I enjoyed playing, and though I was able to read sheet music back then, which I no longer can, I only read it because I had to do it for those lessons. I was bored of playing music from sheets, so what I started doing for fun was using a dust cloth, and sliding it on the piano keys as if I were cleaning them, and making sounds. I would slide the dust cloth over the black keys, and play them so it sounded like a harp. I would also stand on the piano, and play the keys with my feet! When you do this, you get these unpredictable melodies and rhythms. It also sounds nostalgic at the same time, so I had a lot of fun doing that.

The first record I ever bought was in elementary school. It was a Christmas record by a masked wrestler named Destroyer who was from America. Destroyer was his wrestler name, but he just looked like a kind old man who loved children. The cover featured the masked face of Destroyer, but the music was all heart-warming Christmas songs. You would never imagine that it was a Christmas record from the cover. I loved the gap between the cover and the music.

When I was in the sixth grade, I found a record with a really scary cover at the record store. It had a robot on it and I bought it because it freaked me out. But I wanted to overcome the fear I had. It was the first record I ever bought—and it was a Queen record—because I was drawn to the cover.

Back then, I was really into recording vinyl onto cassettes. But I would record the sound playing from the speakers, instead of a direct recording using a cable. I would borrow records from an older guy in the neighborhood, and I would play the sound coming out from the speakers onto a double cassette player that my parents bought me. After recording the Queen record onto a cassette, I recorded myself whispering over the music, because it made me feel like I was a part of the record. So my home recording history started by using this double cassette player.

I also recorded the sound of myself peeing in the bathroom. I kept on layering the sound of myself peeing by bouncing the tracks, and at the end it sounded like an enormous waterfall. I felt so good about myself for recording that sound. I was an only child, so I would stay in my room by myself and do whatever I thought was fun, so I had a really happy childhood.

My mom was always fun to be with and she was like my best friend. I love my mom dearly, and she also had her own history.

She had two older brothers and the oldest one was one of my biggest influences during my childhood. My uncle was a spiritual seeker. He was seriously trying to gain supernatural powers through his own efforts. He wasn't interested in being possessed by another entity and gaining supernatural powers from that. He wanted to have supernatural powers that he developed on his own. Through spiritual training, he was trying to gain the power of remote viewing, healing people's diseases and helping others to fulfill their mission in life.

My uncle also happened to be a collector of jazz records. He loved music, but the way he listened to music was through vibrations. Whether it was pop music or alternative, he wasn't interested in listening to the superficial sounds of the records.

I always loved seeing his reactions when he listened to the music I recorded. He was fascinated that I started playing drums in a band called Boredoms when I went to art school in Kyoto. He always asked me to let him listen to the music when we released an album. He was interested in the sounds I was creating, what kind of people I was performing with, what kind of music was being made, and what dimension the music was coming from. When I was about twenty-eight years old, he predicted the day that he would die, and then he died on that exact day.

When I moved from Okayama to Kyoto to go to art school, I had no idea that I would be playing music with the people I met by chance for years to come. I was frantically just taking in all the new sensations I was experiencing at the time. I met Eye in 1986. I didn't know about Boredoms. All I knew was Eye made music as Hanatarash by using objects that weren't musical instruments. I didn't even know that this kind of music was called "noise" back then. Since I was influenced by my uncle who saw all music as vibration, I didn't see any separation between noise music and piano music.

Eye asked me, "Do you want to play drums?" even though I'd never played drums in my life, nor imagined that I would.

But I was instantly drawn to what it might sound like if I did. So I said "Yeah sure, I'll try playing drums!" From then on, I got really interested in playing in a band. I thought of a band as a space where you can experiment and see what instruments you are compatible with, rather than a place to just play music. The other people couldn't play instruments either, but everybody was interested in seeing what kind of sounds they could make. The conventional approach to playing an instrument is to master a certain technique, make the instrument vibrate and play music. But I was drawn to the simplicity of the drums, where you could just bang on it to make sounds, which was what I also liked about the piano. There was no textbook or manual we followed. From the beginning, we were there to play with sound, just like children.

I completely ignored the musical education I received on the piano, and was excited by the prospect of collaborating with people by playing drums. In 1986, I decided to play drums with Eye and a bassist named Hayashi from Kyoto in a band called UFO or Die, which was my first band. Both Eye and myself loved how Hayashi played bass. He was a fan of Jaco Pastorius, Lemmy from Motörhead, and Sid Vicious from the Sex Pistols. Even though I was a beginner on the drums, he would always say, "Wow, you play so well!" and he would follow my drum playing on the bass. He was such a great bassist. I joined Boredoms in 1988, playing drums and singing on the second album *Soul Discharge*.

Another relative that influenced me was my mom's second brother. My mom's oldest brother was the one who was into the supernatural world. The younger brother was the exact opposite of my "supernatural" uncle. He was someone who was full of human imperfections and loved to sing. He was an eccentric person who loved chubby women, was always sweating, and would sleep naked on the roof to dry his body.

I loved it when this uncle would sing the song "My Way." He would sing in key, but would completely ignore the instrumental track, and would just sing it the way he wanted to, as if he had

67

never heard the original. Whenever there was a family gathering, he would sing "My Way" to his heart's content, and I would just watch him in awe. He was so funny. There was always a sense of not knowing what was going to happen next when he would start singing. He said that the COVID-19 pandemic made humans boring, which made him lose hope in humanity, and he ended up taking his own life.

I also loved my maternal grandmother. She was incredibly good at playing the Japanese board game Othello, and at one point she said that she wanted to go on a journey to find someone who was better than her at playing the board game. My grandma also loved to sing, and became a master of shamisen and traditional Japanese *nagauta* music. She loved to sing traditional Japanese songs, but she also loved my music.

I think it was in 1988 when Sonic Youth came to Japan for the first time, and performed two days of shows at the old Shinjuku Loft in Tokyo with Boredoms. If I remember correctly, UFO or Die played on one day, and Boredoms played on the second day. Sonic Youth and Boredoms were also asked to perform in the Kansai region and did a show at a hall at the Kyoto Institute of Technology.

My grandma said she wanted to see me playing drums live at least once before she died, so my parents brought her to the Boredoms and Sonic Youth show. Later on, I heard from our live engineer that there was an elderly woman standing on a chair beside the PA booth with her arms in the air screaming and having fun. He said that he was worried that the woman might fall from the chair and hurt herself. (It was my grandma.)

Kim: This is blowing my mind to hear! How much were you aware of the Japanese avant-garde growing up? What kind of music did you listen to as a teenager? Did you listen to seventies prog rock like Nights of the Assassins? Were you aware of the punk and underground scene around the Drugstore in

Kyoto? When did you become aware of the No Wave scene in New York? Was it through John Zorn? Ikue Mori?

Yoshimi: Before I entered art school, I went to a summer school to prepare for the entrance exams. During the day I studied sketching techniques, color, and three-dimensional drawings. At night, I would go to clubs to see shows. That's when I saw a band called Noizunzuri from Kyoto, and they had a huge impact on me.

This band played really strange music. It sounded similar to PiL but the male vocalist had a really unique voice, and sung melodies that sounded like traditional Japanese music. I loved the earth-shaking bass, and the percussive guitar that had just the right amount of presence in the music. The drummer was a really beautiful woman, and apparently it was her first time playing drums in the band. Her rhythms had a really sparse sound, and she would sing background vocals while banging on the floor toms.

There was something nostalgic about their sound, but avant-garde at the same time, and it was right up my alley. Later I found out that the first guitarist in Boredoms was the guitarist for Noizunzuri. I later became friends with the woman who played drums for them, but after the band broke up, she stopped playing and got married, leaving her days of being in a band behind.

With Eye and Hayashi I started the band UFO or Die, and began writing songs, doing home recordings, releasing 7"s, drawing the cover artwork, and playing shows. After rehearsing once, I would play the drums at the venue. Back then, I didn't know that you could adjust the height of the drums, so I would leave them as they were after the drummer in the previous band played them. I would be thinking, "Wow, these drums are so hard to play," but would also be thinking, "I can get different nuances out of the drums that I couldn't before," so I'd kind of enjoy the limitations. I relied on my physical connection to the instrument to create sounds. Whenever I would scream and play snare rolls at the same time, my drum playing would get better. I joined Boredoms in 1988 and we started recording the second album *Soul Discharge* right away.

For me, it was never about playing music because I was influenced by someone else's band. I didn't have any interest in the music of Boredoms before I joined the band. But after I joined them, I got more and more into in their music. I'm the kind of person that engages impulsively with whatever is in front of me.

I've never verbalized what punk rock means to me. Everything I do is out of impulse, so I don't know if that's "punk" or "rock." I've always just followed my impulses, and created sounds that emanate from being myself.

I think I first met John Zorn in 1986, as he lived in Japan for about ten years. When John started Cobra, he asked me and Eye to join. John is like my second dad in NYC. He always listens to any music that I release and always supports the music I make. When I went to a record store with him for the first time, I bought Cecil Taylor's *Unit Structures* after he recommended it to me.

Eye was the one who told me, "You've got to buy the *No New York* compilation!" I saw Ikue Mori for the first time on the back of that cover, and DNA became one of my favorite bands.

Before I started playing drums in the Boredoms, the drummers I first admired were Iku-chan from Noizunzuri and Ikue from DNA, and I was listening to their drums instead of listening to the band's songs. Their drumming styles were so unique and stayed true to who they were, so when I was asked, "Do you want to play drums?" I thought, *Maybe I can do this!* Those drummers made me feel that the drums were the coolest instrument on earth.

Seiichi Yamamoto, who played guitar in Boredoms in the nineties, owns a venue called Bears, where Ikue Mori and I met for the first time in '87 or '89. We performed a twin drum show at this club. The performers that day were John Zorn, Ikue Mori,

Bill Frisell, Yamatsuka Eye, and myself. It was a dream come true playing twin drums with Ikue. I don't remember what I played, but I remember toning down my drumming so I could hear more of Ikue. But midway through the show I couldn't hear anything at all.

Ikue and I became very close, and she's like a mother or sister to me. Ikue started performing with a drum machine instead of a drum kit, and she told me, "Since you're around, I'm going to quit playing the drums and leave them up to you." The next time we did a twin drum set was in 2016 or 2017 at Union Pool in Brooklyn with your band, Body/Head, Kim.

Kim: I always loved watching Ikue play drums in DNA and it was my dream to play with her that way. To see you both play together was surreal. Can you talk about Saicobab and Saicobaba? What is the difference between them? How is it different from OOIOO and Boredoms?

Yoshimi: I started a project called Saicobaba (saico = ancient, baba = old lady) where we performed completely improvisational shows. In both Saicobaba and Saicobab, Daikiti Yoshida, a sitar player, is at the core of the group. I met him at a rehearsal studio in Osaka, where Boredoms used to rehearse from the nineties to the 2010s. He used to be a guitarist who was known for a very delicate sound, but when I met him, he was only playing sitar.

He had difficulty making a living just playing guitar, so he also worked as a guitar tech for other professional guitarists, but he got sick of the music industry in Osaka. I didn't know anything about the difficulties of the music industry in Osaka that Daikiti was a part of. That would be obvious, because I don't know anything about the music industry in general in Japan. I only know about the world of Boredoms, which is a space I helped to create, and it's my home. By the time I met Daikiti, he had already started playing the sitar. He impulsively flew to India and found his mentor (he studied sitar from 1996 under Ustad Shujaat Khan, who is the seventh-generation sitar master from the illustrious Imdadkhani school of sitar playing).

Whenever I saw Daikiti at the studio, he would say, "I'm so envious of you because you're always creating music based on your impulses. What you're doing looks so fun and it sounds authentic." He would always smile as he watched me play drums and sing. When I would play guitar in OOIOO, he would always say, "You have such a unique way of playing. How can you be so free?" He is a very technical musician, but he seemed to enjoy my improvisational and unpredictable style of playing.

I didn't take Daikiti's words for granted. I place of lot of importance on improvisation, and my technique is reading the vibe in the room, and creating sounds freely, whether or not I'm listening to what the other musicians are playing. There are some people who fall in love with one instrument and master it, and they become one with that instrument by honing their skills, but that approach is not my forte. My approach to musical expression is about becoming friends with an instrument, understanding its characteristics, and inserting myself into the world of that instrument.

With people like Daikiti and U-zhaan [Shujaat Khan], they fell in love with their instruments, practiced for many years, and became one with their instruments. When I improvise with them, I listen to their sounds, and then layer the sounds that emanate from within me on top of what they're doing.

I seem to be the type of person that can easily ignore the rules of the universe that were discovered by the ancients...But I also know that you need to train yourself to be able to understand the ancient rules of the universe first, in order to be able to ignore them and still make interesting music. I've never been to India or studied Indian classical music, but my approach when dealing with music from another culture is to offer myself as one form of culture, and to layer myself on top of the music.

Saicobaba is a raga band made up of myself, U-zhaan on tabla and Daikiti on sitar. They invited me to join by saying, "Yoshimi, you can just ignore the classical music we're playing and improvise your vocals over what we do." (U-zhaan studied with tabla masters Zakir Hussain and Anindo Chatterjee. He is now the leading tabla player in Japan.)

In the 1990s and 2000s, whenever Boredoms played shows in Japan, we had Daikiti open up with a solo sitar performance. He'd be playing sitar by himself on a big stage on top of a beautiful rug, and when people would enter the venue, you could tell that his performance changed the whole vibe of the space.

With Saicobaba I would never rehearse, but would just show up at the venue and improvise my vocals over their music. For years, I would improvise over U-zhaan and Daikiti's Indian classical ragas using just my raw sensibilities. I would vocalize only when it felt right. In a way, it was my own internal practice, and it was a way for me to get in touch with myself.

While performing with Saicobaba, I got a clearer picture of what I really wanted to do, which was Saicobab (which means "ancient baby"). It was closer to the concept I wanted to work off of. I've been fascinated by hardcore and punk music since my youth, and I was able to find that hardcore element within the ragas.

We would play this ancient music at very fast BPMs and improvise. I asked Daikiti to create grindcore raga music, and use melodies that were based on classical Indian music. I would then practice those melodies, but I would let go of it all as soon as I mastered it. I could find myself in the polyrhythms, and I wanted to understand them in my own way and sing! So in a way, I was the vocalist in a hardcore band! That was the intent that came up inside of me for this band.

Boredoms is a band that attempts to recreate the musical vision that Eye has in his head. So when I play with Boredoms, I am dedicating my performance to the group and layering my sounds over the music. When I say "dedication," it's not a farfetched concept. I am becoming a part of the whole, which is Boredoms.

It's always difficult to explain the different approaches I have for each band. They're all a part of me, and it's hard to put into words.

Kim: I believe that you are expressing yourself in Saicobab in a way that you can't in Boredoms or OOIOO, but what part of you are you expressing? What is the relationship between these three bands, and what is the musical element that runs through all of these bands? Do these bands influence each other in any way?

Yoshimi: I often get asked this question about Saicobab, since the three bands have such a different sound. I don't play music in different bands to fill in the gaps that I'm not able to with other bands. Bands are as different as different countries and cultures. That's also true when you session with different musicians. What direction you're facing when you play together, the humidity in the air, the weather, what environment the other musicians grew up in, what past lives they've lived all influence and change the music. So there's no way to say that there's one definitive approach to a band. Everything feels new to me, and I approach each project as a newcomer. I don't play music unless it involves a process of excavating what is inside of me. Rather than just expressing myself, I want to discover what sounds will emanate from inside of me when I place myself in certain situations. The only thing that these bands have in common is that I am in them, which is not such a big deal.

Kim: I can totally relate to this, Yoshimi, that is so well said. So much of Sonic Youth and other bands I've been in had so much to do with what each person brought to it. Their personalities and music and other influences. I like to think of it as eccentric music, but every band is special in that you take away one person and it changes the vibe and is not the same. I love the fusion of many genres of music in Japanese underground music, and especially Boredoms beyond the New York No Wave scene. Were you aware of other indie bands in America, like the Butthole Surfers? Did you talk about certain bands or was it just an organic process of making music? I feel like Sun Ra must have been a big influence on you and Boredoms...

Yoshimi: I'm the kind of person that doesn't understand how to categorize music into genres. Whenever I play drums in a group, I become a part of that group, and the sounds I create become a part of the band's music, so I'm not conscious of what influences my sound. When I decide to play an instrument, it's not because I'm influenced by some other music. The person that has influenced me the most when it comes to playing in bands is my "spiritual seeker" uncle, who listened to the vibrations of music. We would listen to music together and try to figure out which dimension the music came from.

So it was encouraging to see someone like Sun Ra who came from Saturn, and incorporated Saturn's vibrations into his music. The members of the Arkestra all wore costumes that were styled after Saturn, and when they played their instruments, it became one entity. All of the members followed Sun Ra's vision, and it felt like their music was radiating into the world. It was as if the Sun Ra Arkestra was being influenced by themselves and creating music cyclically.

I witnessed a Sun Ra show at SOB's in NYC...possibly the year that he passed away. I think it was during a Boredoms tour.

He came out in a wheelchair and was placed in front of his keyboards and synthesizers. Sounds emanated as soon as his fingertips touched the keys. It was as if his fingers were already playing music in the empty space when he raised his hands. I'm not exaggerating when I say that it seemed as if the keys happened to touch his fingers, which then produced sounds.

When I witnessed that, I was convinced that music becomes audible when the musician is physically touching the instrument, but the music is already being played within that person.

If the music you hear is made up of the vibrations being emitted from one person, layering multiple sounds on top of each other is an extraordinary phenomenon. Then you have an audience who comes to see that, and they bring that influence home with them. Music is vibration, so it enters people's bodies and souls like light.

In order to be able to make the music audible that is already playing within you, you need to prepare yourself as a vessel to receive the music. You could say that that's my technique. It's all about keeping yourself light and putting yourself in the position to receive, rather than being tense.

I never practice my instruments or even listen to music. When it comes time to perform or record, I become one with the environment I'm in, and enter the state to vocalize or create sound. Right before the moment I'm creating sound, I'm thinking of other things.

The Butthole Surfers were one of Eye's favorite bands back then. He's a record collector and deep listener, and he taught me about all types of music.

When I heard the Butthole Surfers for the first time, Gibby's voice reminded me of Hibari Misora's [legendary Japanese singer] song "Ringo Oiwake." The music had a melancholy sound to it. Paul's guitar phrases reminded me of traditional Japanese folk music. I related to the twin drum set up they had with a male and female drummer. In 1993, when Boredoms did a U.S. tour, King Coffey came to see our show in Austin. We connected with him there, and later Boredoms and the Butthole Surfers performed together in Japan. I remember that I stopped playing drums midway through the show to dive into the audience. I think it was because the audience seemed to be having so much fun that I impulsively wanted to be where they were, instead of playing drums on stage.

Kim: Thank you for your very generous answers. Here is a last one. You come from a culture that has such appreciation for music and musicians, as well as very expressive fans. While I feel grateful that people are interested in what I do, sometimes I feel a disconnect between who I am and my public persona, what people project on me. As you've become more well-known and an inspiration to many people all over the world, do you ever feel uncomfortable with it?

Yoshimi: There is a disconnect there and being in this position makes me feel uncomfortable sometimes. But it's all a part of me. When I create music or art and express myself, in a way, I'm exposing everything that is inside of me to the outside world. As soon as my expression makes its way into the world, the person who receives it interprets it in their own way. The receiver will project themselves onto me, the source of the expression, and create their own mental image of me. All the different people who receive my expression will have different mental images of me, so in a way there are multitudes of "me" that exist. By the time a person receives my expression, I don't exist there anymore. So being the source of this expression, all I can do is be myself and express myself honestly. My job is to expose the sounds that are within me in a way that feels good to me, and be myself to the best of my abilities.

Double-Digit Jukebox:
An Essay in Eight Mixes

Leslie Jamison

Mix #1: NYC vs. LA

When I was a kid, it felt easiest to get close to my inscrutable teenage brothers by loving the things they loved: epic tennis rivalries, the Washington Redskins, Bob Dylan, and the Star Wars trilogy, especially *The Empire Strikes Back*—clearly the best film of the three, they said, a verdict I began repeating to other eight-year-olds with an air of absolute authority.

My brother Eliot, especially, was as mysterious as a locked room, but sometimes I could hear music playing behind his closed bedroom door: Springsteen belting out the thrilling opening lyrics to "Atlantic City," *they blew up the chicken man in Philly last night*; the gruff soul-summoning of Bono's scratchy voice from "Achtung Baby": *when it's one need, in the night*; or the harmonica-jangled charm of Dylan himself, bidding someone a wry, mournful fare-well in "It Ain't Me, Babe." (Did he really tell her to "leave at her own chosen speed"? It seemed so.)

It was hard to crack Eliot open—as a third-grader, I even wrote a poem in the shape of a cereal bowl about how quiet he was at breakfast—and I was desperate for whatever scraps fell off the table of his opaque interior. When he gave me a wallet-sized photo taken at his prom, because I begged him for it, I kept it on my dresser for more than a year, even though his date hadn't been his girlfriend or even his friend, just because it offered a rare glimpse of his life. Even now, almost twenty years later, I can still remember her name, Amanda, and picture the sleek curtain of her straight blonde hair against her gold lace-patterned dress.

In many ways, he was deeply reserved, but I can still remember the delight in his voice when he took me through the lyrics to Dylan's "Fourth Time Around": how Dylan sings about saying good-bye to a woman (again!) by "gallantly hand[ing] her my very last piece of gum," and then—Eliot got excited, explaining this—how the gum *comes back around*, a few lyrics later, when the woman gets upset and the speaker says, "Your words aren't clear, you'd better spit out your gum." Eliot loved the minor plotline of the gum, and he loved pointing it out, and I loved him pointing it out, although I didn't have the faintest clue what the song's weightiest lyrics might mean to him: "Don't forget / Everybody must give something back for something they get." Even if I could not access Eliot's most intense feelings, I could access one of the things that was capable of summoning them. This was the thrill of his music.

When Eliot left home for college, I was just nine years old. In the way of many single-digit people, my feelings were bottomless and capitalized: I was Abandoned and Heartbroken. We lived in Los Angeles, a city my brother had never particularly liked, and he left for college in New York City, a place he loved immediately, more passionately than I'd seen him love anything besides tennis and Dylan. The following summer, he came back from college with a new (New Yorker) girlfriend and a mixtape they'd made together: half the songs were about Los Angeles, the other half about New York. The mixtape was meant to stage a battle—NYC vs. LA, which city had inspired more epic music—but the contest was stacked from the start: in truth, both my transplant brother and his native girlfriend believed that New York was a better city, and that it had inspired better music.

I fervently defended the LA songs, from Tom Petty's "Free Fallin'," *All the vampires walkin' through the valley / Move west down Ventura Boulevard*, to Guns N' Roses' "Paradise City," *where the grass is green and the girls are pretty*...I defended the LA songs not because I liked them more—though I mean, how cool to think of Vampires walking down Ventura?—but because I wanted my brother to like me. My brother's love for New York, his deepening dislike for our home city, felt like a rejection of the world we shared—the sunlit, salt-breeze world of the west—and proof that he migrated somewhere better. So I defended what we shared— our city—because I wanted to share something with him. In truth, I didn't know *what* I liked, because my taste had been shaped around his—like a plant bending toward the light, I bent toward the things he loved as a way of bending myself toward the sense of being loved by him.

Mix #2: Alien

The first boy I ever kissed was also the first boy I ever slept with; he was also the first boy who ever gave me a mixtape, and the first boy I ever fell in love with. You could say I moved quickly, or else you could say I was a late bloomer, depending how you looked at it. All this happened during my senior year of high school.

I'll call him Mark. He had bright blue eyes like chipped shards of sea glass, fine blond hair like a downy fur across his scalp, and a pair of tattoos he kept hidden from his parents. He'd gotten the second one right between his shoulder blades a few days before his high-school graduation, and he spent the whole day wincing as well-wishers clapped him on the back. His arms were covered in cuts he told his mom were cat scratches. I knew the truth. I cut myself too.

I was so crazy about Mark that I'd even gone with him to a 311 concert. And even I—generally so malleable to a man's desires that I could barely discern my own—could tell how shitty their music was. I mean, you didn't have to call information to find their blandly sugar-coated, hacky-sack pitter-patter stoner riffs both grafted and grating. *Amber is the color of your energy?* Not mine!

But Mark's relationship to positivity, as conversational default and life philosophy, was born from root systems of pain that ran deep into his childhood. For this reason, I respected his general desire to "keep it light," musically and otherwise. This righteous forbearance took me all the way to Santa Barbara for a 311 concert where the moral of most of their music seemed to be: This song is impossible to enjoy unless you're stoned. Only trouble was, I generally got anxious and twitchy when I was stoned, which didn't stop me from doing it a fair amount anyway. (See also: malleable to the desires of others.) I was the stoned girl circling the swimming pool, telling the other kids it really wasn't safe to be in there if they'd been drinking—which was pretty much the opposite, I realized, of what being stoned was supposed to feel like.

Anyway, my one true 311-loving love made me a mixtape! This was right before the dawn of Napster and the ascendance of digital music, right before mixtapes started to feel like artifacts of the past. It was also right before Mark and I left for our respective colleges. Just a few days before my flight across the country, he told me he didn't think we should stay together. Long-distance seemed untenable, and he was staying on the West Coast, while I was headed East; which I'd come to understand as the more sophisticated side of the country. At least, it was the coast where all the men in my family kept going. But now, this man was staying. When he said he thought we should break up, I got so angry I went home and smashed a stack of plastic cups against my bedroom wall, then used the shards to cut myself. I called him, basically hyperventilating over the phone, and he said he wanted to come and talk it out but his dad wouldn't let him use the car. Double-digit feelings, double-digit problems.

When I drove to his house the next night, the last night before I got on an airplane to Boston, my heartache was a double-decker heartache: the sting of being rejected, and the shame at how fully this rejection overwhelmed me. It seemed to speak to a lack of inner resources.

As soon as I arrived at his place, Mark told me that he'd made me a mix. It told a story, he said. We lay on his bed and listened: First came the jaunty stuff that represented our salad days, Blink 182's iconic "Josie," *Yeah, my girlfriend takes me home when I'm too drunk to drive*, and the inevitable 311: *I know a drugstore cowgirl so afraid of getting bored*...Then it veered hard into emo songs meant to express the ways we understood each other's darker parts, the secret conversations between our scars, Eels singing: *I am OK. I'm not OK.* The tape culminated with the Bush song "Alien," a power ballad lurking in the shadows of their better-known radio hit, "Glycerine." And as "Alien" played in his bedroom, *And she comes to take me away / She's all that I needed*, Mark told me that he'd changed his mind: he wanted to stay together. It was the most romantic moment of my life. I hadn't had very many romantic moments, but this was romantic enough to make up for all the ones I hadn't had before.

As the chorus bleated its plaintive, earnest gibberish—*I'm an alien, you're an alien / It's a beautiful rain, a beautiful rain*—Mark kept talking: he'd always felt like an alien. I was the only one who'd ever really understood him. Lying on his twin bed listening to Gavin Rossdale's dark crooning, it didn't even matter that the lyrics barely made sense (beautiful rain?). It didn't matter if I didn't like 311. It didn't matter if I actually got a little annoyed when Mark got so drunk and stoned I had to take care of him. (*I wanted to be the one who got so drunk and stoned I needed to be taken care of!*) All that mattered was that I needed him to need me. It all feels impossibly innocent now—believing that saying

I need you could be enough—but I still feel a tenderness for this girl, who needed, so badly, to hear this more than anything else.

Mix #3: Scar Fuel

When I was twenty-one years old, living and drinking amongst fellow aspiring writers in Iowa City—this unexpected midwestern mecca, home to the oldest writing program in the country— my friend gave me a mixtape that was actually a mix-CD, silver-sleek and home-burned. Everything was big in those Iowa days: Big Skies, Big Highways, Big Cornfields, Big Feelings, Big Horizons, Big Strip Malls, Big Buffets. I'd play my music loud and drive around experiencing my emotions as if it were my job. My actual job was teaching undergraduates, which terrified me. Many of them were older than I was, just like the friend who'd given me this mix. Honestly everyone at the Iowa Writers' Workshop— which we called, insufferably, just "the Workshop"—was a little bit older than me. My nickname was "barely legal."

One night in the middle of winter, the friend who'd given me the mix called me after his car broke down and he found himself stranded by the side of the highway. I jumped out of bed and went to pick him up immediately. It was barely above zero. He could die out there! This was January in Iowa! The landscape was suburban but deadly; its stakes high.

Whenever I drove the small highways through fields of corn and soy—picking up a cheap strip-mall mattress, or heading out to the farmer's auction outside of town, taking a friend visiting from New York to the cheese factory in Amish country, where you could buy a tub of squeaky curds (this was pretty much the extent of our tourist attractions)—I loved listening to my friend's mix because it felt like a speculative soundtrack to the life I was embarking on, a roadmap to all the Intense Emotional Experiences I felt destined to have. It was full of songs that seemed like sweeping epics written specifically (of course) about my life.

In "Oh, Mandy!" the Spinto Band rocked out about B-grade cinematic life: *Show me a rerun on the WB / So what's it like to be in it / And move away to the Midwest…* Andrew Bird sang about self-narrating romance even while you were living it, accumulating its particulars like fine details for a short story:

she says I like long walks and sci-fi movies
If you're six foot tall and east coast bred
Some lonely night we can get together
And I'm gonna tie your wrists with leather

But my favorite song was Band of Horses' "The Funeral," whose throbbing melancholy was the soundtrack to pathetic two-mile runs that taxed my smoker lungs, and which I mistakenly believed was actually called "Scar Fuel." I perpetually misheard the song's chorus: *At every occasion once more, it's called the funeral…* To me it sounded like: *Every occasion wants more scar fuel…* I loved the idea of scar fuel! I wanted more of it! In Iowa, everyone seemed to know more than I did about music, about love, about *life*—the stuff of living, which was also, to all of us, the *material*. I needed Experience the way an artist needs paint.

So much of the time, this experience still revolved around men—or at least, the strongest emotions did—which was a source of pride and shame at once. Romance still felt like the realest possible life to me, the most distilled form of experience; but I was also starting to sense the shop-worn edges of this conception of reality. Weren't there other things besides men worth having strong feelings about? It was actually a deep relief when I found myself in a bathroom stall one day crying about a *story*, not a man. Feeling something, at last, about my work.

Mix #4: My Girls

Five years later, I found myself driving back to Iowa once more—listening to different music, with a different man in the driver's seat. I'd been living on the East Coast, but my partner—my great love, my possible soulmate—was starting at the very same Writers Workshop I'd completed several years before, so we were moving back to Iowa to build a life together in a little white clapboard house overlooking a park near the sorority houses. Looking back at my twenty-one-year-old self, my mid-twenties self felt *very* mature. Dave and I were going to be adults. We were going to play house together, make it stick, make it work. Make salad every night. Make cocktails for our new friends and serve them on our porch.

In the meantime, we were listening to a mix he'd put together for our drive. It was all indie music that made me feel cooler: a step up from the pop emo radio hits that I binged on like comfort food. (In my heart, I'd always be a seventeen-year-old smoking and listening to Coldplay's "Yellow" on my headphones.) This mix was full of the Dirty Projectors and Animal Collective, and from the clanging chords of "Stillness is the Move" rose great lyrical truths:

> On top of every mountain
> There was a great longing
> For another even higher mountain

As the School of Seven Bells' "Half-Asleep" carried us across the endless expanse of Pennsylvania—the state was "more than just Philadelphia," we were finding out—and the wind rushed through our open windows, we remembered seeing them play live in a room with walls plush and red as a womb (a womb room!) at the Wellesley Student Center, just five minutes' drive from where Dave had grown up. *If you're six foot tall and east coast bred*...he was both!

But the true centerpiece of our driving mix was Animal Collective's "My Girls," a surging anthem that started with a tinkly pitter-pattering of synth, joined by voices like shamans singing across the hills: *There isn't much that I feel I need / A solid soul and the blood I bleed*...As we listened to them clapping and incanting their declarations: *I just want / Four walls and adobe slats / For my girls*...I heard an anthem for a way of living that was all about the soul and the home. The artist as maker and dweller. This is what we were going to be: Soul Dwellers. Together.

Once we were living that life—which was beautiful, but also fissured with conflict—I'd find myself playing that song on repeat, over and over again, just to bring back the feeling of hope that had swelled in me when I first heard it. Those years would see me struggling to make a relationship work, rather than just leaving when it got hard; they'd see me getting sober, publishing a novel. But I was still so fragile, like a leaf blown around in the wind, my feelings unbearably powerful. And I was still listening to a man's music, still trying hard to please him, to be exactly what he wanted. After blasting Top 40 hits in our car, I'd turn the radio dial to NPR so that when he next started the car he'd think that's what I'd been listening to.

In truth, I'd been eager to adopt Dave's taste in music because it felt far more subtle and sophisticated than my own. It was like preferring sashimi to birthday cake. Even when I genuinely loved his songs, as I came to genuinely love "My Girls," I still loved them wrong, somehow—loved them too much, listening to them over and over again, binging on them like I binged on pastries and wine. I always wanted *too much*—just like I still wanted to get blackout drunk, every night, rather than just enjoying a drink or two; just like I wanted texts from Dave all the time, because otherwise I'd stop believing I was loved. Restraint was never my jam. Jam was my jam: infinite sweetness, infinite feeling, infinite song.

Mix #5: Wounded Mix

During that second stint in Iowa, I also had a day job. Four days a week, I worked twelve-hour shifts at a bakery overlooking the train tracks on the south side of town. When I changed into my uniform in the bathroom by the coffee machine, at the start of my seven a.m. shifts, I was often hungover and/or crying. Mostly it felt like sheer relief to get carried out of whatever I was feeling by facing my production list, always clipped to the side of the walk-in freezer: rolling out shortbread dough and punching out snowmen or pumpkins; icing little green frogs holding tiny valentines; prepping the cold brew for the next morning, pulling espresso shots for (invariably messy) cappuccinos, mopping the floors at the end of the day. I appreciated the regularity and physicality of the work, and our little community in the kitchen; loved getting chased around the walk-in freezer by the baker who'd made a big weird club out of frozen cinnamon rolls stuck together, and loved filling the big sinks with soap suds and washing massive silver mixing bowls with my boss's young daughter, who stood beside me on a stool.

My boss, the owner and founder and manager and *everything* of the bakery, was a wildly funny, straight-talking, brusque but secretly tender-hearted woman with whom I ended up becoming bosom friends, despite feeling—at first—that I seemed to her simultaneously incompetent and overqualified, a sort of absurd figure who darted around the kitchen crying and messing things up. She liked to tease me for being emo. Early on, I'd made the mistake of telling her that my mom and I used to make collages together, and whenever I said I was having a shitty day, she'd ask, "You gonna collage about it?" She helped me laugh at myself, which was honestly what I needed at that point—more than I needed affection, booze, or more texts from my boyfriend—in order to save me from myself.

My boss ended up making a mix for the back kitchen that she called "The Wounded Mix," in honor of my affect and my incessant desire to talk about feelings. The first track? Mazzy Star's "Fade Into You." Just the sound of that opening croon: *I wanna hold the hand inside you…* was enough to make us seek each other out in the kitchen, just so that we could grin at each other above our flour-dusted black aprons. The wounded mix also featured the Decembrists and their dead-earnest time-travel ballads, Beach House and their emo sublime: *There's something wrong / with our hearts / When they beat pure / They stand apart.* Listening to those songs let me ask myself whether it was really necessary for a relationship to feel as difficult, as painful, as mine often did. Honestly, the Wounded Mix created a landscape in which it was okay to feel deep pain and deep love simultaneously, and also—maybe, *maybe*—not take their simultaneity so seriously all the time. Like, welcome to being…anyone.

When I worked on Sunday mornings, I worked alone. I could blast the Wounded Mix as loudly as I wanted. The bakery was closed, but we still baked off a bunch of pastries and cookies to drive to a bookstore café downtown. One bitterly cold winter day, I rolled out cookies while DeVotchKa wailed their lamentations like a holy choir in the empty kitchen: *you already know how this will end.* And that morning, I did know. I knew it would end.

Mix #6: Mixtape for a Rom-Com Villain

More than a decade later—after the end of several relationships, including a marriage—when I found myself living in Brooklyn, single mother to a toddler, I started making mixes on Spotify. One of the first ones was for a man named Tom—a smart, charming man I started dating about a year after my divorce. We went on our first date two days after I'd signed my papers. Tom worked for a hedge fund and lived on the seventeenth floor of a glassy high-rise, in an apartment full of sleek mid-century furniture and a dazzling array of houseplants. He tended to his plants with quiet regularity that verged on tenderness; these green almost-children were how he'd transformed the space into something more than the post-divorce husk it had once been.

On our third date, Tom took me to his favorite plant store, a converted warehouse full of waxy ficus plants, monsteras with serrated, leathery leaves; and prickly, bulbous succulents: a twisting column called a "spiralis," a long penile shaft covered in luminous downy spines, a nested cactus that looked like a green blossoming onion. When Tom pointed to a table of potted plants and asked which one was my favorite, I felt suddenly nervous—it was impossible to know which plant I actually liked best, when I was so overwhelmed by the desire to offer a response that would please him. When I pointed to a rose quartz splashed with pink blooms, he was visibly disappointed. "It's classically beautiful," he said. "But it's not very *interesting*."

In that moment, it was like he'd confirmed some hunch I'd always had about the world: that at any given moment I could say something that wasn't the right thing to say, and someone would give up on loving me. This was a hunch I'd spent much of my adult life trying to convince myself was a tyrannizing delusion. But it definitely felt true around him. Of course, I can also see that he was just a guy on a date in a plant store, trying to make conversation. It's not his fault that he hit the trip-wire of thirty-seven years of baggage. That's part of what can be so mortifying about dating—people who are basically strangers get to trigger all our deepest damage.

After my wrong answer, I surveyed the rest of the plants on the table in a panic, spotting a clumpy, creaturely-looking succulent called the dinosaur-back plant, and thinking, I should have chosen this one instead. It looked like swollen heads of broccoli that had been shaved of their nubs. You weren't supposed to touch it with your bare hands; not so you wouldn't get hurt, but so you wouldn't leave behind your gleaming human oils.

At the end of that night, Tom invited me up to the penthouse lounge at the top of his high-rise apartment building—it was literally called the Sky Lounge—where we sat facing a fake fireplace, our backs resting against a sleek leather recliner, starting at the lights of Manhattan across the river, and the glowing red arms on the clocktower of the Williamsburg Savings Bank. Tom told me that he often described himself as a Rom-Com Villain—the handsome, wealthy, impermeable guy in the romantic comedy that you definitely *didn't* want the girl to end up with. This comment, of course, made me want to stick up for him—because I saw the sweetness in him, the thoughtfulness, the creeping tendrils of vulnerability.

Tom often used some version of this formulation: *the thing I like to say about x is y*; or, *the story I usually tell about college debate is z*—the syntax itself letting me know that we weren't inside an original moment, that he was simply articulating something he'd articulated many times before. Tom had been dating for nearly eight years, since a divorce in his early thirties, and I sensed this syntax rose partially from going through the rituals of self-exposure with so many different women. Of course you developed shorthand phrases. But I also wanted desperately to break his patterns, to make him say things about himself he'd never said before, to make him feel things he'd never felt before.

I wasn't very good at it. Near the end of our dating, Tom told me our conversations were only 80 or 90 percent as good as he felt they *could* be. We were both interesting people; it was like we weren't living up to our potential. In some deep part of myself, I could feel the truth of what he was saying—that there was some core way in which we didn't fully connect—but I was also terrified by the idea that some part of him floated slightly above our conversations, evaluating each one.

But before all that, a few months into our relationship, I made Tom a mix on Spotify. I called it "Mixtape for a Rom-Com Villain," because even a rom-com villain deserved a mix; because maybe every rom-com villain had once been a teenage boy wondering if he'd ever have a girlfriend. Or at least, that was the story I told myself about his vulnerability, how I'd finally be the one to see it and assuage it.

The mix was partially composed of songs we'd listened to in bed, throwbacks to the nineties, a time when we were both teenagers just starting to come alive in the world: Massive Attack's "Teardrop," *black flowers blossom*, or Portishead's "Glory Box," *Give me a reason to love you*. Maybe that's all I was looking for—a reason to love him, this man with whom I made so much sense, who could give me stability, a home, more kids; a semblance of the unbroken life I craved in the aftermath of my broken marriage.

Most of the playlist was an assembly of songs that I'd loved across the course of my life—songs that were not just classically beautiful but somehow *interesting*, like the plants I hadn't chosen: Björk's "Joga," PJ Harvey's "The Wind," and even Eels's "Electroshock Blues," the same song that had been on the mix my high-school boyfriend made for me, held some fragile, aching, vaguely embarrassing part of myself, like a bug trapped in amber. Tom listened patiently when I played it, this song that held the perfect encapsulation of my young sadness. But I could tell he didn't particularly like it. And when he didn't particularly like it, I could see how much I'd yearned for him to like it. In hindsight, the playlist looks a lot like the rest of our ultimately relatively short-lived relationship—like I was trying to take all the parts of myself, my history, and make something good enough for him.

Mix #7: The First One

When I started writing this essay, all the early mixtapes I remembered were the ones made by men in my life: my brother and my boyfriends. These mixtapes were all part of a story I'd told myself about how my musical tastes were shaped: that my taste in music was a microcosm of the larger ways my tastes had been shaped by men; that I'd spent much of my life trying to gain the affirmation of men by loving what they loved, and by creating myself as a person they would see as worthy of love. Many of the authors I loved most were male: Faulkner, Carver, Berryman. Many of the systems I'd tried hard to rise within—schools, colleges, publications—were run by men, and legible to men.

But then I remembered another mixtape. The first mixtape. And it illuminated another story—a very different story, a story that had been there all along. The first mixtape was a gift from my aunt Kelda. Kelda is actually my half-aunt, my grandfather's second daughter from his second marriage—much younger than my father, younger even than my brothers. My two half-aunts were magical creatures to me when I was growing up: they were creative and queer and emotionally expressive; one was an artist and a carpenter, the other a singer. When I went to visit them at the all-female school they attended—a place called Mary Baldwin, in the Virginia hills—it felt like an enchanted world, full of warm, creative women who seemed deeply connected to and excited by one another. During that visit, I heard for the first time many of the female musicians I'd come to love—Dar Williams, the Indigo Girls, Ani DiFranco—and before I left, Kelda gave me a mixtape full of their songs. I can still remember the looping blue scribble of her handwriting, fitting the names of their songs onto the tight lines of the cassette liner: *Both Hands, Galileo, Traveling Again*.

When I heard Ani singing, *Now use both hands, Oh, no don't close your eyes*, I wasn't thinking about lesbian sex, at least, not at ten—but what I heard was a claiming of pleasure, an insistence on keeping eyes open and showing up for everything. Of the two songs by the Indigo Girls, it was "Romeo and Juliet" I fell hard for immediately, *Oh no I can't do anything except be in love with you*. A lyric that's been sung a thousand times, in some form or another: how the overwhelming intensity of love drives out everything else. Some whispered version of this lyric was all I could hear for years. But it was "Galileo" that made me want to dance alone in my bedroom, just a girl making swirling swimming motions with my hands, singing along off-key as two lesbians from Georgia belted out: *look what I had to overcome from my last life / I think I'll write a book.*

That ten-year-old dancing to "Galileo" in her bedroom was singing these lyrics, over and over again, *How long 'til my soul gets it right.* And almost twenty years later—fresh from a divorce, raising my daughter as a single home—I played "Galileo" again and heard this question a different way: perhaps the soul getting it right wasn't about finding a soulmate, but the pleasure of the song itself—which is to say, the pleasure of making. The soul getting it right meant somehow giving up the model of getting it right I'd lived by for so long.

Of course, it was also a song about reincarnation; how we are doomed to being born again, and again and again. How we are lucky enough to get born again, and again and again.

Mix #8: Quarantine Nights

When the Covid-19 pandemic struck New York and the entire city went into lockdown, when I came down with a mild case myself and stopped leaving home entirely, it was just me and my two-year-old daughter in our two-bedroom apartment for two weeks straight. No other adults. No childcare. No leaving. My case was mild. It felt like a regular flu except I had no sense of taste and smell for several weeks. The world was gone in several ways at once: strangers, sensation, streets. My daughter remained. Music remained.

Once I was feeling something like myself again, I made us a mix. I called it Quarantine Nights, but we listened to it all day long. On the daily schedule I'd written with rainbow markers and pinned to our fridge (*10 a.m. storytime, 1–3 p.m. nap,* ha!) I'd carved out a few slots for fifteen-minute dance parties. I didn't make the schedule because I expected we'd ever follow it, but because it kept me from going insane, to think of having a possible structure to follow.

My friend Bri once wrote, *pain makes demands but being felt isn't always one of them.* And that first quarantine spring, the demands my loneliness made were not about being felt, they were about solace and pleasure. When I made our mix, it was as much about dancing as it was about feeling. Or it was about dancing as a way of feeling. As my daughter danced to Loudon Wainwright's "Swimming Song," I heard in the lyrics that survival wasn't about self-awareness or self-reflection so much as it was about motion, and muddling through:

This summer I went swimming
This summer I might have drowned
But I held my breath and I kicked my feet
And I moved my arms around

From the depths of our quarantine spring, summer seemed pretty far off. The trees were budding and blooming beyond our windows, but they made a mockery of spring—its openness, its promise. The sirens blared around us. Tens of thousands of people in our city were getting sick and dying.

This quarantine mix was different to my Rom-Com Villain mix. It felt less like a performance of self for any particular audience— my apartment wouldn't have any visitors for a while, there was no one to perform *for*—and more like a survival pack. The only rule was that songs needed to bring me joy.

After I made it, I found it was largely composed of songs from other women, from friends, other mothers, former students— songs we'd listened to together, or that I'd lifted from playlists they'd sent me. Sure, there were songs that reminded me of the men who'd first played them for me. The Velvet Underground's *Sunday Morning* made me remember waking up in a poet boy-friend's shoebox apartment above a falafel shop, feeling his arms around me on a lumpy futon mattress. Courtney Bennett's "Shivers" made me remember driving through Houston at dusk with my feet on a musician's dusty dashboard, trying to convince myself our love affair wasn't as doomed as both of us knew it to be. But most of the songs had been gifts from women. And in this way, they felt like a continuation of the lineage of that first mixtape from my aunt, and the story it opened up for me—about all the women who had shaped me, my taste in music and maybe everything else, as much as men ever had, as much as all the systems and institutions of male approval I'd tried to be good enough for.

Our quarantine nights were full of songs from women. It felt so good to convene these women through their songs—a kind of spectral gathering after my daughter and I hadn't seen anyone in weeks. When I danced to Q Lazarus's "Goodbye Horses," in my cramped apartment, on my hardwood floor with its tiny jutting nails, with my little daughter dancing beside, I thought of the former student who had sent the song to me; telling me it was part of how she was getting through the loneliness of quarantine. For my daughter, dancing usually just meant running around in circles, sometimes begging me to follow: "Run, momma! Run!" Other songs summoned friends: the clas-sical piece lifted from a playlist my friend Rebecca sent, full of songs Daphne Du Maurier had listened to while she wrote; or songs taken from a playlist my friend Elliott had made when lockdown first sent us all inside: Gillian Welch's twangy "Look at Miss Ohio," *I wanna do right but not right now,* or Nina Simone's haunting cover of "Here Comes The Sun," a song my mother used to sing to me, *Little Darling, it's been a long cold lonely winter.* "Hoppípolla" made me remember going to urgent care with my best friend years before, how she tucked her headphones in my ears as I lay on the crinkling paper of the examining table, and played me Sigur Rós because their songs felt, to her, calming and transporting at once. Gloria's cover of Talking Heads' "This Must Be the Place" summoned the memory of dancing in my friend Anna's living room, with her and her toddler Albert. Albert and my daughter seemed bonded in a deep, inscrutable way, beyond language (they couldn't really speak). They'd often disappear into another room, giggling behind window curtains; and they both loved this song: *Did I find you, or you find me? / There was a time before we were born.*

There was a time before my daughter was born—when I'd smoke on cold stoops in various American cities, listening to music on my headphones and mourning the breakdown of a relationship with some man—but that time seemed long ago. Now I was home with my daughter for as long into the future as I could see, with Gloria crooning, *Home, is where I want to be / But I guess I'm already there.*

Because I'm most at home in words, I often find myself invoking lyrics when I write about music. It's a fumbling, stuttering way to get at what the music made me feel, when of course I know the true pulse of music is the sound of it, the way it moves through your body. Dancing with my daughter during the pandemic, I discovered just how liberating it can be to move beyond the words and live in the sound instead—to seek out music as a source of pleasure rather than simply an expression of pain, or a stage for dark interior unraveling.

The story of my playlists over the past three decades, from seven to thirty-seven, is a story about coming to an understanding of my taste in music as a landscape of pleasure not entirely shaped by men, and my emotional life as a force structured not only by romance—longing and heartbreak—but also by joy, sustenance, friendship, caregiving, and laughter. This was part of what it meant to dance during those quarantine days, and those quarantine nights—to feel the visceral summoning of my body into motion, alongside the summoning of another body beside me: a tiny body, a beloved body, the always-moving body of my daughter.

Love was where I'd always wanted to be. I guess I was already there.

Broadside Ballads
Liz Pelly

In the early 1940s, Woody Guthrie and Pete Seeger lived in a Greenwich Village collective house with their bandmates in the radical labor song group, the Almanac Singers. The Almanac House was 1941's version of what gets called a DIY space now—members of the group met and practiced there, hosted big nightly suppers for traveling musicians and neighborhood kids, and threw rent party performances in the basement every Sunday afternoon. For the weekend gigs, they'd slide every mattress in the house down the stairs for seating. Regular performers included Leadbelly, Josh White, and Burl Ives. Admission was 35 cents; rent was $95/month.

The Almanac Singers was an amorphous, collaborative effort. One day last year, I found myself fixated on an iconic, black-and-white photograph of a six-piece formation of the group, with two guitars, a banjo, an accordion, and all the members singing. I could only imagine what they might be performing from their repertoire filled with old union tunes, jabs at scabs, songs of solidarity and humor and scrappy harmonies. Maybe they were running through their wry, talking-blues guide to workplace organizing, "Talkin' Union," that instructs workers to "pass out a leaflet and call a meetin'." Or maybe they were belting out their high-spirited interpretation of the anti-capitalist tune "I Don't Want

Your Millions Mister," where they would include a verse advising the rank-and-file to stick together in "one big united band... and with a Farmer-Labor Party / we will win our just demands." More likely, though, they were singing an anti-fascist anthem.

One of the most compelling aspects of the Almanacs is how they operated as a collective—they wrote songs together, as a group, and held organizing meetings to make decisions—and yet, staring at that photograph, I found myself curious about them as individuals.

Guthrie and Seeger are well known, but who were their bandmates, what were their stories, and why haven't they been as celebrated? As it turns out, they were equally fascinating: there was Bess Lomax (sister of the storied field recordist Alan Lomax), Lee Hays (later of the Weavers), Millard Lampell (who was also a writer), Arthur Stern (the group's secretary). And then there was accordionist and vocalist Agnes "Sis" Cunningham, one of the more radical among them, and also one of the eldest members.

Sis was in her early thirties by the time she got to the Almanac House in 1941, and at that point, she'd already spent a decade in the singing labor movement as an organizer, music teacher, and performer, spending several semesters at the socialist Arkansas school Commonwealth College, and as a member of a roving musical agitprop troupe called the Red Dust Players. Throughout her life, she was deeply dedicated to the political power of topical songs and underground publishing, decades later co-founding and editing the influential mimeographed magazine *Broadside*, which she launched out of her kitchen in 1962.

She was a legend, but by the early 1940s she was already dealing with state surveillance. Sis and her husband, the leftist journalist Gordon Friesen, came to New York from Oklahoma to flee the intensifying red scare in their home state, where fellow Communist Party members were frequently having their homes raided, being put on trial and thrown in jail. She and Gordon would long be followed by the FBI for being involved in activist projects and for standing up for political prisoners. When the Almanacs started to see some commercial success, and then had record contracts and radio bookings canceled overnight because of their communist connections, Sis was already familiar with the feeling of being retaliated against by the government for her politics.

Because of the blacklist, or maybe in spite of it, Sis and her collaborators knew the importance of creating their own media, of making space for voices obfuscated by the commercial music world, of self-documenting their scenes and songs for future generations. "The big commercial music publishers and recording companies aren't interested in this sort of material," she told Gordon, in the days when they were considering launching *Broadside.* In their joint memoir, *Red Dust and Broadsides,* Gordon explains that one of their primary goals in publishing the magazine was to preserve non-commercial protest songs of the day for future researchers.

Co-edited by Sis, Gordon, and a rotating cast of collaborators, the little homemade magazine would publish one hundred and forty-one issues over twenty-six years, providing a crucial platform for the likes of Bob Dylan, Phil Ochs, Malvina Reynolds, Rev. Frederick Douglass Kirkpatrick, Buffy Sainte-Marie, Janis Ian, Len Chandler, and dozens more. It was "the Bible of folk music," as Lucinda Williams put it. (The first issue's tagline was "a handful of songs about our times.") It provided a springboard for countless names and causes that weren't getting coverage elsewhere. And while it wasn't an explicitly feminist project, Sis's lifelong commitment to movements for justice made it inherently so: "Folk music, like everything else, has always been male-dominated," she told *Ms.* in 1974. "Men are always in the best position to do something with music—not having to worry about kids and housework, and ways to bring in extra dollars. At *Broadside* we've always been conscious of women singers, and we've tried our best to promote women."

Some of the songs featured in the magazine would eventually end up pressed to wax, when *Broadside* launched a series with the early Folkways label, called *Broadside Ballads*, that issued recordings and detailed liner notes gathering material from those homemade mimeographed mags. The seventh entry in that series was a collection of Sis's own recordings, *Sundown*, released in 1976, and listening to them is like hearing a supercut of highlights from her time in music, including songs and stories from her early days in the labor singing movement, as well as her later years practicing the documentary-style songwriting that spun the news of the day into song. She sang tales of class war where the working class won. Some were her originals, some were co-authored with her family members, and some were tunes she learned from other singers over the years.

Sis came from a musical tradition in which songs functioned like musical newspaper articles, documenting and reflecting the current struggles and stories. These were songs that were meant to be shared, rewritten, updated depending on the situation of the day. In their joint memoir, Gordon once wrote that the creators of topical songs took no interest in popularity or poetry; that the artistic quality of the songs didn't need to be any better than a homemade picket sign. "These songs should probably be judged on the same utilitarian level as one judges the durability of the shoes on the marchers' feet," Gordon wrote. "Both shoes and songs shared the same basic purpose: to help the marchers reach their destination." Topical songs "strengthened morale and bolstered determination to keep the shoes moving."

Not everything about the "documentary style" songs of the day holds up today, and even in those days, there were fierce debates about the definitions, purposes, and processes of so-called folk music. But in her stories and songs, in the pages of *Broadside*, in the cracks of *Sundown*, there are lessons about the potential for people's music as a vehicle for political action. Sis and her friends knew what they were against, but they also knew what they were for. They were staunchly DIY but they understood the systemic conditions that required them to be. They didn't just want to describe the world, they wanted to change it. This was not art for art's sake. Songs were meant to be part of the movement. They were songs to be sung at rallies, in union halls, to galvanize the dispossessed to unite and fight.

Even when Sis was running *Broadside* in the early 1960s, her place in the folk music world was somewhat of a bridge—one of the many connective threads between the mass movements of the 1930s and the 1960s. As someone interested in self-organized musical spaces, self-publishing, and the popular resurgence of socialist politics today, I have been drawn to the story of Sis and those she called comrades—and their potential as a bridge into the movements of today.

"She was a true believer," said Sonny Ochs—sister of Phil, friend of Sis, contributor to *Broadside*—when I went to meet with her last spring, to hear her memories of Sis and see her full collection of *Broadside*s. "She just really believed in the cause, and these songs. And about helping poor people. God knows she knew what that was about."

*

Born into a family of poverty-stricken farmers in 1909 near Watonga, Oklahoma, Agnes "Sis" Cunningham saw first-hand the effects of predatory loan lenders and Wall Street grain speculators on rural families. Those experiences stuck with her throughout her life: her most popular song is her Depression-era Dust Bowl narrative, "My Oklahoma Home," co-written with her brother Bill, where she sings from the perspective of a homesteader who loses everything to the wind and dust storms—their home, family, wheat, oats, chickens, pigs:

It blowed away, it blowed away
My Oklahoma home it blowed away
You can't grow any grain, when there isn't any rain
All except the mortgage blowed away.

Like other songs that appear on her Folkways album, *Sundown*, "My Oklahoma Home" deals in matters of life-or-death, but with a winking humor; Bruce Springsteen, who has recorded the track twice, has noted his appreciation for both its "toughness" and its "wit." Listening through her weary and crackly story-songs, her tendency toward matching harsh truths with comic relief plays out like a survival mechanism.

Life was hard in Oklahoma. In *Broadside* #138, under the headline "I Was A <u>Very</u> Premature Anti-Fascist," Sis recounts almost dying of measles and scarlet fever as a seven-year-old. During that bedridden year of childhood, she read *Appeal to Reason*, the socialist texts of labor organizer and five-time presidential candidate Eugene V. Debs, which her father subscribed to. From her father and from Debs, Sis wrote in *Broadside*, "I reached the conviction that humanity can be saved only by a completely socialist world." (In 1979, the year after Folkways released Sis's record, one of her label-mates released a tribute to Debs, a spoken-word "historical narrative" on vinyl. The author? Bernard Sanders.)

Sis felt that her true political education during the 1930s came not from reading books, but from directly participating in the struggles around her. During that decade—her twenties—she would join the Communist Party of the USA and its cultural arm, the John Reed Club; the Southern Tenant Farmers Union, where she recruited members; the NAACP; the League Against War and Fascism (inspired by the Spanish Civil War), to name just a few of the grassroots efforts she was part of.

Sis had played piano since she was a kid, and followed high school by attending a teacher's college and teaching music for years. But it was really her subsequent semesters at the left-wing, pro-labor Commonwealth College that taught her the radical potential of singing and songwriting. In the summer of 1931, she enrolled at Commonwealth and studied Marxism, labor songs, and social theater. Later, in 1937, she taught music at Asheville's Southern Summer School for Women Workers, a socialist school that aimed to teach labor history to mill women and tenant farmers; she'd teach through folk songs, particularly, what were called "zipper songs"—songs where verses could be zipped in or out depending on the topics of the day.

The experience is captured on *Sundown*, with "Song of the Evicted Tenant," a ghostly ballad she performs a cappella. Sis explains that she learned the song from a woman named Myrtle Lawrence, a sharecropper from the Arkansas Delta region, whose eleven-year-old niece made it up after one of the biggest floods they'd ever had in the Delta:

Way down in old St. Francis bottom
Where they call it the devil's den
Where many a poor tenant has lost their home
And me, oh God, I'm one.

*

In 1939, Sis helped form the Red Dust Players, a group that aimed to use songs and skits to educate and galvanize poor farmers, aiding in the organizing drives of the STFU and the CIO Oil Workers. They would travel from town to town in southern and eastern Oklahoma with their sets painted on window shades, which they'd tack up wherever they performed. "Sometimes they'd have a sagging old porch and that would be our stage," Sis says between songs on *Sundown*. "And the headlights of the two cars we traveled in, we'd shine them on there, and that would be our lighting." They'd play in schoolhouses, churches, or just out in a field. The performances were free to attend, and the group would often bring along boxes and baskets of whatever food they could fit. One of their skits depicted a family losing its farm to a mortgage company, which is then saved by the union.

On one occasion, the group got a call from an agricultural union that needed a last-minute program for that evening, to rally sharecroppers around the union medical care plan. Sis wrote five songs in that one day; three of them would later appear on *Sundown*. In an interlude on the record, she explains that the group would set their lyrics to old familiar melodies, "so it would be easier for the folks to learn 'em and sing 'em along with us." One song that best exemplifies this egalitarian sing-song ideology is "Mister Congressman," a three-minute letter to an aspiring candidate, full of demands that those in power listen to the poor sharecroppers and not just the bosses: "You better get the poor folks' point of view / or we're damn sure not a gonna vote for you," Sis sings. "The tenant union is here to stay / we don't care what the land hogs say!" The verses are followed by a playful earworm of a chorus, so sticky and simple, it almost sounds like a children's song.

"No More Store Bought Teeth" is a short but sweet, one-minute jingle promoting the union healthcare plan, in which Sis shuffles through everyday medical scenarios made manageable with a doctor, thanks to the union: "No more store bought teeth / That fall out when you spit / The dentist took our measurements / And made us a pair that fit."

All of this "revolutionary" singing about healthcare and workplace protections did not go unnoticed, as the situation in Oklahoma grew increasingly hostile toward activists. Raids were starting to happen on homes and businesses of communists; some were arrested and jailed. One weekend, when the Red Dust Players returned home from an engagement, they found that one of their homes had been broken into and ransacked. Sis and her bandmates knew they'd be next. Some left Oklahoma; Sis went into hiding with friends out in the country. That summer, in August 1940, the Oklahoma City police raided the Communist Party's Progressive Bookstore, confiscating thousands of pieces of literature, and arresting thirty-five employees and customers. The four booksellers were put on trial for violating the state's laws against "criminal syndicalism" ("whatever that means," Sis once wrote) and sentenced to ten years in state prison plus a $5,000 fine. Gordon documented the trials in detail in a pamphlet published a year later titled *Oklahoma Witch Hunt*: "They burst into the Progressive Bookstore, and without discrimination arrested everyone present, and visitors who came in later," he wrote. "They pillaged the store and carted away some 10,000 books, papers and pamphlets."[1]

A 1941 FBI report confirms they were after Sis, too: "Would have been arrested in Communist Party raids if she had been located," reads the document, under the headline "Suggested For Custodial Detention...Cunningham, Agnes," per the comprehensive reporting of the 2020 book *The Folk Singers and the Bureau: The FBI, the Folk Artists and the Suppression of the Communist Party, USA—1939–1956.*

Sis and Gordon met around this time, quickly married and fled town. In October 1941, they boarded a bus for New York with two suitcases, Sis's accordion, and Gordon's typewriter. They stayed at first with Sid Grossman, a documentary photographer who had passed through Oklahoma and taken photographs of the Red Dust Players. There were two other New Yorkers who Sis had met when they passed through Oklahoma in the Red Dust Players days: Woody Guthrie and Pete Seeger.

*

Industrial Workers of the World (IWW) organizer and songwriter Joe Hill once said that, "a pamphlet, no matter how good, is never read more than once, but a song is learned by heart and repeated over and over. If a person can put a few cold, common sense facts into a song, and dress them up in a cloak of humor to take the dryness off of them, he will succeed in reaching a great number of workers who are too unintelligent or too indifferent to read a pamphlet or an editorial on economic science." That was the thinking that informed the types of songs Sis played at socialist summer camps and with the Red Dust Players. It was also the type of thinking that informed *The Little Red Songbook*, the IWW's "songster," the phrase for little folk song booklets of the time.

"That book right there was a major, major influence on the Almanac Singers," explained Smithsonian Folkways archivist Jeff Place. "They did tons of things out of that book." By the time Sis joined the group at the end of 1941, the Almanacs had already released its debut album, *Songs for John Doe*, and its collection of labor classics, *Talking Union*. The latter's 1955 reissue, *Talking Union and Other Union Songs*, is perhaps the group's most enduring record: the fullest snapshot of the songs they would play in union halls and at house parties, the record sounds like listening in on one of those events, with group-sung labor classics like "Solidarity Forever" and "Casey Jones (the Union Scab)."

Sometimes a single Saturday night would turn into a mini citywide tour. "We almost always accepted every invitation to sing anywhere—we needed the money too badly to turn anything down," remembered Bess Lomax Hawes in her memoir, *Sing It Pretty*, "and thereby managed to double- and even triple-book ourselves on popular evenings, forcing us to dash wildly from Queens to Brooklyn and far Yonkers, sometimes dividing ourselves in two..." They'd pool all the fees, but it was never enough. As Bess remembered it, the arrival of Sis and Gordon to the Almanac House was vital to the group's continued existence, a combination of their "picket line" experience, "strong musical repertoires" and general wisdom: "They brought the group a grown-up stability that was very important during the later years of the war, when so many of the fellows in the group were drafted..."

There was a moment when it seemed like the Almanac Singers had a future in music—there were record contracts in the works, bigger bookings happening, and at one point they even auditioned for the Rainbow Room at Rockefeller Center. But "the ink on the contract wasn't even dry" when an exposé on the group ran in a New York newspaper revealing their various members' political ideologies, and it was all swiftly canceled.[2]

Sis and Gordon moved to another apartment on Hudson Street, and for a time, Woody lived with them. Multiple nights a week, musicians and friends would come over and play: Leadbelly, Sonny Terry, Brownie McGhee. "I am the king of twelve-string guitar, Sonny is king of the harmonica, and Sis is queen of the accordion," Leadbelly proclaimed at one such jam session. They'd go until two or three in the morning, until the landlord complained.

Despite the onset of their blacklisting, the Almanacs recorded their final album with Keynote Records. *Dear Mr. President* features Sis's accordion playing and her solo cut, "Belt Line Girl," in which she encouraged women into factory jobs during World War II. When Sis and Gordon briefly moved to Detroit in 1943, and Sis found a job in a factory, the NYC communist newspaper *Daily Worker* ran an article under the headline "'Belt Line Girl' Gets a War Job": "Sis Cunningham, accordionist of the Almanac Singers, has taken her own advice," they wrote.

*

Through the 1950s, Sis all but disappeared from music. She did some work with the newly formed group People's Songs, but mostly focused on raising her two daughters and trying to make ends meet. The family slipped further into poverty, and faced ongoing battles with sickness, depression, and the welfare office.

They were also feeling the effects of the blacklist—what she called a "death" she and Gordon only lived through because they "had a pretty good idea of what was happening in the county and the world." In March 1945, Gordon was questioned by the FBI. But they knew what was happening to them was not their fault.

Sis didn't have the same clarity around her dwindling music life. "I saw the trouble as stemming from something within me instead of two primary outside forces: working-class oppression and women's oppression, both killers," she wrote in her memoir. "The circumstances of the blacklist was for me only the final pull into silence."

"They just barely survived through that 1940s period," remembered the historian Ronald D. Cohen, who worked with Sis and Gordon on *Red Dust and Broadsides*, and has helped preserve their archives. Through the 1950s, Sis and Gordon were involved in a bit of left-wing political organizing, but not much. "That's what's amazing. After all that hardship and struggle, they decided to put out a magazine."

*

One of Sis and Gordon's odd jobs during that period was handling Pete Seeger's correspondence. Pete dictated his letters to tape and sent them to Gordon and Sis to type them up. One day there was a letter from Malvina Reynolds to Pete about the need for a new topical magazine specifically dedicated to new political and protest music. Malvina didn't think *Sing Out!* was publishing enough material like this; she considered starting the magazine herself, but wanted to focus on songwriting and performing.

Sis thought it was a good idea. She knew how to transcribe music, and Gordon was a good writer. Maybe they could do it. Sis called up Pete; not only did he encourage the idea, but he and his wife Toshi offered to fund a telephone and the supplies they'd need. Pete sent them a Revere reel-to-reel recorder. They also had a hand-cranked mimeograph machine they'd inherited from the American Labor Party when a local branch shut down.

Broadside was a zine before zine culture existed. It was supremely DIY: a few sheets of 8.5 x 11-inch paper with two staples. It was made in the kitchen of their low-income apartment in uptown Manhattan's Frederick Douglass Housing Project. "We cleared the dirty dishes off the table and went to work cutting stencils on a manual Underwood typewriter, or I would set up the scope and do the music," Sis remembered. For the first issue, they made three hundred copies and sold them for thirty-five cents. In that issue, the opening editor's note explained that the aim of the publication would be "not so much to select and decide, as to circulate as many songs as possible and get them out as quickly as possible."

"When they lived in public housing, she had to sneak the *Broadsides* out in the baby carriage to take them to the post office," explained historian Ronald Cohen. "Because you couldn't have a business, living in public housing. So they would mimeograph those early *Broadsides* and then put them in the baby carriage and sneak them out."

They got some submissions in the mail, but for the most part, the magazine's material was gathered at monthly meetings held at their little apartment, where musicians would show up with their guitars, and everyone would go around the room playing songs into their reel-to-reel tape recorder. Then Sis, Gordon, and Gil Turner—who worked as the emcee at Gerde's Folk City—would together decide what to include. "Sis would sit at her piano and transcribe all of the music," said Jeff Place. "Their daughters and all of them would sit in their kitchen and paste up these booklets." Upon the release of the first issue, radical NYC newspaper *The Worker* anticipated *Broadside* being "an interesting venture in popularizing political and social songs as hot as the roll of a newspaper and considerably more truthful than most," under the headline "Topical Singers Get Organized."

*

Turner helped them recruit musicians for the meetings. One person he brought through was Bob Dylan, who kept turning up at the meetings for over a year, along with his girlfriend at the time, political activist Suze Rotolo, who immensely influenced his early work. Phil Ochs—also a regular meeting attendee—kept coming by the apartment even when monthly meetings ended. The zine's early issues were heavy on songs by Dylan, Ochs, Malvina Reynolds, Tom Paxton, Len Chandler, and Peter La Farge.

"We had meetings in a crowded room," Ochs remembered in a 1971 interview with *Rolling Stone*. "And there's Pete Seeger and there's Bob Dylan and a bunch of people, and Dylan would sing 'Masters of War' into a tape recorder, because that was his song for the week. Very bizarre." Over the course of its 186-issue run, *Broadside*'s most frequent contributor was Ochs, submitting over seventy songs and also writing articles. The apartment was like a second home for him. "She pretty much became his surrogate mother," Sonny Ochs said. "He would sit with Sis and Gordon for hours."

"It was underrated. Look at it, it looks like a high-school project," Sonny added, flipping through piles of her own *Broadside* collection. "But when you start looking at it…this is a treasure trove." Sonny, who had co-hosted a tribute concert to Sis in 1997, in many ways still embodies the spirit of *Broadside*. As we sat at her kitchen table perusing her full collection of the magazine, we listened to her community radio show dedicated to underground political folk singers, and she told me about the performance space she helps organize at her local library.

Flipping through a stack of *Broadside*s is indeed a joy. Songs featured over the years included Malvina Reynolds's "Little Boxes" (#20), Nina Simone's "To Be Young, Gifted and Black" (#103), Lucinda Williams's "You Don't Have to Hustle Me" (#140), Buffy

Sainte-Marie's "Now That the Buffalo's Gone" (#152). The types of groups covered ranged from El Teatro Campesino, the musical group of California's United Farmworkers, to the Fugs, the protest-singing avant-garde rock band from New York.

"They didn't get caught up in personalities," explained archivist Jeff Place, who co-curated and compiled the massive retrospective boxset, *Best of Broadside 1962–1988: Anthems of the American Underground from the Pages of Broadside Magazine*, released in 2000. "They put songs in there where they believed what was being said in the lyrics. I remember one issue Gordon was talking about how he was really into the song 'War Pigs' by Black Sabbath, which is not something you would imagine they would be into. But the lyrics are the things that really got him." One of the central purposes of the magazine was to inspire young songwriters to write about local issues. They'd sometimes publish a newspaper clipping covering a pressing story of the day as a writing prompt and encourage musicians to submit songs around specific issues.

One of the many volunteers who helped crank the mimeograph machine was Josh Dunson, who started showing up at Sis and Gordon's place when he was twenty-two, after his mom came across an advertisement for *Broadside* in the *Daily Worker*. He eventually became a contributing editor.

"There was a culture there that sustained all of it," Dunson said. "Everyone was so excited about the topics. Everyone else there, including myself, and Sis and Gordon, considered ourselves as part of the civil rights movement, and a mass movement. And that was very different in the early 60s because the last mass movements really were in the 30s. And that was before everyone in that room was born, except Sis and Gordon." Dunson said "the best meeting ever" was one that took place after a group of Broadsiders had just returned from the Atlanta Sing for Freedom, where they met Southern singers who were helping lead the civil rights movement.

And though the meetings were always a tight squeeze in that tiny apartment, "people would angle their guitars so they would not get in anybody else's way," Dunson recalled.

Publishing *Broadside* was not without its struggles. In issue 138, where Sis described her health issues, she went on to explain a number of her heart irregularities and their related miseries: "I attribute these new difficulties to the strain of putting out *Broadside* combined with the anguish of having to leave out for lack of space the many fine songs being sent to us by our loyal contributors and trying to convince them that this country's musical world, as well as the rest of its media, is controlled by stupid and illiterate capitalist pigs."

*

In my early efforts digging around online for what I could learn about Sis, I stumbled upon a track in the depths of YouTube. "But If I Ask Them" is a ballad where she sings in a voice that's tired but sure, sweet but weathered, from the perspective of a hard-traveling, truth-telling woman whose song has become popular, while she remains poor. This narrator, "heard but not identified," watches on in awe: *The song became no longer mine / They're singing it now and their clothes so fine!*

It sounded like it could have been written yesterday. In a monologue introduction to this song, Sis dedicates it to the Appalachian folk singer and coal miner organizer Aunt Molly Jackson. "But If I Ask Them" was specifically written from Jackson's perspective, but it feels like a timeless indictment of the music industry at large, taking aim at the record label thieves who "cashed in on another's grief" as folk music became increasingly commercial. When Sis took on Aunt Molly Jackson's story as subject and recorded it for *Sundown*, it was fifteen years after Jackson had died, "penniless and exploited," as Sis wrote in her album's liner notes.

The song was inspired by a letter Jackson had written to *Sing Out!* magazine in 1960, just before she died, chronicling how "people would come to her for her songs, but if she asked them how she could get a few pennies for her songs, they'd say they didn't know." Aunt Molly wasn't the only one who endured such experiences. (And surely did not experience the worst of it, as a white singer in an industry that had long profited off appropriation of Black culture.) Listening to "But If I Ask Them" now, though, it is striking to remember just how long grassroots artists have been struggling to locate the pennies they're owed. Sis's resulting song was one of *Sundown*'s most powerful.

> Schedule's kept and deadlines met
> They see nothing they regret
> Promoter's paid, producer's praised
> Champagne poured and glasses raised
> Round the ring, a toast is said
> All too soon they pronounced me dead.

Sis's entire solo album plays out like a document of the radical musicians and labor organizers she met along her many journeys; ones who didn't become household names but who had their own songs and stories. In her songwriting, much like she did through her publishing, Sis documented the everyday people and voices she encountered, not just in order to reflect the times, but to provide tools for organizing and to inspire action. The archives of *Broadside* are similarly rich with people's music history. During a tribute program filmed toward the end of Sis's life, Matthew Jones, the civil rights activist, member of the Freedom Singers, and field secretary of the Student Nonviolent Coordinating Committee, called Sis "one of the greatest women in folk music."

Like many others represented in those pages of *Broadside*, though, Sis's own songs and impact matter not because anyone else needs to be put up on a pedestal like so many have put big-name folk stars of generations past. Instead, it matters because Sis's story is a reminder that history is made on the margins, by those who maybe never get famous, but who stay on the ground organizing with workers, opening their homes for meetings, letting the musicians crash on their couch, transcribing lyrics, printing and mailing the zines.

---

[1] Gordon Friessen, 1941. *Oklahoma Witch Hunt.* Oklahoma: Oklahoma Committee to Defend Political Prisoners. https://issuu.com/worker33/docs/ok_witch_hunt.

[2] Agnes "Sis" Cunningham and Gordon Friesen (1999). *Red Dust and Broadsides,* edited by Ronald D. Cohen, p. 222. Amherst: University of Massachusetts Press.

My Brilliant Friend

Maggie Nelson

The news of Lhasa's death on New Year's Day, 2010, sent me
to the couch to howl like an animal. I curled up with my face
against the fabric wall, needing the privacy one needs when
stricken. I hadn't even known she was sick. How could I not
have known.

Breast cancer, age 37, said the *New York Times.*

The days passed, and I found I had questions. Lots of questions.
With no one to direct them to, they festered. After a year, I took
the risk of sending them to one of her sisters, whom I'd known
slightly in high school. She kindly promised to answer when she
had time, but I never heard back. Who could blame her?

So I turned, instead, to YouTube. There I could find montages
of still photos of Lhasa set to her music: Lhasa leaping over
railroad tracks in an overcoat, Lhasa dunking under seawater
in slinky silk, Lhasa performing in a black spaghetti-strap dress
surrounded by fancy-looking bassists and harpists. I read the
comments in English, French, and Spanish, most of which offered
some variation on *Puto cáncer. No te olvidaré jamás, dulce ser.* Mostly
I watched her last recorded performance, shot on April 11, 2009,
at what appears to be a house party in Montreal, by filmmaker
Vincent Moon. I scoured Lhasa's face for signs of foreknowledge,

acceptance, fatigue, anger, resolve. I tried to discern if she'd had a mastectomy. Her hair was short, her skin tone changed—signs of chemo? Or illness, or age? I watched and watched, but mostly saw nothing but Lhasa, pretty much as she always was: bearing down on each word, deep in song.

And then, out of the blue, days before the tenth anniversary of her death, I got an email from a music journalist named Fred Goodman, who said he had recently published a book titled *Why Lhasa de Sela Matters*, and would I like a copy. I sensed, correctly, that many of my questions were about to be answered.

I last saw Lhasa in the winter of late 2004. I was living in an industrial loft in Williamsburg, the kind where snow wafts in through the walls. It was a trapeze loft, managed by a friend in circus/performance art/cabaret. I had fallen into living there after a breakup that had caused my status in New York City real estate to plummet—I'd gone from living in my own one-bedroom, rent-controlled apartment in Boerum Hill for $790 a month to occupying a fifty-square-foot corner of a leaky, loud loft occupied by multiple others for $850 a month. Squatters and strangers abounded; one queen who spent the night with someone moving out the next morning just stayed on, burrowing atop a plywood platform. For weeks, before any of us got up the gumption to insist he leave, he cooked in our kitchen wearing a turban and apron printed with strawberries, as if our den mother. It was my first year out of graduate school, and my first working as a "professor," which meant trying to live on $3,500 a semester and struggling to correct papers to the sound of trapeze rehearsals and rowdy sex at random hours. "You're really *living the life*," Lhasa said over tea in the loft's communal kitchen, which housed a clawfoot bathtub full of dirt and dozens of large plants hanging from the rafters. This was high praise, from Lhasa. I was glad, as always, for her approval.

Lhasa knew many amazing people in her childhood and adulthood, and I'm not writing this to insert myself into that canon. What Lhasa meant to me is hugely outsized compared to what I meant to her. I accept that, and suspect it is true for many others. That happens commonly with renowned people— old friends and acquaintances try to stake their claim. I liked Elena Ferrante's *My Brilliant Friend* but had a hard time making it through once I realized that I was more Lenù than Lila—Lenù being the plainer, more obedient, less magical friend who grows up to become a writer, Lila being the truly brilliant friend who suffers more grievously, has her genius go unrecognized, and eventually disappears. Lila burns her writing, while Lenù's stories— about Lila, of course—become the book we are now holding in our hands, the homage paid by the high-functioning mediocre to the fast-burning extraordinary.

Now, none of this is really the case with Lhasa. The world came to know her genius, and her music lives on, is beloved. But she did disappear. I still do not understand how this is possible.

We had met fifteen years earlier in high school, at the Urban School of San Francisco. Before showing up at Urban, Lhasa had been living in a school bus with her family in Mexico; after her parents split, she moved with her mother and a constellation of siblings into a railroad apartment on Harrison Street in the Mission. I didn't know it then, but her mother had just come off kicking dope, birthing six daughters in quick succession (two of whom she no longer had custody), surviving a near-fatal car crash, and fleeing a string of rough relations, the last of whom was Lhasa's father, a nomadic Mexican philosopher-mystic. (From Goodman I learned that Lhasa's mother retained a connection to money through her own mother, a volatile actress who had starred in Elia Kazan's *America*, and was unhappily married to a corporate titan of New York City. But proximity to money doesn't guarantee money, or stability; certainly that was the case here.) I, on the other hand, was the second child of rule-following, ambitious, voted "most likely to succeed" white Midwesterners who had moved to San Francisco in 1969 not for the Summer of Love, but for my father's job in labor law. By the time I got to high school, however, things had taken a bit of a turn. When I was eight, my parents split; when I was ten, my father died, abruptly. The suddenness and mystery of his loss had filled me with dread, and my older sister had begun to slide, bringing drugs, older boys, and troubled friends into our shared basement life. Before long she would become a runaway, spending time in juvenile hall and reform schools; I would stay at home with my mother and stepfather, struggling to distance myself from the more frightening of her woes while trying not becoming a total nerd or goody-two-shoes. (The latter felt a distinct possibility, as, almost despite myself, I cared deeply about my studies. I was also fearful that, were I to misstep, a 250-pound bald guy in a car with child-lock doors might come for me as well.) In eighth grade, I read *I Never Promised You a Rose Garden* repeatedly, and experimented with splitting myself into two: Maggie, who got good grades and gravitated toward light and life, and Margaret, who was sick with grief and anxiety and actively wanted to die. By high school, this struggle had become visible in my fashion: ankle-length, flower-printed hippie dresses with tassels, Renaissance Faire amulets, China flats, a mop of bleached blonde hair and heavy eye makeup modeled after Ann Carlisle's character in *Liquid Sky* (whose name was, of course, Margaret).

Lhasa showed up dressed like a gypsy with a dash of *Alice in Wonderland*—headband holding back straight, waist-length hair, floor-length pleated skirt with a cinched waist, leotard top with a ballet sweater or scarf to cover her ample chest. More rarely, she wore jeans—low-slung faded Levis—with a black rayon shirt, boat-neck collar. Her face in high school looked exactly as it looked later, so if you Google her, you'll know. People with strong faces like Lhasa's tend to have them their whole lives. Lhasa knew her face—its high cheekbones, its almost clownishly wide smile—very well. In printmaking class, in ceramics, in painting, she reproduced it over and over again, like Richard Dreyfuss sculpting that butte in *Close Encounters of the Third Kind*. It's a mythic face, but it's also just a family face, her family face. Sometimes it seemed like the only face she could draw. (I was unsurprised to see it show up on the cover of her first album, 1997's *La Llorona*.)

I wish I could convey the magic of Lhasa and her sisters, two of whom were also enrolled at Urban. They were stunningly beautiful; surely that was part of it. Ironically, as a teenager (was Lhasa ever a teenager?), she wasn't considered the most beautiful of them. Her eyes were narrower, like her father's, whereas some of her sisters had wider eyes, like their mother's, which made for a more classic movie-star look. This may have worked in Lhasa's favor in the long run (or at least, for as long a run as she got): "Beauty without imperfection is just…*'pretty,'*" she later told an interviewer with disgust. I knew the feeling: my older sister was also known as a great beauty; on more than one occasion, I found out that guys I had crushes on were actually enamored with her, and using me to get closer to her legendary beauty and badness.

For Lhasa, who'd been home-schooled on poetry, fairy tales, and mythology, enrolling at Urban was an unsteady compromise with normativity. For me, it was my best shot at ditching it. I wanted to get as far away from the BMWs and aging deadheads of Marin County, and as close to the movie *Fame* as possible. Urban was housed in an old firehouse on Page Street between Ashbury and Masonic, in a purple and gold Victorian, the word GUMPTION carved on the double wooden firehouse doors. Inside was a two-story space organized around a hole where the firehouse pole used to be, wherein an enormous ficus now sprouted. At breaks we sat around the pit and let our feet dangle down. There was no shortage of yuppie kids—it was a private school, after all—but it wasn't yet the cleaned-up college pipeline it later became. We had to do a lot of community service, which is how I found myself, at thirteen, taking care of a retired Irish priest in a Tenderloin hotel each afternoon. "Bless you, my child," Father Andrew would say as I helped him in and out of his ripped easy chair, two purple, zipper-like scars running down his knees. The Haight of the 1980s was also in a fashion crisis reflecting spiritual unrest: young skinheads in suspenders and Doc Martens roamed the streets, kicking hippies slumped under Mexican blankets, some of whom had been there for the past twenty years, surely wondering when a Gap had sprouted on the neighborhood's most famous corner. At recess you could buy speed in the backroom of Double Rainbow, patchouli oil from the tarot shop, or wall-size silk flags of the *Dark Side of the Moon* album cover at the head shop. Lunchtime brought warm sesame bagels with scallion cream cheese from Holy Bagel; avocado, alfalfa sprout, and jack cheese sandwiches on coarse wholewheat from the health-food store by the free clinic, or massive, perfect burritos at Chabela's, near the entrance to Golden Gate Park. Incredibly, we were allowed to smoke, albeit not right in front of the school (we smoked around the corner, on Ashbury, where several stand-up ashtrays had been installed for that purpose).

Lhasa's itinerant, iconoclastic, and occasionally indigent past distinguished her from many of the kids at our school. At the same time, I can think of few friends from that time, rich or not, who had what one might consider a "normal," functioning household. Barely anyone's parents were together; most were hardly ever seen. There were kids already living on their own, kids involved in Survival Research Laboratories, kids enmeshed with the Pickle Family Circus. The circus thread lacing the school—circus being an available class option—would prove life-changing for several of Lhasa's sisters, as well as for Lhasa herself. At some point Lhasa and I absorbed into our friendship a delight-ful transfer student who seemed closer to sixty than sixteen, with arcane intellectual interests and utterly absent investment banker parents. Like Lhasa, he was a man-out-of-his-time, enraptured by ancient literature and lore; he introduced us to the Marquis de Sade and whippets (later, he became a historical archeologist). Our art history teacher was a wry, willowy visionary who taught us about Jung's anima and animus, converted us into docents for an exhibit of New Guinea totems at the de Young, and had us read Joseph Campbell's *The Power of Myth* before scouring our lives for "peak moments." Our Spanish teacher was a demanding force of nature whose extravagant passions rivaled those of Lhasa's family; when she died in 2005, her obituary read: "Born in Barcelona, Spain, she survived the Spanish Civil War, her father fighting for the Republic, her mother haranguing Fascist soldiers. In 1970, she became a teacher at the Urban School of San Francisco, and spent the next 34 years teaching Spanish and Latin American literature to adoring (and sometimes slightly frightened) students." RIP, Joana.

There might have been someone at our high school romantically interested in Lhasa, but generally speaking, she seemed untouchable. Some people—even in cool, progressive high schools—are simply above it all, not because they're arrogant, but because they levitate above the gross vicissitudes of adolescence, their soul having already ascended to the next realm. Lhasa was like that. Even her figure was mature. She had a great sense of mirth and laughed often, but she was also deadly serious, which led to many clashes with the stoner dudes who aggressively instructed us smart and serious girls to relax. (I will never forget the ratty-haired surfer who popped several of my birth control pills "just to see what happens" during a class hike in an old-growth redwood forest, all the while telling me to *chill the fuck out*.) But some of Lhasa's untouchability was also literal, and had to do with her decision to remain a virgin, a situation we discussed at length.

It was exotic, to be a virgin in that environment. Lhasa said she was waiting for a "real man," not a silly high-school boy—a

Prince Charming she imagined was out there, waiting for her, too. I, on the other hand, had taken the *Little Darlings* route: convinced everyone around me was fucking like crazy (my sister had already had an abortion by ninth grade), I felt mortified by my virginity, and by fifteen, had taken active measures to remedy it.

Lhasa's Prince Charming stuff made me nervous. I worried she thought too highly of men, even the good ones. Certainly she was impatient with creeps and sexists, but there was a certain reverence when she talked about men—especially *handsome* men—that I didn't share. She revered powerful women—indeed, she was one, and would become even more so. But she could also be brutal about women she considered weak, complainy, or insufficiently serious. (Years later, after touring with the Lilith Fair, she would tell an interviewer that she had no more time for "whiny" female singer–songwriters who only wanted to "pick at the wound and see how much it hurts.") I had a few friends who tilted that way, and I could feel the burn of Lhasa's disapproval when I palled around with them.

Lhasa's apartment on Harrison felt unchaperoned and sexual. Languid young bodies in shiny leotards stretched on mats and practiced circus tricks in the rooms off the railroad hallway (her three sisters were training to become a tightwire walker, a contortionist, and a trapezist, respectively). Then there was the mystery of Lhasa's mother, who emanated sensuality and children (in addition to Lhasa and her three sisters, there were two adult half-sisters who showed up from time to time, as well as, inexplicably, a new pixie boy toddler). While most in the house slept on messy mattresses on the floor, Lhasa's bed was a loft, a bastion. We lay there chastely side by side, discussing the pros and cons of unrestrained passion—save for one night, when Lhasa's mother was away, when I spent a particularly lustful night with my high school boyfriend in Lhasa's mother's bed. What was Lhasa thinking that night, up in her loft? Should I have been up there with her, taking turns reading aloud from Lawrence

Durrell's *Justine*? Was sailing through pack after pack of birth control pills the right path, or did Lhasa's romantic withholding put her in touch with a more mystical, transcendent realm to which I pitifully lacked access?

As with sex, so it was with politics: Lhasa and I were adamant about our convictions, perhaps Lhasa even more so. But whereas she was big on passionate, outraged speeches, I wanted to be in the nitty-gritty action. So, after my time with the priest, I started working at CISPES, the Committee in Solidarity with the People of El Salvador, headquartered in the Castro. It pains me now to imagine myself, a sixteen-year old blonde from Mill Valley waltzing into the CISPES office, full of righteous anger at death squads and imperialist injustice, ready to cold call and Xerox. But I was utterly convinced of the cause, and enjoyed working somewhere the FBI cared enough about to raid, overturning our empty cardboard boxes of printer paper and Cafix.

What were Lhasa and I into, together? The soundtrack from the movie *Time of the Gypsies*, composed by Goran Bregović. The Kronos Quartet's recording of Terry Riley's *Cadenza on the Night Plain*. Heavily steeped blackcurrant tea with milk, and the spidery plants that grew up her living room walls. Billie Holiday (of course). Fyodor Dostoyevsky and Paul Celan. Stevie Ray Vaughan's version of "Voodoo Chile," to which we danced our fucking guts out at a concert of his we attended together a few months before he died. The I Ching—O Lord, the I Ching. (I still have the I Ching I procured with Lhasa, introduction by Jung, leavened by a black and blue embroidered pouch holding pesetas from our 1989 trip to Spain.) My 1976 silver VW bug, in which I could take us places blasting *Electric Ladyland* and stuffing the car ashtray with Camels and Ducados. My reversible Korea jacket, blue velvet with embroidered tigers on one side, faded red and white silk stripes on the other, which Lhasa and I took turns wearing (and which I tragically left behind on an airplane in 1994, ending an era). Lhasa taught me that it was important to have one nearly perfect version of every necessary item: one good knife, one good teapot, one good coat. This is one of the many lessons from her that I have carried with me all my life.

In high school I knew plenty of kids who wore woven socks with leather soles and listened to Led Zeppelin and baked pot brownies while gearing up for the Harmonic Convergence (this describes me at times). I also knew plenty of goths who wore motorcycle jackets, dabbled in dope, and pledged undying love to Nick Cave. But Lhasa was my first and only truly bohemian friend—someone for whom being an intellectual was the essence of cool. She was completely unafraid of dorkiness or hokeyness so long as it was in pursuit of wisdom, truth, or beauty. She later told an interviewer that awkwardness, being uncomfortable with ourselves, is how we retain our dignity. Somehow, she knew and lived by this principle in high school, a time when awkwardness feels to most of us not like dignity but like dying.

Our junior year, we studied together in Spain, at La Universidad de Zamora, chaperoned by our ferocious antifascist Spanish teacher, who taught us to say *Me cago en Déu*. Our daily instructor in Zamora turned out to be a shockingly sexist teacher named Angel, who wore crisp white button-downs and a leather jacket draped around his shoulders like a little cape. He smoked through class while lecturing to us about why women shouldn't hold positions of power. *Es simplemente a-n-t-i-n-a-t-u-r-a-l*. I can still hear Lhasa huffing in outrage. Angel was forced into pedagogical camaraderie with the most disaffected kid in our class, a guy who was treated with apprehension back at home, but in Spain found an outlet for his closet machismo. It was frightening to behold, his first red-pill high. Every night Lhasa and I talked and smoked, smoked and talked, at a whitewashed bar decorated with broken cobalt tiles situated near a crossroads with a sign pointing to Portugal. Stands of cottonwoods rained fluff on us as we stumbled home, though I never saw Lhasa lost in liquor. If you told me this place was a dream, I would have believed you, except that I just found it on the internet: Trabanca.

When Lhasa began to sing, it was thrilling and agonizing. Thrilling because there, all of a sudden, was her voice, booming in the church gymnasium we rented for All School Meetings on Fridays. Lhasa wasn't just showcasing her voice, but the profundity of her investment in both the song at hand and life itself. To stand up in an auditorium full of teenagers, even sophisticated, arty teenagers, in your floor-length skirt and headband, and showcase this investment via an unhurried, a cappella version of "Good Morning Heartache," demands bravery. The first few meetings at which she sang, she kept her back turned to us. When she started turning around, she had all the tics I behold now in her YouTube videos, repurposed, as happens, into starpower—the repetitive tucking of her hair behind her ears, her side-to-side rocking, her breathy introductions, her giggling apologies when she erred. She was good, so good, but she wasn't perfect, and the combination of all that intensity with occasional swerves could be excruciating. No one knew where all this was going. But everyone knew something big was happening. On weekends we looked for cafes where she might be able to sing, her doggedness in the face of her stage fright challenging me to equal bravery, though I didn't yet know what to be brave about.

After graduation, Lhasa invited me to visit her in Mexico, where she would be spending the summer with her father. I don't think I've ever felt as free in my life as I did then, at age seventeen, boarding a plane for Mexico to find my brilliant friend in her legendary habitat, with a handwritten note in my pocket as to how to locate her. The house was more like a shelter—half exposed to the elements, dirt patios between kitchen, bathroom, and sleeping areas. We slept on mats in an elevated area under a thatched roof, around which we sprayed circles of poison to repel scorpions. By day we'd pile in Lhasa's father's van and drive to resort hotels, where he would instruct us in how to pretend we were guests to use their pools. At sunset, Lhasa's trapezist sister would perform on a hilltop to an audience of neighborhood kids, disseminating the family magic.

I saw more of Lhasa's body on that trip, spent more time with her at dawn and dusk, than ever before. I even snapped a nude photo of her in the shower—a true transgression, as she was so modest. She smiles at me in it with half-feigned outrage, covering her breasts, strong tan lines arcing at the tops of her thighs. I also have a photo of her in a sleeveless pink nightgown, smoking a morning pipe, and another of her over drinks, holding two cigarettes (one mine, so I could take the picture). One indolent afternoon, her trapezist sister drew me naked, lying on my side; I took a photo of the charcoal drawing, which remains the only evidence of what my naked body looked like at seventeen.

In the fall I went east to college. Coming on the heels of Mexico, the Haight, CISPES, and Lhasa, my liberal arts school in a depressed New England town felt alien and paltry. I had chosen a place that people told me was maximally nonconformist and politically active; once there, I felt surrounded by jocks, legacy kids, bad diner food, and stodgy East Coast traditions and architecture that meant nothing to me. There were even fraternities! Why hadn't anyone told me? Politics meant sobby Take Back the Night marches on the library steps, holding candles. Lhasa would have been appalled. I tried to impress my "frosh" dormmates by playing them my beat-up cassette tape of Lhasa singing "Willow, Weep for Me." *That's my friend from home. Isn't she amazing?*

The first creative essay I wrote in college was about my summer in Mexico, as I felt sure that Lhasa and her family were the most interesting things that had happened to me. I wrote about the day her father took us to an abandoned glass factory littered with piles of broken blue glass, a place that gave me the inspiration, on the spot, to write a book in fragments about the color blue. Twenty years later, I wrote it. I always aimed to send it to Lhasa—I thought it might be the first book of mine she might really like, as it was an unabashed ode to beauty flush with heterosexual pathos. But somehow we ran out of time.

Who taught you to write like this? my professor wrote on the back of my essay. I thought she meant it in a bad way, until I realized that she didn't. When I realized, something inside me began.

Lhasa went off to college as well—St. John's, in New Mexico. I think she liked the idea of "studying the works of history's greatest thinkers," as its website now advertises; less imaginable is that she would take part in "established traditions that date back decades or longer, from signing the college register...to taking part in senior prank days before graduation." Within months she had dropped out, and moved to Montreal to be near her sisters.

By the time I visited her there in 1991, things out east had looked up for me. I'd fallen in love with a woman, the first woman I'd ever fallen in love with (if you don't count Lhasa), and managed to escape the banality of dorm living by moving into her off-campus home. This woman was deep into a totally other mythology—one based in the East Village, involving Patti Smith and Cowboy Mouth and the Poetry Project and Eileen Myles and Lydia Lunch and David Wojnarowicz. It was the age of AIDS, and New York was alive with ACT UP, Lesbian Nation, kiss-ins and die-ins. I was taken.

In Montreal I found Lhasa with a shaved head, experimenting with the occasional mosh pit. Over blackcurrant tea in her kitchen, where spidery plants grew up the walls just as they had on Harrison, I told her about my female lover, and my newfound revelations about bisexuality, the plasticity and fungibility of organs and desire. I could be misremembering through the lens of my own phobias, but I don't recall her having a particularly warm reaction. Who knows what she really thought—sometimes I suspected that Lhasa reacted strongly with snootiness or disgust when she hadn't yet determined what she thought or felt about something. (She would, after all, later come to worship Chavela Vargas.) But I remember leaving Montreal with the feeling that our friendship had suffered a blow from which I wasn't entirely sure it would recover.

In reading Goodman's book, I learned that Lhasa's struggle with messy, everyday engagements with messy, everyday people—her difficulty in accepting them as something other than comedowns from the exalted world of myth, allegory, or fairy tale—extended well into her adulthood, even after she began to have full-fledged relationships. "Lhasa said that when you're in love and in a relationship and things are working, it's actually really a series of disappointments," one of her friends told Goodman. Worldly success offered no relief: as another friend said of her post-fame life, "She had turned herself into this great singer and, in her mind, into the princess. And still no prince appeared. And, in fact, some of the men in her life held her status and grandness against her. They would punish her in little ways here and there." Reading this made me angry; I also recognized the urge. Whether out of jealousy or self-protectiveness or some combination thereof, often I felt myself flickering between defending my importance to her and keeping my distance. "I've seen her flush people," a longtime collaborator, Patrick Watson, told Goodman. "[S]he flushed me." Not staying too close was one way to avoid the drain.

And the drain was always a possibility, especially given our differences. In addition to my retaining the stink of the Marin County bourgeoisie (a stink which, I eventually realized, only intensifies with denial), the truth was that, no matter how many hours we spent throwing the I Ching, I harbored a deep distrust of archetypes and omens, Lhasa's principal nourishment. (One of her ex-boyfriends later told Goodman that Lhasa deeply believed "that she was being guided, that the universe cares. There were people in her life pushing her in that direction. I tried to get her to read existentialists because I believe in the absurd and that the universe doesn't give a damn about any of us... And that would piss her off so much that she would throw me out of the house and not speak to me for a while.") A lot of the art—perhaps most of it—that I felt compelled by, Lhasa would likely have considered trash. She valued beauty and craftsmanship more than I, and had a much higher threshold for melodrama and whimsy. A little of the circus aesthetic went a long way for me; at times I found her relentless sincerity exhausting, at times bordering on the comedic. A painter friend of hers told Goodman, "We used to argue about art a lot. *A lot*…She went all the way! It drove me crazy. And one day when we were having this conversation, I just walked away. But that was us. Two days later, we're right back—it's love again, no problem." Lhasa and I never had such fights; whenever I saw her again after a long interval, it was always love again, no problem. But the intervals grew longer.

After college, I moved to the Lower East Side, where I got very into postmodern dance, especially of the contact improv variety. I took classes at Movement Research, religiously attended dance performances at the Judson Church, no matter how godawful, and took part in weekly contact jams at PS 122 that my boyfriend at the time disparagingly referred to as "touch club." I was becoming increasingly dedicated, in dance and in writing, to immanence rather than transcendence—to specific bodies rather than "the body," to mantras such as "after the ecstasy, the laundry." Yet in my personal life, I remained drawn to charismatic people who knocked themselves out to have mystical, dramatic experiences. Often, this meant substances. One of my first boyfriends in New York—the guy who made fun of touch club—was a distinctly Lhasa-esque figure—larger than life, full of magic: the way we sat around drinking heavily steeped tea in his drafty Victorian at water's edge, talking about Kierkegaard and listening to early Dionne Warwick, the way he kept house (he too knew the rule about having one perfect iteration of each object), all reminded me of her. We even threw the I Ching. But his eyes were pinned, and his magic was dark. You can't always have one type of magic without the other, I know now. But you can learn to lean.

Another guy I hung around with for a while was a Montreal-based dancer with whom I had begun a lackluster threesome affair at a summer dance festival where he had been my teacher. After the festival, he maintained an interest in me, which was kind of flattering, and also kind of not; given our age differential, it was all a little typical. Not having anything better to do, however, and wanting to see Lhasa, I accepted his invitation to visit him in Montreal. I think I thought, since this guy was kind of a clown—literally—she might be impressed. We went to see her sing at a café, and it was my first time watching her perform with a musician, fully engaged with her audience. Not long later, she put out *La Llorona*, which promptly made her a star.

The attention was what she'd been angling for all along, but once it came, it freaked her out. A short time later, she left Montreal for France, to be, once again, with her sisters.

While she was in France, we exchanged letters. Someday I'll find them. They're no doubt sitting in a little white shed on my mother's property, along with the rest of my correspondence and diaries from age sixteen to thirty-three. I used to be someone who kept meticulous diaries, made collages and mixed tapes, wrote friends and lovers long letters, took Polaroids, and made poetry out of cut-up newspapers. Now I sit here in front of my Mac like everyone else, and hope that my thinking hasn't become as homogenized as my technology. If I were to bust out the rubber cement now, it would be performative nostalgia. I don't know if those modes of expression are unique to one's teens and twenties, or if magic has simply seeped from me. The older I get, the less open I feel to magic, or the less compelled I feel to make it or seek it. I don't know if this is has to do with sobriety, or depression, or happiness, or age.

I think I pretty much know what our letters were like, anyway. I know she told me all about the city of Marseilles, the performances she was doing with her sisters' circus, and a failing love. I know they were written in her meticulous, upright printing in blue ink, with sketches of the city, and that face, in the margins.

By the time Lhasa visited me at the trapeze loft, she was done with France, and was touring her second album, *The Living Road*. She had performed in Park Slope a few nights earlier, and I had brought a writer friend to the show. This writer friend was unusually alive to magic, and I had wanted him to see and feel everything in her that I felt and saw, as if sharing the magic might make it grow. On stage that night Lhasa was generous, beatific, stunning. She knew it; I'd never seen her know it. I wouldn't have been shocked if she'd emerged from the green room afterward in furs.

After our tea at the loft, we walked around Williamsburg. It was freezing, so we had to hustle up and down Bedford to keep warm. I told her all about the book I had just finished, about the 1969 murder of my mother's sister, Jane. She told me all about a dress she had recently purchased for a music awards ceremony. It was clear that Lhasa's fame had exceeded, had perhaps even vaulted over, New York City, a place which was my everything, but which now seemed provincial in her presence. (This may be because New York City—and the United States in general—never received Lhasa as she was received elsewhere, perhaps due to our national tendency to dump all non-English singing into "world music." Someone even told me the other day that Apple Music had her listed under "soft rock.") I had never seen Lhasa excited about fashion before. It moved me, to hear her describe her dress. It was *so beautiful*, she said, her breath puffing white in the cold. *Like I wouldn't believe.*

And that was it. That was the last time I saw her.

I've been reading a lot of Thomas Bernhard lately, whose novels often feature a masculinized version of the Ferrante plot. There's often a genius figure—a dead man—around whom the narrator rotates: the narrator has to go through the dead man's papers, account for his last days, reckon with the friend's unfinished opus.

Like Wittgenstein—an intimate player in Bernhard's universe—Bernhard acts a kind of magician: by writing in and around inexpressible, unfinished genius, and by allowing his narrator to be a kind of dufus—someone who parses and perseverates—Bernhard creates his own work of genius, i.e., the novel we hold in our hands. I used to think, if I were a novelist, I might try for something of the same. I would write about someone like Lhasa, letting my narrator exhibit her own paucity of magic, her spiritual shallowness, her lack of charisma, her comparative cowardice, her defensive recourse to irony. The narrator would be the Freudian to her Jungian, the Beckett to her Joyce, the unbeliever to her faith, the average-looking to her great beauty. Yet somehow the reader would come to appreciate the narrator as well. Neither would triumph. They could just be themselves.

For ten years I had imagined that, when her *New York Times* obituary said she'd battled cancer for two years, it meant that Lhasa had sought any and all means possible to stay alive. I had imagined that, all options finally exhausted, her huge family had rallied around her, with siblings and relatives flying in from all over the globe to be by her side. But Goodman's book told a different story. As Goodman tells it, after her diagnosis, Lhasa basically froze. "I need some time to think," she told people. For months and months, she took that time. No mastectomy. No chemo. No treatment, save special diets, and a visit to a Brazilian healer. "Lhasa remained guarded about her condition," Goodman writes. "She gave out very little information about her condition, even to her family. There were a few months when she wasn't even sharing her status with them." After a lifetime of seeking and embodying wisdom, Lhasa seemed lost. Those who advocated for treatment got shut out. Her friend Watson told Goodman: "We were not allowed to say goodbye. It leaves it raw."

Of course, stage 3–4 is stage 3–4; there's no telling what treatment would have mattered. But many people who loved her were angry. "I was mad at her," Watson told Goodman. "This

Vitamin C bullshit. I can respect romance and the bubble. But there's a time to call a spade a spade. Smarten up and go get chemo." Her last boyfriend put it a little differently: "I don't know if I would qualify it as denial. That wasn't the quality of it. She didn't quite spurn treatment—she reasonably approached Cancer Inc. the way she did everything, not taking it on gospel. And she definitely sought alternative treatments. I think it was closer to being a personal and private struggle for her."

Upon learning all this, the shame I had felt about falling out of touch, and the anger I had felt about not having known she was sick, evaporated. In their place, I felt more tenderness for my friend than I ever thought possible.

The Mahabharata says: "Of all the world's wonders, which is the most wonderful? That no man, though he sees others dying all around him, believes that he himself will die." To write about a dead person risks showcasing this error. It has a certain smugness to it, the smugness of the still-living. I wish I could stamp out this smugness as I write. But then I might also stamp out the wonder.

In one of my favorites of Lhasa's songs, "Is Anything Wrong?," she asks if time will make us wise. For the past few years, I've been literally praying for it to do so. I don't want to grow old, or older, with the same, festering neuroses that have tortured me, if not made me, this far. I want to abandon my habitual churning, the confines of my own bubble. For my own sake—and also for that of my son—I want to model a certain form of acceptance, a willingness to take life on life's terms. If time alone makes us wise, then I wouldn't have to *do* anything to achieve this acceptance. But that's not what the song says. The song asks a question.

Near the end of Goodman's book, I found the answer to what I somehow most needed to know. And that is that Lhasa's dying was hard. Very hard. Goodman describes her as being, at the end, blind, unable to walk, restless, unaware of what she was doing.

He doesn't give any more details, and he never mentions pain. He just quotes her sister Gabby, one of the handful of people who was there to witness Lhasa's final decline: "I wish *like hell* that she had decided to end her life by her own choice several months earlier than go through what she went through...I don't know if there is value in watching someone that you love suffer so horribly. I don't think there's value in it. And that's my takeaway."

I read these words in my dark office in the early morning hours, before the sun comes up, before anyone else is awake. As if it might evacuate their pain, I flip back to YouTube, and mindlessly scroll the comments by her videos: "now she twinkles high in the heavens like the star we already knew her to be," "She's in Heaven now, a welcome addition to a choir of angels," "R.I.P., my goddess." They say what I always wanted everyone to say, yet today I find them enraging. Lhasa *was* a star, an angel, a goddess, if there are such things. But she was also a goofy, struggling, often lonely human who, near the end, had apparently become fed up with certain of her stories, her bubble, and was looking for new ways. "I don't think she ever wanted to let go of the castles in the sky. And she was starting to," a friend told Goodman. Her last boyfriend echoed this assessment: "She was done with churning in her own solitary romantic sufferings. She was really done with that."

Was she done by April 2009, at that house party in Montreal, memorialized in video by Vincent Moon? By June of that year she would start to get headaches, which would soon become seizures. The video pans over the hipsters lined up against the wall, squatting on the floor, all intently watching her body. I think back to all the eyes fixed on her during our All School Meetings, and I want to break into the frame, protect her from all the prying eyes, all those voyeurs to her swan song. But I know by then she was a star, and could handle any crowd.

Awake again before dawn, I find that Goodman has sent me a new video, also from April 2009. It's another Moon piece, this one produced for the tenth anniversary of her death, containing rehearsal footage for a tour she would never take (for her last record, the self-titled *Lhasa*), along with snippets of an interview with her no one has ever seen. The video is dark, dark light in the dark of my office. Her face looks like it's struggling to emerge from the shadows; it unnerves me. At the video's end, she gives a long description of her song "Going In," in which two unborn souls—*deux ami*—are sitting on a ledge, discussing the pros and cons of jumping off a cliff, into life. The jump would be the moment of conception, of choosing to be born, no matter what's to come.

That story is familiar enough. But Lhasa's "going in" isn't just about choosing life despite its inevitable suffering. Her narrator—which, she makes clear, is also her—is going for "intentional blindness." "It's like I am choosing to dive into life and to lose my lucidity, to lose my wisdom, to be blinded by life. It's as if life were a sort of loss of vision…that's somehow what it is." The narrator-friend tells her listening-friend that it's worth it to walk *away* from God, *away* from Truth, in exchange for a life spent seeking such things. "Just for the trip!" Lhasa laughs, impressed by her friend's valiant idiocy.

Diaphoresis

Margo Jefferson

1957–59

I stare at the album cover: BUD POWELL: JAZZ ORIGINAL.

When I'm alone I take it out of the record cabinet and stare, whether or not I intend to play it. Sometimes I put it back unplayed. And think on that face, that dark, sweating face.

The camera has presumed to walk up and stare. He's closed his eyes. His face is shadow and smoky light against a gray and muted-black night expanse. His hair and mustache are black. There's a patch of white shirt and striped tie, a patch of suit. He could be floating alone in a cosmos of his own design. His lips are parted. (Humming, breathing, as he sweats.) He's possessed by his music. In a state of ecstatic—let us use the Greek word for sweat—*diaphoresis.*

I was eight, I was nine, and I'd learned to slip the record from its jacket, hold it by the edges and avoid breathing quickly when I placed it on the spindle and pressed ("don't hit, *press*") PLAY. I would choose records for the whole family to hear but I'd always find separate time to listen alone on the living room couch, sometimes rocking back and forth. When I played Bud Powell's records, I thought his piano was like Ariadne's maze, fingers winding into runs, angling into chords, lucidity racing virtuosity across every beat and turn. I was reading Greek myths then. I made him Theseus of course, the hero wresting beauty and harmony from a monster's grasp, his right hand unspooling the red thread of coherence, left hand scrutinizing, probing, assessing his progress.

I couldn't admit, not yet, that he was the Minotaur too, half-man half-bull, of cursed and sacred origin; despised, feared, locked up, and turned into a ravenous monster whose task was to kill the young and beautifully human. Bud Powell was a genius-monster, made a genius through hour on hour of ravenous music listening and practice; made a monster by years of cop beatings, medications, liquor, breakdowns, electroshock treatments, heroin, and forced confinements in mental institutions. Half-man, half-beast—the designation assigned Blacks and enforced by law and practice, the punitive ire of rulers who imprisoned them in institutional labyrinths where their task was to destroy other prisoners and thereby demonstrate their own debasement. The famous story, the legend: Powell, playing the piano keys he had drawn on the wall of one such place, asking a visitor, "What do you think of these chords?" Don't pity him. He'd crafted the tool he needed to flee brick and concrete for the glass enclosures of his music.

Brave monster, lead the way!

Give us headlong runs; give us cheeky headstrong chords and titles. "So Sorry, Please." "Tempus Fugue-it." "Un Poco Loco."

Then suddenly my preteen heart would need the more tranquil strains of unimpeded romance.

The evening breeze caressed the trees... Tenderly.

I loved Erroll Garner's version of "Tenderly." It was written as a waltz in 1947, the year I was born, a waltz of flowing upward lifts and downward sweeps; even when jazz musicians made it a 4/4 ballad they acknowledged its mood of suave rapture.

Erroll Garner *bestowed* that rapture. His piano led you into the luxe abandon of post-war romance. He was a buoyant, lavish sybarite.

Powell's wary notes withhold the arch and ache of the song's opening, letting (or making) us find our way to the melody, pausing to let notes that seem about to become impetuous circle and almost stutter; withholding, testing runs and letting us have a few measures of rapturous dynamics, chords "kissed"—here they're almost battered—"by sea and mist / Tenderly." A few quiet treble runs, a few self-contained arpeggios, a dissenting interval.

Impossibly elegant ("Parisian Thoroughfare," "Strictly Confidential") you slay the monster and triumph—in the world—in yourself. He was a brave and blazing monster, defying with his harsh left-hand chords, his right hand probing, constructing, sometimes repeating those emphatic beats in measure after measure like a willfully aggressive speech pattern. Don't pity him.

"The evening breeze caressed the trees…Tenderly." Erroll Garner's "Tenderly" cushions you, so as to guide, usher you into the stately lavish mansions of a love affair. Powell disguises that path with pristinely thoughtful notes, restraining his runs, permitting only a few measures of chords "kissed by sea and mist…"

As I write I play Powell's "Strictly Confidential" Suave and cheeky. Harlem nonchalance. I play "Parisian Thoroughfare." Allegro Brillante with flâneur ease.

My father had told me a bit about Powell. The musicians he awed night after night at Minton's on 118th Street.

Now I'm playing "In Walked Bud"—Monk based it on the chord changes of "Blue Skies." In walked Bud and scattered particles of light gathered into skies of boundless blue.

He was a genius, my father said. He went mad. I heard it as he blazed through unsanctioned notes and chords. What was it like

141

to blaze and blast through unsanctioned states of mind? My father always spoke gravely of our menaced and martyred race giants. He'd begin by talking to me—I felt respected—and he'd end staring into a silence where the weight of elegies, past, passing or to come, was his alone.

"If it were possible, I would gather my race into my arms and fly away with them." Years later when I read these words I almost dropped to my knees. Ida B. Wells could have written them for my father. He'd longed to be a jazz musician, not a doctor. He'd played the trombone and he'd worshipped Duke Ellington. Oh to be what Lawrence Brown was, the Duke's chosen trombonist. To heal with art.

"Why did you choose pediatrics?" I once asked my father.

"I wanted to find out what was wrong with people who couldn't tell me themselves," he said.

He wanted to be a rescuer. He became one.

But he wanted more to be rescued.

They could enrage me, these valorous, wounded men. I was a child. Why did I have to absorb all this? Why couldn't Bud Powell find a way to be Theseus, I thought—slay the monster, defy the men who'd made him one, and outwit the monster inside himself?

Why couldn't my father find time to gather me in his arms each day and take solace in my company?

He took pride in my brightness, my school successes, the talent my piano teacher Muriel Rose said she saw in me. A contributor, not a martyr, Miss Rose had studied with Florence Price (recite it together, children), the first Negro woman to have a symphony performed by a major symphony orchestra (the Chicago Symphony Orchestra). Miss Rose had been a composer before she became a teacher. What sacrifice, what quiet martyrdom lay here? Had she abandoned composing as my father had abandoned his trombone?

Maybe he hadn't wanted children—he was already caring for so many. But maybe having no children would hurt a pediatrician's credibility... So even if he didn't want them, he might have felt he needed them for professional reasons.

A child decides: I cannot, I should not have to take all of this in. "I will turn these confounding dangers, these losses into a workbook of behaviors I can manage." Scenarios to follow; reactions to memorize and absorb. Preventive pedagogy. I will quash what's unbearable. It's a long-playing record to be returned to the cabinet.

*

I've reached an emotional stalemate. I want to dilute, possibly delete this "Ah the lifelong wounds of childhood" climax. I feel a little ashamed.

"Sometimes it is better to be a little ashamed rather than silent"
Czesław Miłosz

Should I go forward to the vistas of adult life?
   No. Let's stay where we were.

The record has gone back into the cabinet.

I take out an Ella Fitzgerald LP...

On her album covers Ella Fitzgerald dresses tastefully. On the cover of *Ella Sings Gershwin* (1955) she wears chic nightclub attire: a ranch mink stole beneath which we glimpse a dusky rose gown in a fabric shimmering discreetly. No lurid outsized jewelry. On *Ella Sings the Duke Ellington Songbook* (1957) she wears a smart black middy blouse with a white sailor collar and white cuffs. Her left hand holds sheet music; a sleek ladies' wristwatch is also visible, as is a gold wedding band. She is as much matron as musician.

On a spinning black disk she sounds like all I could dream of. She's a romantic comedy heroine with perfect pitch and varied pace. Mischief, longing, quicksilver charm.

In the 1980s when my best friend (white) is writing about thirties romantic comedies I play at a game of appropriation and compensation; I match her white Hollywood stars with my Black jazz ones: Ella is Jean Arthur and Carole Lombard; Ivie Anderson is Claudette Colbert; Billie Holiday is Barbara Stanwyck with Bette Davis touches.

The black disk is spinning through the late 1950s and early sixties, back to my preteen-girl state. Like most preteen girls I long to be physically desirable; like most Black preteen girls I long to be physically desirable while also being physically impeccable. Her tastefulness does not make me enjoy looking at Ella Fitzgerald's album covers. She is portly. Forever, perpetually portly. The first lady of jazz never sheds pounds dramatically, never transforms herself against all metabolic odds and sashays for the camera, the set, in form-flaunting outfits. The way Judy Garland does. The way Oprah Winfrey will.

She can't lose weight. And when she sings on television she sweats.

Black women of achievement with ambitions need to be wary about their public relationship to sweat. (If you're Althea Gibson or Wilma Rudolph, it's understood that you must sweat to succeed. But don't bring it out of the locker room.) Historically, sweat is for workers who have no choice but to labor by the sweat of their brows, the sweat in their armpits, the sweat that soaks through their clothing, making it stained and smelly. "Work and sweat, cry and sweat, pray and sweat!"[1]

Ella Fitzgerald sweats in concert halls, in nightclubs (are there sweat stains on that dusky rose gown when she's through performing in it?), on national television shows. On television sweat dots her brow and drips, even pours down her cheeks. Sweat dampens her pressed and curled hair. Sweat runs into the stones of her dangling earrings. Like Louis Armstrong, she uses a white handkerchief. Louis Armstrong, Satchmo the Great, dares to sweat before multitudes. He knows many of his white fans think it's happy sweat. Smile and sweat, laugh and sweat, play music, sweat! Onstage and on television he's never without his white handkerchief, wiping the sweat from his face, wiping the spit and sweat from his trumpet valve. His African mask of a face (the beaming-grimace smile, the fixed popped eyes) makes this a ritual though, not a necessity. His ritual of artistic diaphoresis.

Who makes fun of his girth, his dark skin, in public? He wipes his sweat vigorously, proudly; she dabs at hers quickly, almost daintily. If one *dabs* at sweat it becomes more refined. It gentrifies into euphemism; it becomes "perspiration." White women, even white ladies, are permitted to perspire. But on television white women singers do not perspire. Which means that, even as she swings, scats, and soars, Ella Fitzgerald's sweat threatens to drag her back into the maw of working-class Black female labor.

To her years on the streets, alleys, and sidewalks of New York: To age fifteen when her mother dies of a heart attack and her stepfather gets abusive, when she flees, first to an aunt in Harlem then to the streets. The once-excellent student cuts school day after day.

Does courier duty for a number racket.

Does lookout duty for a brothel.

Earns small change with bits of song and dance.

Gets arrested.

The charge is truancy and the courts dispatch her to the Colored Orphan Asylum in Riverdale, New York. Why is she sent upstate to a reform school a few months later? Who has she angered, what has she done? Is this asylum—the only one in New York to house colored children—hopelessly overcrowded?

Ella Jane Fitzgerald is sent to the New York State Training School for Girls in Hudson, New York, a reform school for white and Black girls, and the only such racially integrated institution. Seven of the ten the Judge sentences that year are Black. Most of the inmates, whatever their race, have been convicted of nothing but truancy—truant (noun) means "beggar, vagabond"; *truant* (adjective) means "wretched, miserable, of low caste"; *truant* (verb) means escaping, rebelling, despairing, raging in perpetual motion. All of these girls, thirteen to fifteen years old, arrive bearing the weight of words like "wayward," "morally impaired," and "incorrigible." Ella, in the words of the Judge, is "ungovernable and will not follow the just and lawful commands of her mother." Thank you for your careful attention to this case, Judge. Her mother is dead.

Once they arrive at the school, the girls are housed in squalid cottages and often—we can assume regularly—abused in various ways by various members of the staff. This would be the place to note with rue that at least there was a choir for Ella to sing with. There wasn't: only white girls were allowed in the Training School choir.

She is, however, singled out for solo beatings in a locked basement.

A year later she makes her escape. By what means? Does someone help her? (An inmate pal? A sympathetic cook or janitor?) Who leaves the basement door unlocked?

Ella Jane Fitzgerald flees, walks, runs, craws, and hitchhikes the one hundred and twelve miles from Hudson, New York, to Harlem.

Over valleys, streets and alleys, winding trails,
Over highways, rocky byways, through hills and vales...[2]

She is making her bid for whatever self-governance the streets will allow. Scuffle, shuffle, warble; stand outside the doors of nightclubs and theaters (or squeeze your way in to listen); do what you must with whoever provides you a night's meal and board. You will rassle up a future or join the anonymous thousands who live and die trying.

At last it's 1934! At last it's time for this seventeen-year-old runaway to walk onto the stage of the Apollo Theater, and into her destiny as the Swing Muse of Harlem. She will win its fabled Amateur Night contest; she will be noticed, introduced to important bandleaders. But she's still the brown-skinned girl in the raggedy clothes: Fletcher Henderson won't hire her. What about Chick Webb, the bandleader whose drums rule the revels at the Savoy Ballroom? He must be persuaded; she's too ugly he protests the first time around—he of the hunched back, the tubercular spine, that will kill him five years from now—does he worry that the sight of two plain people on stage, one malformed, one gawky and chubby, would presume too much on the good will/ask too much of his merry-making audience? But he's persuaded. And rewarded. Three years later Ella is responsible for the band's first nation-wide Number One hit record. The words and tune are hers, as is the idea. *It was a game I played in the orphanage*, she says lightly, and says no more.

I started to brood about this in 1996. Every December the *New York Times Magazine* dedicated an issue to the celebrated who'd died that year. I was asked to write about Ella Fitzgerald. I'd reviewed Stuart Nicholson's 1994 biography; I sat down with it and with all my albums. Then I wrote:

Ever since I found out about the horrors of Ella Fitzgerald's youth I've wanted to protect her from the scrutiny of critics and fans like myself, who have always inflected the pleasure we took in her singing with patronization. Sweet Ella, we said when she was alive, she's wonderful but she has no emotional depth. Poor Ella we say now; she did suffer but she denied it—banished it from her life so she could dwell in a pristine musical wonderland.

*

She is twenty-one. From her mother's love untimely ripped she tucks an elegy inside/into a nursery rhyme.

The standard nineteenth-century version:

A-Tisket A-Tasket
A green and yellow basket
I sent a letter to my love and on the way I dropped it.

Ella's 1933 version:

"A-Tisket A-Tasket the *wrong*-colored basket!" jokes *New York Post* columnist Earl Wilson, for Ella has made the song's green and yellow basket brown and yellow. But how could brown be the wrong color for brown-skinned Temperance Fitzgerald, who left Newport News, Virginia with her daughter Ella Jane circa 1920 and settled in Yonkers, New York where a better life could be sought and found?

The Original:

I sent a letter to my love
And on the way I dropped it

Ella's sends hers to the "mommy" she lost at fifteen, the mother of the fairy tales she must have read in her Yonkers elementary school, the "mommy" of Cinderella, and Snow White, who dies too young to shield her daughter from neglect and cruelty. (Ella's voice curls into near-baby talk when she sings the word "mommy.")

The Original:

> I dropped it, I dropped it
> And on the way I dropped it
> A little boy he picked it up
> And put it in his pocket

Ella makes the thieving boy a "little girlie" like herself—a gleeful doppelgänger, who goes "trucking on down the avenue" (make it Lenox Avenue); who goes "peck-peck-pecking all around / Until she spies it on the ground." (As Chick Webb's drums voice Lindy Hop chicken peck moves, Ella's second self steals the letter, missing nary a beat.

Abandon hope all ye who enter the sphere of a child's despair.

> She took it she took, she took my yellow basket
> And if she doesn't bring it back I think that I will die!

It's a child's wail kept in check by the implacable, impeccable beat. The orchestra's a congenial but watchful guardian: it insists on the good behavior of a snappy riff and major key.

Which Ella Jane rejects with a minor key retort and a defiant unresolved note. Do not deny a child her despair.

> If that girlie don't return it
> Don't know what I'll do!

Here's the point I suddenly realize—she's becoming the song's auteur. Coding, shaping, her future as a soloist, a band member, a leader and a collaborator.

It's a stringent discipline even when it's ebullient and joyous. The band indulges her with eight bars of major–minor call-and-response. When her voice curves around the beat, heading for a lament, their chorus keeps her firmly upright and uptempo.

> Oh gee I wonder where that basket can be...
> (So do *we* so do *we* so do *we* so do *we*
> So do we!)

> Oh gee, I wish that little girl I could see.
> (So do *we* so do *we* so do *we* so do *we*
> So do we!

The legato balm of saxes will sweeten her next outburst.

> Oh why was I so careless with that basket of mine?
> That itty-bitty basket was a joy of mine.

But "itty-bitty basket" is a wail. If she'd been a perfect child, would she have lost her mother? Futile to mourn, says the band. You're a grown girl now. You're an errand girl for rhythm. Pulse and syncopate.

> A TISKET! (March!) A TASKET! (Yes!)
> I lost my yellow basket!
> Won't someone help me find my basket
> And make me happy again a-a-gain?

Ella slips a quick blue note into that last triplet. The band's acknowledgment is a few minor key measures and then they all hit the swing playground for a jaunty call-and-response finale.

> Was it red?
> NoNoNOOONo
> Was it green?
> NoNoNOOONo
> Was it blue
> NoNo   NOOO No
> Just a little yellow basket!

A snappy four-beat salute from the band. A snappy repeat from the singer. The record spins to an end and hurtles up the music charts.

TOP OF THE WORLD, MA! This twenty-one-year-old orphan is a star who will live and flourish for fifty-eight more years, securing her reign as the First Lady of Song and the First Lady of Jazz. And for fifty-eight years she will not speak of her past. Ever. She will offer no pained or ruefully tranquil admissions, no touchingly unguarded confessions. She will refuse our scrutiny and our pity.

I know nothing of this when I am an anxious preteen taking Ella Fitzgerald LPs out of the record cabinet in search of a pristine musical wonderland. Only her sweat and heft give me intimations of the Black female destiny she has thwarted, banished. It's a destiny that every hour, day, and year of my young life has been plotted to prevent. And in this swathed and sheltered life, I am squeamish about the public evidence of her sweat and size.

When I return to Nicholson's 1994 biography, a folded-down page marks this excruciating item from a 1938 issue of *DownBeat* magazine. "220 pounds of songstress" goes the headline, then:

Portly Ella Fitzgerald was a bit late for a recording date last week when she was caught in the escape hatch of an elevator. The infernal machine stalled between floors and Ella, already late for a recording date, endeavored to escape through a trapdoor in the top of the cage. It took three strong men to rescue the 220-pound songbird. Ella opens March 28 at The Blue Note.

(Sixty years on I want to beat them around the head and ears till they cry "Uncle!" and beg her pardon.)

In the fifties and sixties, when her status as the First Lady of two realms is assured, do ardent fans politely call her "big" or do they just go ahead and call her fat? (Not without pity—and it's such a lovely voice, they quickly add.)

Are her Black fans more courteous than her white ones?

Whatever their race, however much they respect her musicianship, do male musicians who work with her talk this way? Do they joke, fifties and sixties-style, that she probably started sweating even more once she entered menopause? Not to her face, no, but behind her back, when she can't control them with her ravishing, diaphoretic musicianship?

We—multiple we's—always called her Ella. I'll call her Miss Fitzgerald now as I study her album covers. Miss Fitzgerald, you dress with such alert and tasteful care, your choices always appropriate for club, concert, festival, or television. When you perform you sometimes cup your cheek to hear yourself more precisely. You were never at ease with TV show patter, staged spontaneities; you'd clasp your hands in your lap and gesture a bit uncomfortably after the scripted retort, the obliging response to a joke or pleasantry.

Your earrings were always distinctive without being show-offy. Sometimes you had a semi-natural cap of frizzy curls—that was in the fifties and how contemporary and smart, how unashamed it looks now. The young singer Camille Thurman says she watched all your videos, feeling so proud, taking such pleasure in your appearance, which for her was inseparable from your performance.

Ella Fitzgerald, you worked hard for your sweat.

You earned it like Bud Powell, like Louis Armstrong. And here I can't stop Yeats from entering my head, the lines from "Adam's Curse" where the male poet labors to make beauty and the female muse labors to be Beauty. I can't—why should I?—stop them from entering my head; I can stop them from doing the same work they were doing when I first loved Yeats in college.

Ella Fitzgerald Rehearses

I said, "A line will take us hours maybe"
Yet if it does not seem a moment's thought,
Our stitching and unstitching has been naught.

Ella Fitzgerald Flees Caste Servitude for Music Service

Better go down upon your marrow-bones
And scrub a kitchen pavement, or break stones
Like an old pauper in all kinds of weather

Ella Fitzgerald Claims Her Artistry

For to articulate sweet sounds together
Is to work harder than all those.

Ella Fitzgerald knew what any woman ever belittled, ignored, or punished for being not-beautiful knows in her beauty-pauper bones.

To be born woman is to know
Although they do not talk of it at school
That we must labor to be beautiful.

That we must labor to make beauty, each one as she may.

At the end of your 1960s Berlin concert, you took hold of that sweet and lovely standard, "How High the Moon," and built it anew as an explosive eight-minute swing-bop expedition into popular music archives, "popular" including Charlie Parker, Ferde Grofé, Harold Arlen, Slam Stewart, Rimsky-Korsakov, and your own "Tisket." Parenthetical phrases, melodic digressions, harmonic insertions—it would be profligate if its proportions weren't flawless (at critic Will Friedwald's last count, you drew on forty-five pieces for your extended, mostly-scatted solo). You ended with the opening lines of "Smoke Gets In Your Eyes," that resplendent Kern and Harbach lament. *They asked me how I knew / My true love was true"* you sang like a bugler sounding a wake-up call. *"I of course replied, Something here inside..."* and then, then, instead of singing Harbach's *"Cannot be denied,"* you declared your victory with the words:

SWEAT GETS IN MY EYES

After that it was easy, just a matter of scanning an octave and letting the final four "moon"s take off like the four stages of a rocket.

Your mind is your music laboratory, stocked with compositions you broke down and recombined. Melodic or harmonic phrase inserted, interpolated; digressions and decoys. Or maybe it's a version of a dressmaker's swatch book; each song ("Flight of the Bumblebee," "Night in Tunisia," "Darktown Strutter's Ball") a piece of fabric you assess, display or join to other swatches for that final glorious garment.

Ella Fitzgerald, you labored to be beautiful.

You earned your diaphoresis day by day, night by night, rehearsal by rehearsal, tour by tour.

People should have begged for the elixir of your sweat.

I do.

I beg for it.

---

[1] Zora Neale Hurston, 1995. "Sweat," *Hurston: Novels and Stories*. New York: The Library of America.

[2] "Lonesome Swallow," J. C. Johnson, Andy Razaf, sung by Ethel Waters.

Sonic Seasonings: The Genius of Wendy Carlos

Sinéad Gleeson

We open, with an opening:

A vast lake of black or silver depending on how the light catches, the shade an indication of its depth; surface all glass. Alongside, a car travels an isolated road, bisecting an immense forest. It cuts a strange, man-made trough through a sea of firs. We track it overhead: olive treetops tinted white by autumn sun, casting shadows as the camera stalks a yellow Volkswagen with Colorado plates. The shot broadens, revealing the vast snow-capped spires of the Rocky Mountains. The film's famous title appears in blue font and both the typographic choice and idyllic landscape are not visually typical of horror. What makes it so creepy is something else; the lushness is accompanied by a unique, menacing sound. Low electronic notes boom; orchestral, drone-like. By the time the car reaches a tunnel through the mountain, a slow purr begins, building into a ululation of terror. It's one of the most memorable soundtracks in film history, and its creator—who turns eighty-three in 2022—remains one of the most enigmatic composers of the twenty-first century: Wendy Carlos. For a time in the 1970s and early 80s, she was the go-to auteur for directors looking for futuristic scores rooted in apocalyptic electronics. If you wanted sounds that no one else was using, Carlos was the person to call—as Stanley Kubrick did, for this famous opening scene, as well as for *A Clockwork Orange*. Carlos was an outlier, a maestra in her field, but little has been heard of her in recent years. Her last album was released in 1998, and the bulk of her work is out of print. Anyone uploading her music to YouTube quickly finds themselves on the receiving end of a legal takedown. As time goes on, there is a real fear that her legacy will slip away. It's one she has total control over, but chooses not to be public about. Fans all over the world are protective of Carlos, and I know I'm not the only person who has typed and deleted an email to the webmaster address on her charmingly retro-looking website. The price of being an artist who connects with so many is an audience's desire for ownership; for visibility and engagement, which they have no right to. Until then, there is only the work, the corpus of an unparalleled practitioner.

*

Wendy Carlos was born on November 14th, 1939, in Pawtucket, Rhode Island. Aged six, she began taking piano lessons, but the family couldn't afford an actual piano so her father drew the keys on a sheet of paper for her to practice on. Later, she mastered the organ, and by ten had composed her first piece of music, "A Trio for Clarinet, Accordion and Piano." She built a hi-fi system, and later won a science scholarship for constructing her own computer. By the time she was a teenager, *playing* music wasn't enough: Carlos wanted to know how to create it—not just the physical instrumentation, but how to record it—make something new. In the basement of her parents' house, she experimented with reverb and constructed a tape machine.

Later, studying at Brown University, Carlos moved from a single subject degree to a combined one of physics and music—two subjects she excelled in, and which for her were inextricable.

The science was in the music, and the music was possible because of technology. To subsist, she took work scoring short films, which taught her about synching music to film, and got a job at Gotham Recording Studios, creating jingles for ads. In 1962, Carlos undertook a Masters in music composition at the Columbia-Princeton Electronic Music Center (CEAM), home of the vast RCA Mark II Synthesizer. There, she learned how to record each sound onto a section of tape, which was then laboriously cut together in order. There's a tactility and precision to this process, requiring infinite patience, but Carlos was committed. Her mentors—Vladimir Ussachevsky and Otto Luening—were pioneers in using tape to make electronic music, and had an interest in avant-garde composition. Carlos was less enthralled by the latter, or by serialism and twelve-tone music, and in an interview with composer Frank Oteri, she described it as: "non-rhythmic, non-melodic and non-harmonic."

At CEAM, she opted for a graveyard shift, working on music projects through the night when she was unlikely to be interrupted. Listening to the later midnight shifts; as if working through quiet, dark hours alone, impacted on the kind of tones and sounds she made. It would be another decade before Carlos worked in film, but the eerie, nocturnal atmosphere of those nights must have stayed with her, seeping into the compositions.

After Ussachevsky and Luening, Wendy Carlos met two other people who would have a life-changing influence on her. In 1967, Rachel Elkind was working for the head of Columbia Records, who were about to launch "Back-to-Bach," an attempt to reinvigorate their classical catalog. Contemporary composers and artists were approached to update the work of the German composer, and Elkind landed Carlos a commission. Finally, Carlos would get to release music, even if it wasn't wholly her own compositions, it was the beginning: an opportunity to see what the modular synth could really do. While Elkind championed and kickstarted Carlos's career, it was meeting Bob Moog that steered her creative process in a whole other direction. He recognized the depth of her technological genius, and without her, Moog's life's work might have been considerably different.

The Moog name is now synonymous with coveted synths and ubiquitous plug-ins, but in the mid-sixties, its creator's journey in sound equipment was just beginning. In 1964 Carlos attended the Audio Engineering Society conference in New York, and found Moog manning a stand of his complicated synthesizers. Comprised of voltage-controlled oscillators, with switches and cables for patching through notes, it resembled an old telephone exchange; a bulky sentinel of sound requiring a lot of space. The meeting was fate—and mutually beneficial. Bob Moog wanted to make his synths more accessible to the public, but the early prototypes were cumbersome, expensive, and often sold as separates. Carlos bought her first Moog—a 900 series—and agreed to compose music to showcase what the synth could do. In return, Bob Moog provided her with discounts on future Moog purchases. Carlos also began offering technical advice on developing the equipment further, and Moog began incorporating these suggestions into the hardware. It quickly became clear that his new collaborator had a serious compositional gift and could achieve things with the Moog that he simply couldn't. He was in awe, and Carlos was similarly effusive about him. "[Bob] was a creative engineer who spoke music: I was a musician who spoke science. It felt like a meeting of simpatico minds."

*

A few feet from where I write, there are several synthesizers, including a Moog Voyager—a later, more compact model, nothing in the realm of the bulky 1960s prototypes. The control panel is upright, with rows of dials and a small olive display screen for presets. My husband, S, is a composer, producer, and musician, and a long-time admirer of Wendy Carlos: of her ethos and commitment to technology, the sounds she painstakingly eked out of non-touch-sensitive keyboards, the catalog of sublime film soundtracks. In interviews about his own work, he regularly cites her as an influence, advocating for the vision of her process. Over lockdown, we replayed her albums and talked through the technical difficulties of her chosen process. Early Moogs were monophonic—the user could only play one note at a time—and without a computer, sound was produced note by note. It was a tedious and time-consuming graft to make the most basic melody. Nearly fifty years later, in the dark of a Dublin lockdown, we rolled through notes on the keyboard, bending the pitch, playing with filters and I can hear what intoxicated Carlos all those years ago.

*

When RCA produced its first synthesizer in 1955, the *Harpers* magazine reviewer, Edward Tatnall Canby, described it as having "a grotesquely inhuman quality…there is, indeed, everything in this synthesized sound but life itself." For Wendy Carlos, the experience couldn't have been more opposite. The synthesizer represented not just the future, but possibilities outside main-stream music and a means of assembling sound in a new way. *Switched-On Bach* was recorded in the basement of Wendy's apart-ment on a customized 8-track tape machine and the Moog synth. There were no pre-sets, sequencing, or instant patching options, which meant the entire process was grueling and repetitive. Ten Bach pieces were played entirely on the Moog, and the end result borders on carnivalesque; the notes a prophetic echo of early Nokia ringtones, even if some dismissed it as kitsch. The most famous piece, "Air on a G-String" has a poignancy that's less obvious in the orchestral original, but what's immediately clear is the power Carlos has over the instrument. Despite the early Moog limitations, she wrings every possible tone out of each note, playing with pace. Listening to it now, there's a long list of music that has borrowed from it: wacky squelches so beloved of nineties drum and bass; the frantic energy of "Prelude and Fugue No. 2" is vintage rave before the break drops. What can never be stated enough about Carlos is how ahead of her time the composition—and experimentation—was. The music wasn't for everyone, but if Columbia, Elkind, or Carlos hoped there was a niche market for *Switched-on Bach*, they vastly underestimated the response. It was an instant hit, selling over a million copies. It topped the Billboard Classical Albums, won three Grammys and was the biggest selling classical album of the decade. Glenn Gould applauded its "unflagging musicality" and it became the ultimate crossover record. But its success overwhelmed Carlos, and was possibly at the root of her later unease with fame and the attention it can bring.

A listener at home can easily forget how *physical* the act of making music is. Many times at a live show, I'm struck not just by the songs, but how much of the experience is created by the body: a voice for singing, lungs working the woodwind, hands on keys. Bob Moog knew that owning complicated, costly equipment was one thing, but finding someone with the skill to demonstrate its possibilities was essential to its success: "All synthesizer music is made by musicians," he said. "Synthesizers can make sound patterns: only human beings make music."

Every possible effect a musician, producer, or DJ could hope to eke out of a synth exists these days. Carlos not only persuaded Bob Moog to modify how chords were triggered, but also made advances in touch display, multi-channel audio, and quadra-phonic sound. She was a brilliant technician and, crucially, both a musician and engineer who understood the possibilities of sound and how to achieve them. Over the course of a year, Carlos built her own four-keyboard Wurlitzer II and outlines the intricate process on her website. It's a fascinating, extremely technical account, demonstrating an endless curiosity about sound waves, hardware, pistons, and couplers.

*

If Carlos's work and chosen medium was quite singular, she wasn't alone in her field. Other women—Eliane Radigue, Laura Spiegal, and Suzanne Ciani—were working with diverse elements of sound: analogue and modular synths, tape loops and programming, often collaborating with galleries, outside of the mainstream. In the world of music, Kraftwerk (formed in Düsseldorf in 1969) were contemporaries and certainly influenced by her. Their 1970 debut album featured mainly traditional instruments—guitar, flute, and violin—and while they were still a long way from "Autobahn" and "The Robots," they also used drone sounds. It's possible they missed *Switched-on Bach* in the late 1960s, but given how little synth music was around in the early 1970s, they certainly heard the *Clockwork Orange* soundtrack. In 1972, *Kraftwerk 2* still stuck with conventional instruments, but pointedly moves toward an electronic aesthetic. The production nods distinctly to the mechanics of tape-based avant-garde, using pitch changes in speed and echo effects. The first track, "Klingklang" (later the name of their Düsseldorf studio), uses a preset organ beatbox for percussion, but the opening moments operate in a cosmic space—a kind of intergalactic symphony, the precursor of their futuristic sound. Kraftwerk advocated for the concept of the man machine, using robots as stand-ins when performing their track of the same name. The hybrid musician/machine designation could apply to Carlos and the modular synth. She was the machine, and the machine was her: a sort of sonic symbiosis.

Echoes of Carlos's work didn't end with Kraftwerk: her 1972 album *Sonic Seasonings*—themed around the four seasons and comprised of Moog and field recordings—is one of the earliest examples of ambient music, pre-dating Brian Eno's *Discrete Music* by three years (Eno's mid-seventies work also made use of synths and tape delay). On the *Aladdinsane* tour, David Bowie's used "Ode to Joy" from *A Clockwork Orange* as his stage entrance music. Producer Giorgio Moroder cited Carlos as a key influence and a Moog modular synth features heavily on Donna Summer's "I Feel Love." In the same decade, Stevie Wonder was interested in working with Carlos, but when he visited her apartment, she pretended she wasn't in. She was intensely private and knew that high profile collaborations would bring more attention. In the 1980s, Vince Clarke (Depeche Mode, Erasure), The Human League's Phil Oakey and others championed not just her musical influence, but how she had made the synth into an instrument in its own right, not just a hardware sound tool. From Daft Punk to Mount Alaska and Octo Octa, her influence is still felt.

All through the lockdown, I returned to her albums and scores. As Dublin's streets remained quiet and remote, I listened again and again to *The Shining*, its dark lake, the roadside ululations. It felt apt. Carlos has a gift for tonal register, switching from sinister to melancholic, and the score suited the dystopia, my torpor, the sense that the world once familiar, would never be the same again. *The Shining* is not just a horror assemblage of blood elevators and telepathy, of dead twins and eerie hotel corridors: fundamentally it concerns a family cut off from the world, and the terrifying impact of isolation on the psyche. In the first lockdown wave, people were encouraged to stay home, and keep away from others. In the only room at home available to me to work, I listened to those droning loops. The building sense of dread in each note. Sometimes it transported me; other times the sounds were a dark cumulus, gathering over the house as the days spread identically into one another.

*

The visual, what's on screen, is the core of any director's practice, but Stanley Kubrick thought *a lot* about how *The Shining* should sound. He didn't want just any opening music; but something that would set the tone for the entire film, unnerving audiences before they'd met the characters or arrived at the Overlook Hotel. Carlos suggested "Dies Irae" ("Day of Wrath") by nineteenth-century French composer Berlioz, specifically "Dream of a Witches Sabbath" from Symphonie Fantastique. The piece traces an artist's obsession—Berlioz had been rejected by an Irish actress he was in love with—and the symphony moves through anger, nightmares, and visions of murder (possibly why it appealed to Kubrick given the breakdown of his central character Jack Torrance). Carlos wanted to recreate part of the sound with synths, but Kubrick was adamant about using an orchestra. In London, where the film was shot, Carlos and Rachel Elkind hired thirty-six musicians and recorded for seven hours (this was very much Carlos' work—she claimed that *Switched-on Bach* took more than one thousand hours to record). Kubrick, wedded to the idea of an orchestral score, used only two of her pieces on the final soundtrack; the rest were by Polish composer Krzysztof Penderecki. But it is the iconic "Main Title" opener by Carlos that makes the soundtrack iconic. A stark, intense symphony that hint at the horror to come.

*

If you are a pioneer and outlier, there is no one to compare yourself to, and no one to compete with. So where do you position yourself if your work is singular, sui generis, even? A practitioner who has preceded a movement can find it difficult to either assimilate, or remain outside of it. Carlos opted for the latter—not just to forgo being bracketed, but to allow absolute autonomy over her music and legacy. In the past, Carlos gave interviews that were packed full of tech-speak, but warmed up by her manner and sheer enthusiasm for her craft. Now she no longer talks to the press, or posts on her website, but she, or a team, pays attention to how she's represented in the world and has gone to great lengths to protect her material. Whenever the music appears online unauthorized, a DMCA (Digital Millennium Copyright Act) takedown is issued. In the past, Carlos made prophetic and sensible comments about the nature of music distribution and its impact on artists, but trying to find her work—legally—is frustrating. It's not for sale via her website, or through online retailers. Most of the albums are out of print, which means judicious and regular trawls of eBay and Discogs are necessary to find them. This withholding is an artist's choice, even if it serves to render them less visible. There is a danger of simply disappearing from the culture, particularly to a new generation whose main access to music is streaming. In a world where it's possible to play almost any song instantly, Carlos's work remains unique, ground-breaking, talismanic—but is slipping away into the locked vault of the past.

During lockdown, I bid online for a vinyl copy of *The Shining* soundtrack and the price kept rising like the ghostly drone notes over that opening shot of the lake. At €300, I opted out, and managed to find used CDs of other work instead, ruefully aware that it's the second-hand seller—not the artist—who recoups the cost.

*

Almost a decade before *The Shining*, Carlos's first foray into film was *A Clockwork Orange*. Again, Stanley Kubrick was the director, and wanted arrangements of classical standards, including Rossini's "William Tell Overture," which Carlos presents as playful and dizzying. In opposition to this is the opener: Henry Purcell's "Music for the Funeral of Queen Mary" made darkly somber because of the Moog. In "Timesteps," whistles, bells, and disembodied voices build into something bordering on tribal, capturing the film's violence (Kubrick only used a few minutes of the track, but Carlos released her own version of the score after the film, containing an epic fourteen-minute version). The album is lauded for another reason: on "A March," from Beethoven's ninth symphony, Carlos programed a vocoder, using Rachel Elkind's voice, to sing "Ode To Joy," perfectly suited to the film's otherworldliness. It's hard to assign gender, age, or nationality to a vocoder. It evades dualities and binaries—organic/electronic; male/female (and other gender identifications between and outside of this). It's a seminal moment in audio, as one of the first uses of vocoder on film, but is also a defiant mode of ungendering.

*

In the early 1970s, Carlos had never publicly spoken about her decision to live as a woman. At the first meeting with Kubrick, she dressed and presented as male. In one interview she revealed that the director casually asked questions to "feel out" if she was gay. In the year before *The Shining*, she agreed to a long interview with *Playboy* magazine, ostensibly to talk about her work, but partly to reveal that she was a trans woman. The result was an in-depth feature that—reading it now—borders on intrusive. Despite Carlos's frequent attempts to steer the conversation back to music, the interviewer fixates pruriently on her gender, sexuality, and sexual experiences. In the very first question, Carlos talks of her fear—of the moralists who will judge her, of an industry that might no longer take her seriously, and is candid about her early memories: "I remember being convinced I was a little girl, not knowing why my parents didn't see it clearly. I didn't understand why they insisted on treating me like a little boy." Carlos hid her feelings until adulthood, grappling with depression and dysphoria. Many times, she considered suicide using the knife she used for cutting magnetic tape. Everything changed in 1967, when she read Dr. Harry Benjamin's book *The Transsexual Phenomenon*. For the first time Carlos realized she wasn't alone and that there was nothing wrong with her. By 1968, she was taking estrogen, and from mid-1969—months before her thirtieth birthday—she began living permanently as a woman. In the interview, there's a painful recollection: of having to do a TV appearance with the St. Louis State Orchestra dressed as a man, wearing a wig and fake sideburns. Terrified, Carlos recalls crying in her hotel room. Understandably she is wary of the press, who have been disrespectful, focused on her gender—or, I suspect a worse crime in Carlos's eyes—quick to view her innovative work mostly through the prism of her transness. (On her website is a "Black Leaf" award system, for those who have been cruel to her.) The record company continued to release albums under her deadname, even on reissues of earlier work, despite her transition. But there is a notable and defiant moniker on the credits, suggested by Elkind: TEMPI—Trans-Electronic Music Productions Inc, which works not only as a musical acronym (tempi, plural of tempo) but as a subtle acknowledgment of Carlos's status as a trans woman. It wasn't until *Switched-On Brandenburgs* in 1980 that "Wendy Carlos" first appeared prominently on one of her album sleeves. The *Playboy* interview contains many sobering moments, particularly when Carlos is asked what would have happened if she hadn't opted for surgery. Bluntly, she replies: "I'd be dead."

Wendy Carlos has only ever wanted to make music and live the authentic life she is entitled to; to have her work stand alongside her contemporaries without constant footnoting in relation to her transition. In a 1985 interview with *People* magazine, she spoke of the response to living as the person she knew herself to be: "The public turned out to be amazingly tolerant or, if you wish, indifferent…There had never been any need of this charade to have taken place. It had proven a monstrous waste of years of my life." It's not up to Carlos to be a figurehead in the trans movement; declining such a role is her prerogative, when music has always been her main priority. And yet, her visibility as a trans person undoubtedly made it possible for a generation of artists like Sophie, Ah-Mer-Ah-Su, Octo Octa, Arca, and Jasmine Infiniti.

Each person is a multiplicity of influences: music, technology, and composition are Carlos's tools to enact a creative life, but her interests outside the studio give a sense of other preoccupations. She is a keen astronomer, enamored of the solar system (see *Digital Moonscapes*) and an eclipse enthusiast. Carlos saw her first full solar eclipse in 1963, and between 1972 and 1985, she combined another of her pastimes—photography—with capturing every total solar eclipse on Earth, from Siberia to Kenya and Australia. Such is the standard of the images, that NASA have used her pictures, and they've been published in notable astronomy magazines. When she was recovering from a car accident, Carlos became interested in cartography, and began making her own map projections of the globe. The music itself may be aural, and technology itself manipulated manually, but so much of the visual world underpins Carlos's compositions.

*

Throughout the 1980s, Carlos continued to compose, releasing a handful of albums, but there were fewer film commissions, and none as high profile as the work with Kubrick. Other film scores from that era—*Blade Runner, The Thing*—may have been even more impressive tonally, sonically, if Carlos had been the composer. The last major feature she worked on was *Tron*, Stephen Lisberger's (then) futuristic gaming flick. For the soundtrack, she wanted to capture not just the gladiatorial games but to be as full of color (in audio terms, this relates to timbre) as possible. Several sections used atypical time signatures, some of which could not be played by an orchestra, so a synth was used. In 1988, Carlos collaborated with Weird Al Yankovic on a re-imagining of *Peter and the Wolf*. 1984's *Digital Moonscapes* was composed for a digitally synthesized orchestra, using a library of sounds to replicate the sounds of an actual orchestra. Carlos and the science fiction writer Arthur C. Clarke were friends (who also worked with Kubrick, co-writing the screenplay for *2001: A Space Odyssey*) and she wanted to borrow the title of his novel *The Songs of Distant Earth* for an album. Released in 1986, it was eventually called *Beauty in the Beast* and is entirely synthesized, influenced by world music, incorporating her own specific tunings. All hugely different projects, but united by risk-taking and an indefatigable sense of experimentation.

*

Throughout the lockdown, late at night in the studio owned my husband, S, we kept returning to Carlos's music. Connections to other musicians showed up. The familiar Berlioz notes from *The Shining* appeared out of the speakers one night on "My Death," a Jacques Brel song by Scott Walker. The more we listened to Carlos, the more curious I was about how she actually made all those sounds. On the Moog Voyager, S showed me how the different oscillators work in relation to each other; how to control the tone with ADSR (Attack Decay Sustain Release), the expanding possibilities of the notes, ways to bend and decay the sound. It was easy to get lost in all the different permutations, in the eerie effect of manipulating pitch.

One spring evening, after a winter of rain and isolation, we sat in the sun and listened to 1987's *Secrets of Synthesis*. Carlos provides commentary in her cheerful Rhode Island accent, outlining practical tips, while moving through *musique concrète*, hybrid timbres and the alternative tunings she believes represent the future of music. Listening to the notes and her upbeat monologue, there it was: a subtle but palpable mood change, a sudden sense of possibility. Summer was not far away, and with it a reemergence; maybe even the chance to hear music in a field, or a bar, or someone's kitchen. Two weeks later, I got my first vaccine shot. The days got brighter, museums and galleries reopened. Two artists asked me to write a response to a piece that centers around a map. The project then became something else, something outside of words, and my husband turned it into an audio soundscape to be played in another room in the gallery. Carlos had been a part of our lockdown life, and because the artists' work was rooted in landscape, I sent them the opening of *The Shining* and explained how the lake and the Moog had worked their way into the piece.

Her last album, *Tales of Heaven and Hell*, was released in 1998. In 2005, she accepted the Life Achievement Award from the Society for Electro-Acoustic Music (a SEAMUS award given to those for outstanding achievement in the world of electroacoustic music) but otherwise, she has been out of sight. In the past, Carlos regularly updated her exhaustive website, but hasn't in over a decade, and only did so recently to object to a recent biography of her life.

Wendy Carlos deserves wider recognition: more listeners, and a greater acknowledgment of the unique contribution she has made to sound and modular synthesizers, and to composition and film scoring. Her legacy remains intact for now, but risks slipping away from future generations. She does not owe the world an audience, or her visibility. Instead, she continues to be her own kind of eclipse: frequently remote, but a phenomenon nonetheless.

Losers

Megan Jasper

It was October 1989 and the Comet Tavern was its normal, sticky self. The air was heavy with the sweat of young men in desperate need of a cleanse, external and internal. The combination of human steam with alcohol meant that more booze was required just to make the stench tolerable. In one year's time we'd call that smell Grunge Juice (a joke) and in two years' time, we'd simply call it Teen Spirit (also a joke, kind of). A pack of men were pressed up against one another at the bar, thirsty. They had long hair, wore flannel, leather jackets, and dirty jeans. One by one they peeled themselves away from the pack like a dingy fruit roll-up, bringing their new and full pitchers of beer back to one of the tables.

The wood tables were also sticky, having been marinating in Rainier and microbrews for years. I always tried not to touch them. Each one had names and initials carved into the wood. Some of those names I came to know as friends in the days and years ahead. One of them introduced herself to me that night. She pointed to a group of guys a few feet away and said, "See the dudes at that table? Those are the Cat Butt guys. Don't fuck any of them. They just got off tour with L7." Another reminder not to touch the wood.

L7 and Cat Butt had embarked on the Swappin' Fluids Across the Nation tour a month earlier in September, when I began my internship at Sub Pop Records in Seattle. I sat on the floor of the company offices, listening to Erica Hunter, Sub Pop's one-person marketing team, call college radio stations in the hopes of them playing more Mudhoney. I was immediately amused by her strategy. "Hi. Is Robbie there? No? OK, can you please tell him that Erica Hunter from Sub Pop called? Yes, Erica *Hunter* as in *Man Hunter*." I loved Erica straight away and as I stuffed Cat Butt's new record—*Journey to the Center Of*—into mailers for college radio stations, I knew I'd found my place.

Sub Pop's offices had an energy that was constantly abuzz. The main lobby was daubed with graffiti and looked like a New York subway in the mid-eighties. The Dwarves spray-painted "You owe the Dwarves $$" on the floor. There was a colorful chaos of posters and stickers on the walls and piles of records, music magazines, cardboard boxes, and mailers everywhere. The phones rang off the hook, the few employees ran back and forth between offices, and there was always music playing. Sometimes the music was loud and heavy like Tad or Poison Idea and sometimes it was the soundtrack to *Twin Peaks* or Lou Rawls, something begging to create balance amid a grunge windstorm. Mostly, it was Tad and Poison Idea.

My desk was front and center in that lobby since I had been immediately promoted from intern to receptionist, a job that paid me $5/hour. I felt like I had struck gold. Charles Peterson, our then-UPS guy who became an internationally famed rock photographer, brought me an old wooden desk from the seventies. It was shaped like a kidney bean and had a red top. I found every sticker in that office and started covering the desk. On the very front was a sticker that said "I hate your band." It must have been during one of the quiet morning hours that I had the time to write in a thick marker "I have grunge in my pants" and "Anal leakage rocks" on it. I started out as the girl who answered phones and I couldn't have been happier. I had no idea that I was about to embark on my own "journey to the center of" and that one day I'd be calling the shots.

One of the first rules I learned was to never say no Mudhoney: they were the main reason we had jobs. The band had a sludgy, distorted, loud, heavy grind going and Mark's raw scream could cut through all of it, his hair flailing wildly. The band was blowing up and for good reason, they were fucking great. Mudhoney was *the* band. They had smarts, rebellion, humor, and confidence in spades, and they were seemingly unstoppable. Their shows were selling out in the United States as well as overseas. "Sub Pop is the house that Mudhoney built." That was the line we used when we gave tours to journalists and tourists when they dropped in, which was often.

The second lesson I learned was that Mark's last name wasn't really "Arm." Mark had called and told me that he needed money to pay for the band's practice space. Bruce Pavitt and Jonathan Poneman—Sub Pop's co-founders—were both overseas, but Jonathan had called in to make sure that everything was OK at the office. I told him that Mark needed $200 and I was given permission to write him a company check and to forge Jonathan's signature. I was proud of my John Hancock "artwork" and brought the check home, where Mark's dad stopped by to pick it up. His dad opened the enveloped and gasped. "Mark *Arm*?! He can't cash this check. His last name is McLaughlin!" Mark Arm was such the embodiment of an underground rock star that it never even occurred to me that he'd have a normal name. I was mortified and the memory still makes me cringe. It wasn't just Mudhoney, it was *Mark Arm*. Thankfully I had keys to the office to make it right.

The bands stopped by our offices all the time. It was pretty common to have Mudhoney, the Screaming Trees, the Walkabouts, Nirvana, and Tad all come in during a week. And it wasn't unusual for them to get to work while they were there. We needed to turn our singles around quickly. Our small warehouse looked like a grunge factory as Mark Lanegan, the Connor brothers, Tad Doyle, and others quickly inserted vinyl singles into jackets, protected with plastic sleeves. The process often took a few days, and the bands were paid $5 an hour to kick out the jams.

Tad stopped by the office with his girlfriend and infant son, Elvis, before one of his shifts. I never knew if Elvis was his real name or a nickname, but the name fit him just as perfectly as the black leather jacket he wore. I had only ever seen Tad backstage or on a stage. In both settings, he had such a massive presence; he commanded immediate attention with his heavy guitar-playing, humor, and snarling vocals. Seeing Tad walk through the office with Elvis in his arms was heart-melting. Tad was soft-spoken, gentle, and so nurturing. It was clear how much he loved that kid. That this same man wrote a killer record called *God's Balls* made me love him even more.

The guys in the Screaming Trees stuffed singles the same way they rocked. Lee sat at that table, focused and with purpose, Van was almost always smiling and making people laugh and Mark would come in once everything was set up, sit as far away from Van and Lee as possible, and split immediately once he was done. I always felt bad for him if he had to wait a little bit longer to get paid; standing around and waiting once the gig was over was never his happy place. The tension between the members was felt but I didn't realize until years later just how bad it really was (and apparently still is). A tweet from Mark Lanegan just a couple of years ago says it all, "I don't know how many ways I can say it but any Screaming Trees reunion, show, rehearsal, lunch or fistfight will not include me." Full stop. I feel bad that things are still strained between them but that quote makes me laugh.

One afternoon when I was stuffing singles upstairs at my desk, Krist Novoselic called. He needed to talk to Jonathan, who was on another call. He told me that one day he wanted to live on a farm, one with enough acreage to not have close neighbors but close enough to one house, where hopefully Kurt would live. For a band that spent so much time stuck in a van together, stopping and playing in cities for weeks and months at a time, I found his desire to live in the country, close to his best friend, sweet.

Krist and Kurt grew up in Aberdeen, aptly nicknamed "The Hellhole of the Pacific," a small coastal logger town in Washington state. The Fluid, a high-powered Denver-based punk band signed to Sub Pop, were playing in Tacoma and a few of us went to the show. Tacoma wasn't my favorite place to go. The city was known for its smell, the Tacoma aroma, due to a paper mill that created a horrid stench of egg farts that would punch you in the face while you were driving through it on the highway. The Fluid were worth it though. The band's visits were always an event, and everybody showed up for them; their shows were transcendent, and they were really fun people. After a predictably killer set, a bunch of us were hanging out in the empty venue. There were a couple of massive cable spools that looked like they were being used as tables. Krist turned one on its side and started to roll it back and forth. Without hesitation, Kurt wrapped his skinny body along the spool's middle cylinder and Krist pushed it across the room. It rolled across the entire venue at a surprising speed and someone managed to stop it before it crashed into a wall. Kurt stumbled out, struggled to find his land legs, and then jumped back in again. When he landed back near Krist, he fell out. Somehow Krist managed to wrap his six-and-a-half-foot body into it and a wobbly Kurt pushed him across the venue. The spool rolled at a slower pace but when it reached the other side of the room, Krist's body slowly unraveled onto the floor. He looked lifeless for a moment but managed to get up once help arrived. And by "help" I mean the only thing that could work that kind of nauseous play, more beer.

Nirvana practiced in Tacoma and I went to a barbecue they had after one of their practices. The band had just parted ways with their original drummer, and Chad Channing and Dan Peters from Mudhoney had been sitting in with them. A few of us drove down to see how things were going. Tracy, Kurt's girlfriend at the time, was there with their pet rabbit. The rabbit seemed a bit "off," dragging its butt on the floor. Kurt came up next to me and started patting it. "She has a prolapsed uterus," he said. "If it comes out, you have to reinsert it."

"Do you reinsert it *yourself*?" I asked.

"Yeah, with the eraser tip from a No. 2 pencil."

A dirtbag with a gentle touch, I liked that about him. I never looked at a No. 2 pencil again in the same way though.

In the Sub Pop offices, all of the staff perfected the art of hustling. We rushed to get the word out that Nirvana and Tad would be touring in the UK and Europe in October 1989, a massive opportunity for both bands at the time. We blasted the incredible news that Mudhoney's first full-length record was the #1 most added record on CMJ. And we quietly and secretly stuffed a bonus Soundgarden 7", "Room A Thousand Years Wide," backed with "HIV Baby," as a surprise for the faithful subscribers of Sub Pop's Singles Club, a mail order club that sent limited edition, colored vinyl 7" singles by bands like Nirvana, Fugazi, Sonic Youth, and so many more to its members. Soundgarden first recorded for Sub Pop and had just recently released their first major label record, *Louder Than Love*, on A&M records. The Singles Club members were fucking psyched that month.

Although the hustle worked to promote the bands and their music, there was a constant struggle for cash. Sub Pop didn't have budgets for any of our projects and we constantly scrambled to make ends meet. So many of the phone calls I answered were people asking for or demanding money that they were owed or that they needed: people who made T-shirts for us, artists who were heading into the studio, credit card companies, phone companies, vinyl manufacturing plants, printers. The list was endless. And curve-ball lawsuits and cease and desist letters didn't help matters. Pepsi filed a lawsuit against Sub Pop for copyright infringement when we used an image that was too similar to their logo for a TAD CD single called "Jack Pepsi." We also needed to immediately stop selling TAD's highly anticipated *8-Way Santa* album because we used a found photo from the seventies of a smiling couple. The man in the photo was grabbing and holding the woman's right breast. The image quickly made its way to the woman, who had since become a born-again Christian and remarried. Understandably, she wasn't very happy. We immediately replaced it, after numerous copies had already shipped to customers and stores, with a photo that Charles Peterson took of the band at the Puyallup Fair the previous summer.

Being the first person in the office had its advantages, especially every other Friday, which was when our paychecks arrived. A number of my co-workers would show up early so that we could run to the bank when it opened in hopes of successfully depositing or cashing our paychecks. It was never a given that the checks were good and they often bounced if we tried to deposit them rather than just cash them out. I found a couple of my old pay stubs with "NSF" (Non-Sufficient Funds) stamped multiple times on the face during an office move and they now hang framed on our office walls.

The bands knew that the label's finances were shaky but there were so many other people who believed the hype. The label ironically marketed itself as a record company with endless cash reserves driving full speed toward world domination. Somehow we *were* getting toward world domination but on an empty tank. A car horn was honking wildly one day while I was walking. Johnny Kessler, who had a fanzine called *Northwest of Hell*, was waving the back cover of his new issue. "Don't Believe the Hype!" was spelled out in block letters. It felt like the ground beneath us could give at any moment. The good days were great but the stressful ones were unbearable. Quitting never felt like an option though. Something was going to happen and we were all determined to find out what it would be.

Where Bruce had ideas, Jonathan had dreams. He arrived earlier than almost everyone else, besides me. We would walk to get coffee in the morning, and he'd tell me what the previous evening had looked like or how the day could unfold. Most days ended with us sharing a cigarette on the roof garden. During one of our smoke breaks he said, "I think that Seattle could become a city that attracts musicians from all over the world." From his lips to God's Balls.

The grunge wildfire spread with an intensity, speed, and heat that felt mega, and Sub Pop was right in the center of it. One night I was walking to a downtown bar with a friend when a car pulled up next to us. A woman in the passenger seat rolled down her window and pulled out a piece of paper from the pocket of her flannel jacket. "Do you know where the Crocodile Café is?" She was only one block away from the venue. The driver leaned toward me and asked, "Do you know who's playing there tonight?" I didn't. The passenger looked at her cheat sheet again. "Do you know where the Offramp is?" That venue was a few blocks in the other direction. Please don't ask me who's playing there. They agreed that they'd go to Croc. "That's where the grunge bands play." That said it all; none of us used the G-word unless it was a joke. Our city was changing so quickly.

Jonathan and Bruce were desperately trying to hold the label together, but its finances were falling apart. The bills piled up and hung over that office like the dark clouds Seattle is known for, and Bruce's dances couldn't make it rain money. Every single band seemed to be on the road swapping fluids and getting laid, and all I got was laid off, with most of my co-workers, in July 1991, days before Mudhoney's *Every Good Boy Deserves Fudge* album was released and two months before Nirvana's *Nevermind* took the world by storm.

I was heartbroken to lose my job. That time was magical, and those days had a raw beauty. Anything and everything felt possible in a way that was equally thrilling and terrifying. Sub Pop's offices were filled with a savage, creative energy that I'd never experienced before and have never known since. Our crew was the most beautifully bizarre pack of misfits. We were Sub Pop's losers, winning even when we were losing.

Jonathan called me one fall morning in 1992. The *New York Times* wanted to talk about grunge for an exposé they were putting together. Specifically, they were looking for a lexicon. Jonathan told me that I might have more fun with their request, and he suggested that they chat with me instead of him. I believe I was finishing my third French press coffee when the phone rang. I was buzzing hard, and excited to break up my normal morning routine; this call would be way more fun than jotting down sales orders.

Rick Marin introduced himself and told me that the feature was for the newspaper's style section. It would focus on grunge and the Seattle movement that was taking over the world. They were covering the recent Marc Jacobs Grunge Collection, which showcased beanie-topped models on the runway sporting torn clothing, Nirvana shirts, flannel, and big-ass clunky black boots. And apparently, they wanted to take a deeper dive into Seattle's underground culture.

At the time, the national spotlight on Seattle felt exhausting. I was excited to break up the workday and I was also excited at the thought of having fun with the journalist. And by "having fun" I mean dishing back the absurdity in a fun "fuck you" kind of way.

Rick asked if I could share the lexicon that we, grunge people from Seattle, used. I was a bit perplexed and needed a minute to understand exactly what he was looking for. "It's tough to just rattle off language," I said. "What if you give me a word and I'll share the grunge translation." He liked that idea.

I immediately started writing down random words and phrases so that I would have a quick "cheat sheet" in front of me. I thought that the cheat sheet would help me to quickly provide a grunge translation—and that the quick timing would make it more believable to the writer. Some of the words rhymed, some were just straight-up nuts, and some were random phrases that I used with some of my friends in the skateboard world.

"Let's start with fashion or regular clothing," Rick suggested. "What would Kurt Cobain call one of his cardigans?"

OK, he's pitching me a softball. "Fuzz. He'd just say 'Give me my fuzz. It's cold.'"

"Great. What about big boots that you'd wear to a show?"

Almost everyone I knew wore sneakers or construction boots. OK. "Kickers." I figured I'd go easy at first and make it seem believable.

"What would a guy call his hot date?"

"He'd call her a tuna platter." I was already getting tired, even after all that coffee.

I decided to make every answer more outrageous than the last in hope that he would realize that it was a joke. I figured we'd laugh, call it good, and he could get back to sniffing out real news. Oddly, even as I was telling him that "Cool" translated as "Okey dokey artichokey," there was no laughing. The only sound I heard was the desperate tapping of keys on a keyboard as he tried to ensure that he transcribed the language of grunge accurately. *Catch you on the flippity flop, Rick.*

I nearly lost my mind when my mom called me a few weeks later and told me how proud she was that I, her daughter, was in the *New York Times*. Some of the translations made it into print, some didn't. All the news that's fit to print.

- **bloated, big bag of bloatation**—drunk
- **bound-and-hagged**—staying home on Friday or Saturday night
- **cob nobbler**—loser
- **dish**—desirable guy
- **fuzz**—heavy wool sweaters
- **harsh realm**—bummer

- **kickers**—heavy boots
- **lamestain**—uncool person
- **plats**—platform shoes
- **rock on**—a happy goodbye
- **score**—great
- **swingin' on the flippity-flop**—hanging out
- **tom-tom club**—uncool outsiders
- **wack slacks**—old ripped jeans

Those years can only be described as surreal, squared and then squared again. And they all came to a screeching halt on that gut-wrenching day in April 1994 when Kurt Cobain died.

After losing my job at Sub Pop, I found myself in the world of music distribution. I worked at Caroline Distribution for a year and then in 1993 was hired as the northwest sales representative for ADA, a new distributor that sold music from Sub Pop, Matador, Merge, Touch and Go, and other mostly independent labels. I was sitting in the offices of Fred Meyer, a West Coast chain of hypermarket superstores, tending to my largest account. The music buyer, Don Jensen, never talked about grunge but he knew it sold in the stores. Don sat in a big brown leather swivel chair. He wore a button-down shirt, and his thinning hair was tied back into a scraggly ponytail.

That look seemed to be the uniform for the middle-aged chain store buyers. The swivel chair and a copy of *Billboard* magazine were the key accessories. There were hundreds of these men at every NARM convention, an annual gathering for U.S. music retailers. I often felt like such an oddball, being a young woman in a sea of older men twirling their ponytails and talking about their stores.

Don's secretary often warned me about his mood before I was called into his office. Today I was told that his mood was "short," which wasn't unusual. It was normal to move through our meetings quickly and I always had to spend a little extra time preparing for those pitches. I had my paperwork and promo CDs ready for him. I was looking forward to having this meeting behind me because many of my co-workers were coming in from different parts of the country to celebrate Sub Pop's sixth anniversary the following night. I was going to meet a few of them at the airport immediately after leaving Don's office. I was happy when he called the front desk and asked them to send me back to his office.

"Did you hear that Kurt Cobain's dead?" asked Don in his gruff voice. I hadn't. I was speechless. Don turned up the radio. The commercial rock station was reporting the few haunting facts that were known. There was a body in Kurt's garage with a self-inflicted gunshot wound. I'm not sure that I said much at all during that visit. My mind was reeling and I was trying to hold my hands together in an attempt to hide their visible shake. In shock, I went through my rehearsed pitches and soon walked out of the office and to my car through a gray Seattle drizzle holding, in my still-shaking hands, the biggest order I've ever taken as a salesperson, thousands of Nirvana *Bleach* CDs. My heart was heavier than the order and it didn't feel right that Kurt's death had immediately translated into sales. The order felt dirty.

I took a moment to gather myself before going directly to Sea–Tac airport. I was worried about so many people, especially Jonathan, and I wouldn't have the chance to check in with anyone until I got home. My co-workers were also in somber moods when I met them at their gate. I remember hearing a stranger say, "Seriously? He killed himself? What the fuck did he have to feel sad about? He's a millionaire." I felt sick to my stomach as we all headed to my car.

I went to Linda's Tavern that night, the last place Kurt was seen. The bar was filling up with friends, musicians, and music journalists who had flown in from all over the world to cover the story. I vividly remember one UK writer complaining about how unfair it was that Everett True had an all-access pass that day. "He'll get the better story," she grumbled. Everett was at Kurt's house with Courtney, in shock and mourning the loss of his friend, whom he loved.

Sub Pop decided to carry on with their party that next evening. The Crocodile Café lined the inside of the windows with brown paper, which seemed smart since a massive number of reporters were gathered outside of the venue and windows ran along more than an entire wall of the business.

As I walked into the venue, a bright light from the cameras hit my face and a reporter jumped in front of me with a microphone. "Did you know Kurt Cobain?" he asked.

"Yeah. I fucked him," I responded. That wasn't true but it was the politest "fuck you" I could muster. I walked through the blinding lights and was relieved to get away from the hungry mob of journalists.

Artists new to Sub Pop, Velocity Girl, Pond, and Sunny Day Real Estate, all performed but the gathering felt more like a funeral reception than it did a show. And although it seemed odd to watch live music, the togetherness that it offered felt right. It was comforting to see friends, to check in with people and to hug them. Kurt's death seemed impossible to process. It impacted so many people both personally and professionally and it all felt disturbing, tragic, heavy, and unsettling. It still feels that way. Kurt often complained about chronic stomach aches and I always felt bad that he was in pain. I could only ever find a small sliver of peace in knowing that those pains were gone.

It took a long time for that smoke to clear and once it did, the landscape looked and felt so different; the forest had been scorched and the trees had finally stopped screaming. There was a stillness that was daunting and large. Going to a random show provoked something like an allergic reaction and large groups of strangers in thermals, flannels, and leather looked like a collective loneliness and emptiness, at least to me. Time slowed down, tribal tattoos started to fade, and a lot of folks removed their nose rings. Even Mark Arm cut his hair short. It was time to hang up the wack slacks and make room for skinny black jeans. My friend Chris Takino, the founder of Up Records, and I called them Cha Cha pants because it's what the younger musicians were wearing, the ones who worked at Seattle's Cha Cha Lounge.

I needed a change as well. I loved selling music but I missed working in a more creative environment and I felt a pull to work more closely with artists again. I was feeling inspired by new music after a long stretch of time that seemed like a post-Kurt, post-Nirvana identity crisis in our city and our industry. I was surprised and excited at the thought of returning to Sub Pop as the label's Senior Product Manager. Jonathan had called me to ask if I might be interested in the gig. Bruce, who was emotionally deflated and exhausted by the joyride, was living full time on Orcas Island and left Sub Pop to burn it clean, island-style. Jonathan was still looking for solutions and I felt honored to help him find them, especially in these new times.

Seattle's post-grunge superbloom had decided it was time to show itself in all its glory. Built to Spill, the Murder City Devils, Modest Mouse, Love as Laughter, 764-Hero, and other bands were breathing a whole new life into the city's scene and music became exciting again. After an extended remix of flipping and flopping, Sub Pop settled into a whole new groove. After so much emotional and financial hardship, we were all eager to look forward and move forward. We were always looking for that next new thing, something upside-down and inside-out original, something with a signature bite, something that felt so of-the-moment *today*.

In early 2000, Zeke Howard from Love as Laughter handed a burned CD to my co-worker, Stuart Meyer. It was music from Albuquerque, New Mexico, a band called the Shins. "It's really good," is all he said. It was really all he *needed* to say; it was great. The songs were catchy, exceptionally quirky, and the lyrics were masterfully weird. For all of us at the label, it was love at first listen.

Within weeks of hearing their music, Jonathan and I flew to San Francisco to see the band play at the Great American Music Hall in San Francisco, where they opened for Califone and Modest Mouse. Isaac Brock, Modest Mouse's guitarist and songwriter, was a huge fan and had been singing their praises. The band's set was far from perfect but there was a magic to their songs, to James's voice and to the dynamic between all the band members. We were all in and so thrilled for "New Slang," the band's hit song, to become our new lexicon. Stuart Meyer and Shawn Nolan, my two co-workers, flew to Albuquerque to seal the deal.

The Shins brought more than great music to Sub Pop. They brought a heightened togetherness and a purpose that was desperately needed. They also brought levity and laughter. James, Marty, Jesse, and Neal were game for anything. On one New York City visit, when the band was staying at the Gramercy Hotel, Marty, the keyboardist, Neal, the bassist, and I spent hours hanging our heads out of the fourth-floor windows of their room while we dropped small pieces of bagels on the heads of passers-by. When we ran out of bagels, we used cream cheese and when we ran out of cream cheese, we used half and half. We laughed until our sides split like boiled hot dogs, three degenerate wieners living our best lives. It didn't take much to have fun and it wasn't the typical type of bonding that most general managers of record companies had with the artists. That band was a B12 shot that made every color brighter and every moment special. Our world turned inside out and landed us in a spot that brought profound rewards, both personal and professional. And it put us on a solid path that carried us forward. What a fortune it was to experience that *Oh, Inverted World.*

Sleater-Kinney came to the label in 2005 when they released *The Woods.* Before coming to the label the band had already established itself as one of the best and most relevant rock bands of our time, as well as one of the smartest and most politically outspoken rock bands. They formed in 1994 at the tail end of the riot grrrl scene in Olympia, Washington, and they addressed everything from rape culture and patriarchal systems to income inequality with a ferocity and punch that was inescapable. They were punk rock feminist royalty and I was ready for that kind of reign.

Carrie, Corin, and Janet took themselves out of their comfort zone and placed themselves literally in the woods in upstate New York during the cold winter months to write one of my favorite records ever released on Sub Pop. While so many other artists were writing a softer style of music, Sleater-Kinney emerged from those woods with a hard-hitting and brutally raw record. The songs, like the women who wrote them, were powerful and ambitious. They addressed inequities, disempowerment, economic struggle with equal parts angst and heart. The band knew that it might be a polarizing record for their audience, and they gave zero fucks.

I stood in the hallway of the old KEXP office in Seattle as Sleater-Kinney were interviewed and performed songs from the new record. As I listened to these three women talk about their songwriting process, as well as their politics, I felt a different and renewed sense of pride and hope. They were about my age, and they rocked harder than almost any other Sub Pop band, past or present. I related to them as a woman and as a music lover. And I was grateful to be in the company of other women. Although I always appreciated working with compassionate and thoughtful people, it hasn't always been easy being a woman in this industry. I found comfort in knowing that they understood me in those ways. And I found myself learning from them, as a woman and as a leader, questioning myself more about how I draw lines, when to cross them, when to speak and when to shut the fuck up. The band spoke, wrote, and performed with a precision that was stunning and they were addressing issues that had become important to all of us. We were ecstatic when they secretly reunited in 2015 and made another record, *No Cities To Love*. I remain overwhelmed to have had the privilege of running the record label that they recorded for.

Sleater-Kinney's music had a sense of urgency that rivaled that grunge tsunami, and it was delivered with a confidence that comes from experience, determination, and an understanding of oneself. Their years at Sub Pop transported the label to a place that almost felt full circle. We were once again immersed in rock and tomorrow seemed boundless. Some things were so different, though. We had all grown up a bit, we were on firmer ground, and were a bit more aware of the cultural, emotional, and financial wake we left behind.

Being one of Sub Pop's losers has been one of the greatest wins of my life. I would never have imagined that I would have been planted in the epicenter of a cultural shift that rocked the globe. I would never have known that I could grow from that girl answering phones to the woman who is now CEO. I get grossed out when people refer to me as the label's "mom," I relate so much more to a simple "motherfucker." There is some truth, though, to the fact that we are all just flawed humans trying our best and needing a nurturing energy.

So many of these artists come into our lives young. They're fine-tuning who they are as artists and as people. They're building their communities filled with other artists and creating their own weird families. They are filling up pitchers of beer, going on tour, reinserting a pet's prolapsed uterus, dropping food on people's heads, fighting the patriarchy, rocking hard and all the while, changing this crazy fucking world. They play, they fuck up, they grow, they succeed in so many different ways, and they often leave that home that Mudhoney built to see what else awaits them in the world. And sometimes they come back home. The return address of every package sent from our warehouse is listed with its sender, Mark Arm, our warehouse manager. He prefers to be busy in between touring.

As for me, I am still learning my place in this world and I am still loving this crazy, colorful, creative universe I stumbled into. I still find myself trying to make sense of it and I can't help but wonder if that's even the point. Mudhoney are probably right: *let it slide.*

Valentina

Ottessa Moshfegh

I sang before I talked. I sang *instead* of talking, really. I was very expressive as a musical entity. I sang cheerful songs. "Can we stop for ice cream?" was a song. "Where are my shoes?" "I'm tired." "I need to pee." These were all songs. I'm sure it was very annoying for everyone in the family, although my mother says it was the only indication I gave that I was happy. Otherwise I was a serious-looking little girl, glum. People often asked me if I was OK. "Are you sad? Are you sick?" Maybe I had what we'd call "resting bitch face" now.

I think my singing was a way to self-soothe. Existential terror struck me very young. It's an experience I recall often: I looked at the clock while sitting on the rug during story time in kindergarten; saw the second hand tick, tick, tick; looked around at all the children, then at my aging kindergarten teacher, saw how she licked her finger to turn the page of the picture book; and I became suddenly, devastatingly aware that I would die one day. That we all would. It was a powerful, empty, selfless feeling, and at five, there was a gauzy, sad wonderment associated with the flimsiness of reality. I understood then that there must be something beyond this realm of carpeting and ice cream and shoes and clocks and teeth that fell out and grew in; and yellowed, fingers

191

that wrinkled, books to keep us hypnotized until the bell rang. What was that other realm? It was ineffable and miraculous—call it "heaven" or "the imagination." Call it "God." Maybe this moment on the carpet was the birth of my artist self, the entity that needed desperately to sing in order to assure itself of its own existence. But I didn't sing for much longer.

I grew up in the classical music world in Boston. My mother was a violist and my father was a violinist. They met in a music conservatory in Brussels; they both had the same teacher, a man who, I understood, took my parents on as their spiritual father. When I talk to my mother about how this teacher guided her and empowered her as an artist, the wisdom he relayed, the confidence he imbued in her, I feel like he was my teacher, too. I'm a descendent of those teachings. My mother was the kind of virtuosa maniac that would have done anything for her art. She was assigned to pick six out of twelve pieces to perform at her final evaluation for her diploma. The jury asked her which six she had chosen. She had prepared all of them—an insane task—and said casually, "You pick." I love that kind of aplomb. I wish I had more of it. I believe that my mother could have had a fabulous solo career as a concert violist, but war, motherhood, a bunch of things got in the way. In 1980 when my parents moved to America, they became teachers. I grew up with kids squeaking "Mary Had a Little Lamb" in the sunroom, their parents ringing the doorbell to pick them up every half hour. I hid upstairs after school and did my homework, or jumped rope and watched movies in the basement. I had to be quiet when I snuck snacks from the kitchen. In the evenings, once the house was empty of interlopers, I practiced piano.

My mother believed that a child's mind must be exercised and exhausted by education in order to grow strong enough to withstand the collective force of stupidity, conformity, fascism, and hatred that threatens to derail her the moment she relaxes. Music was the force with which she herself had battled through the muck and mire. There was no such thing as "too young" to start building up a forcefield against the evils of the world. So I started taking eurythmics when I was three. I joined a chorus for adolescents at age five. I could read music before I could read English. I took music theory lessons and had a private solfège teacher. I could sing every part of a Mozart quintet (*do re mi fa sol,* etc.) and analyze all the intervals and key changes and time signatures, every little thing. Apart from the piano, I studied many other instruments. Violin, classical guitar. I even played the recorder. I don't mean I squeaked on a plastic recorder in first grade with all the kids at my elementary school. I mean I had an esteemed recorder teacher, Gisela. She was a specialist in Early Music, and she played every kind of recorder and the harpsichord. Yes, I studied advanced recorder repertoire. I was not great at it.

From age five until I graduated from high school, I spent every Saturday at the music school, the day of the week the school dedicated to its Preparatory Division students. My parents taught private lessons all day, so I was left to navigate my own schedule of classes alone. I had chorus for two hours in the morning. Afterward, I knocked on my dad's door, interrupting his lesson, and he gave me five bucks to go eat lunch in the cafeteria. The school was a university every other day of the week, so there were older people around. There was a school library, concert halls, grand marble hallways, spiraling staircases, and an old-fashioned elevator. But mostly there were practice rooms where teachers taught privately or where chamber groups met, and where I hid and practiced piano and daydreamed when I had time to kill.

This was in a rough part of the city. There was a lot of gang crime in Boston in the eighties, shootings nearly every day, the police were totally corrupt. It was not a safe place for a kid wandering around between her lessons while her parents were busy teaching, but nobody messed with me. I've always felt kind of immune to random attacks. I've never been mugged. But one Saturday night when I was five, my mother got mugged at the

Burger King across the street from the school. Despite being hugely pregnant with my little brother, she ran out after the thief as he got into a getaway car. I just watched through the darkened windows as she wrestled with the man. I had no idea what was going on. I thought, "This is my life now, living alone in this Burger King." I kind of accepted it. When I look back on this event, I wish I'd been screaming and pounding the windows. "I had fifty dollars in that purse," my mother said when she was back inside. She was furious. As a family of musicians, fifty bucks was a lot. "It was a beautiful tooled leather purse I got in Belgium," she said. I remember the haunting darkness of the city streets after that, my lonely shadow as I passed under a yellow streetlamp—what lurking menace might reach out from the shadows—and I imagined my mother stabbed, bludgeoned, left for dead on the crowded corner. Nobody outside had intervened to help her. This was a profoundly influential turn for me. Life was not only an existential illusion. It was also something that could be violently wrenched away. My friend Kristine McKenna likes to point out that in every novel I write, the protagonist's mother is remarkably dead.

My piano education was pretty typical at first: exercises, scales, arpeggios, sonatas, preludes and fugues. When I had prepared a piece sufficiently, I played it in a workshop judged by a teacher on the faculty of the music school. If I passed the workshop, I got to perform the piece at a public recital the following Saturday. This was all very stressful for me, and the stress felt like a shameful secret. I kept a straight face, though, and learned to look passive, especially when my interior was vibrating at a maddening frequency. As a young person, I was very dramatic on the inside, but stoic, placid, almost grim on the outside. I was nine when I started taking piano seriously, as though it were a necessary stress. Music was not a hobby or something my parents forced me to do; it was a path to follow. At some moments, it overtook my life, at others I felt it ruined my life, and at others still, it was my only salvation. Performing was always an out of body experience for me. Once I got on stage and sat down, I knew my conscious brain was of no use. The music had been memorized, and I had to surrender to it as it came through me. If I started thinking about what my fingers were doing, I would make a mistake. Sometimes I performed with my eyes closed. My little brother used to make fun of the way I moved my body at the piano, cranking his neck back and forth like an overexcited turtle. I wasn't vain about it. I didn't care how I looked when I played, which was a relief. I went into a trance, which felt exactly right. The spirit of the music moved me and came through me. All the practicing was in effort to make that possible.

My seriousness about the piano coincided with finding a new piano teacher, Valentina. She must be in her nineties now, but even when I was a teenager, she felt ancient, an immortal creature of wisdom. She proved to be my soul-charmer. She was very petite, Russian, had short curly black hair and a naïve yet flamboyant way of dressing that contrasted sharply with her size and reserved demeanor. And she always looked exactly the same. Someone once told me that style is always looking like yourself. Valentina was like that. She is still, for me, an icon.

I cried in every lesson with Valentina. Not because she was mean (she wasn't), or because I felt terrible (I did), but because the lessons were so intimate and respectful. And I was moved by the music, by my limitations, and by an overwhelming sense of the perilousness of life. I felt subtly doomed as a pianist, hovering on the tragic cusp of greatness, but never quite stepping inside. Valentina's room at the music school was a safe place for me to shed my tears, a rare thing for me as such a stoic kid. She didn't ignore my tears; my feelings were acknowledged, but there was no alarm associated with crying. Valentina never shamed me or asked me what's wrong, never called my mother to tell her I was emotionally unstable or anything like that. She understood that music elicited deep emotions, which is absolutely true. It's impossible to learn something like a Bach invention, for example, and not feel anything. I could compare it to going to school to be a priest or something. If you can master the material technically, then you can understand how transcendent it is. Music is, essentially, a call to God, after all. I appreciated that I didn't have to ascribe my tears to shame. I could cry deeply, reverently. I could shake the tears from my eyes and start again. "Tempo! Tempo!" Valentina cried, clacking her pencil with precision against the edge of the piano lid.

During high school, my lessons with Valentina increased. I would see her on Saturdays at the music school for our allotted hour, and sometimes for two hours during the week at her home. She lived alone in an apartment not far from the school. She had an upright piano in her bedroom. Until I started visiting her there, I knew almost nothing about her: we never had chit chat, she never asked me about school, I never asked her personal questions. But I gathered from her apartment décor that she liked to travel—she had an enormous bookcase of tchotchke souvenirs, little art things, dolls, paintings—and I knew she was from Moscow and had studied piano there. Lessons at her apartment were far more intense, more private than at the music school. With nobody walking by, we dug deeper into each piece I studied. Valentina taught me more than how to move my fingers across a keyboard; she showed me how a piece worked, how to consider every decision the composer had made. She invited me to come up with my own story for each voice, each phrase, melody, progression. Even the pedal had a personality. She encouraged me to imagine characters, to pose questions, to enact the drama of a piece as though it were an expression of my own imagination. Is this phrase a temptation? Is this sforzando angry or miraculous or clownish? I was the one interpreting the music; Valentina was teaching me how to play it the way I saw it.

I became more and more ambitious about the piano as I battled through high school. I think that's because I was getting in touch with who I was and my own misery and the hunt for my own salvation. Practicing piano was a calculable suffering, in contrast to everything else I couldn't control. I was a complicated teenager. I had chronic pain, as I do now, from complications of scoliosis; I kept a tight seal on a vicious eating disorder; I was immeasurably manic through periods that pushed me to go running at night, burning and seething with so much backstopped fury and ecstasy that I couldn't really talk; and I was desperate to leave home and simultaneously terrified to grow up. I applied to colleges like everyone else. My dream was that I would move out of my parents' house and suddenly live in a trance state, with no consciousness to torture me. It was wishful thinking. Practicing piano was a way to allay the anxiety around all of that. And still, practicing was painful; I was trying to play something that I couldn't play yet, and to play it would mean to be a vessel for God. To be divine. It was like practicing for salvation. That's how seriously I took it. To play a piece badly was wicked, it was shameful, it was so disrespectful that you might as well not play at all.

The music school had a concerto competition every year. Students of all instruments would compete with a single movement of a concerto, and the winner of the competition would play the entire concerto with the school orchestra at the end of the year concert. To win was an enormous achievement. In my senior year of high school, I prepared the second movement of a Chopin concerto. Second movements tend to be slower than the first or third, so I needed less technical agility to pull it off. Technique was always my weakness. My facility was very good, but up against the kids who were forced by their parents to practice seven hours a day, I couldn't really beat them technically. I wasn't an athletic musician. But I could compete musically, emotionally, and dynamically as a performer. And I really, really wanted to sing my heart out at this competition. This was the first time in my life I ever had a mantra, and the mantra was something very humble, like "please let me play this well," or something like that. That Chopin concerto became very important to me. I saw Valentina several times a week for extended lessons as the competition loomed ever closer. I practiced with an accompanist who played an arrangement of the orchestral part. I dreamed in Chopin. I floated through schooldays tapping my second movement on my textbooks. I was completely obsessed. On the morning of the competition, my sister told me something I will never forget. "Shit like this," she said, "is over as soon as you get in the car." But it wasn't. I got into the finals and went back to play another round the next day. I didn't win. In fact, nobody won that year. I guess the judges didn't find a single one of us worthy of the prize.

My dad was a collector of instruments. There were violins piled all over the house. Cellos. Bows. One day, when I was around twelve, he bought a clarinet and asked me if I wanted to play it. I don't know exactly why I said yes. Becoming a clarinetist was certainly not a creative ambition of mine. Still, given that my parents had some standing at this music school, they finagled me in, as a total beginner, with the best clarinet teacher there. This is a man I now wholly despise. He was also a teacher for the university students, and he was a flirt, an egomaniac, a bully, and a pervert. He had a lot of Asian female students he seemed to be grooming; during every lesson with him, at least two young women would come knock on the door to say hello and he would ask them to go buy him lunch at Burger King or a cup of coffee or something. He had no qualms about interrupting my class time as much as he wanted. He said that I was wasting his time anyway—although my parents paid him—because I was not good enough at the clarinet. He loved that I wasn't good, I think. He liked to humiliate me, he liked telling me I was worthless. He used to say that I was less significant than a crumb of dust lodged into the nubs of the ratty old carpeting on the classroom floor. He would tell me to get down on my knees and look up close at the carpet. I wouldn't do it. I didn't cry. I just glared at him. Maybe I laughed. But this perverse cruelty was extremely disturbing to me. And the next moment he would make some comment about my appearance. He would get up close behind me as I played sometimes and rub himself against me, pretending to be fixing my posture. I never saw him with a boner or anything like that, although he probably would have hidden it from me because he knew my parents. But that didn't stop him from saying things like, "You look good in that short skirt, you should always wear short skirts."

I don't know why I kept going. I could have quit any time. Maybe studying clarinet with that jerk was how my pubescent self got to experience being sexualized, to play on the dark side, to be angry, to embrace my disgust, to feel myself hurting in a way that could be contained and pointed at, like the cut of a razor. Maybe it was empowering to me that I got to be in relationship to a man in that way. Although I found him unattractive, I still sought his approval, like a game. I wonder now, if I had never started playing the clarinet, would I have become a pianist? He drilled into me that I was a failure as a musician, beyond hope. My playing was an insult to his ears, he said. Better to sit quietly and be admired for my tight sweater, was the takeaway. I remember that I often went to Burger King to binge after a clarinet lesson. I needed something to make me as sick as I felt. Maybe some dark spirit would come snatch me from my seat and take off in a getaway car. Maybe I would die a gruesome death. And somehow, this would afford me victory, I thought.

I did not win. I did not die. And I did not become a musician.

I went off to New York for college when was seventeen. I had music that Valentina had given me and I'd told her, "I'll come back to see you when I'm on school vacations." I tried to practice on the shitty piano practice rooms they had at my college. They were never tuned, so everything clanged terribly. The sound was really depressing. The few times I actually went to see Valentina when I was home from college were depressing too. Something had been lost, something was gone. I knew I wasn't a pianist anymore. And I was never going to be a pianist again. Perhaps this was what had made my relationship with piano so intense the whole time: I had always known it was temporary. I was a writer. I was not a musician. So I quit. I never told Valentina I was quitting. I just kept canceling my lessons during winter break. "I'm not prepared," I said. "I'm sick," I lied. "I have to go back to New York. I guess I will call you in the spring."

To say goodbye to the piano was excruciating. It was excruciating to the point that I couldn't even listen to classical music for about fifteen years. It brought up too much emotion in me. It was painful, not just because I couldn't play piano anymore, but because the music rang a bell that was so loud, it made everything else seem meaningless in comparison. I credit a lot of this to my arrogance. If you've experienced the ecstasy of playing a Chopin concerto, how do you then go and have a chitchat over coffee with a friend and talk about school and dorm rooms and boys? One becomes addicted to the intensity of the experience of music, and everything else seemed so stupid. So I was a total asshole in my late teens and early twenties and late twenties and early thirties. Maybe I still am.

I did keep in touch with Valentina. She surprised me once at an award ceremony in Boston for my first book, *Eileen*, in 2015. A friend took a picture of me crying when I saw her. Valentina looks exactly the same in the picture, like always. And since then, she's come to two readings I gave at the bookstore in Harvard Square. She probably has no idea how important she was in my life. There are a lot of things I would like to not remember about my childhood, but my time with Valentina is not one of those.

The last time I saw Valentina, weirdly enough, was in an airport in Florida. I randomly got to this airport three hours early because I had been feeling anxious in my hotel room. It was like I'd been sitting on the rug in kindergarten: time was ticking slowly toward death as I was waiting to zip my suitcase and order a car. I couldn't concentrate. And the hotel room reminded me of what I had come to Florida to do: to read a story for a crowd of strangers. Like I was the kindergarten teacher.

With so much time to kill at the airport, I tried to take a nap on the floor near my gate. Finally, while I was sort of half-dreaming, I thought I heard Valentina's voice. I looked up and there she was, trying to get a seat on a flight back to Boston. In a daze, I went to her. And when she saw me, it was as though she expected to see me, like, "Oh, Tessi. There you are." I helped her negotiate with the airline employee. I held her bag as she waited in line. She said she was in Florida to visit her son and grandchild. I didn't even know she had a son or grandchild. That sort of anonymity is, to me, the mark of a truly generous teacher. She had no agenda beyond her love of music and carrying that onto others. She showed me that I had the capacity to feel and to think and make, and to move others with what I make. She saved me from doom. Without her, I don't know if I would have become a writer.

Country Girl
Rachel Kushner

I always said the Wanda Jackson I preferred was the country Wanda, not the rockabilly Wanda. It wasn't just a way to push back on the obvious, the thing that others were crazy about in the late 1980s and early 1990s, when Wanda Jackson had a huge resurgence thanks to bands like the Cramps, X, the Blasters, and the Clash, and rockabilly fans who dressed like she had in the 1950s but added tattoos and piercings. I preferred the version of her artistry that was cloaked in the older, more constrained tradition, even as you could hear in her voice something subversive and strong.

That voice is in my head all the time, singing the opening lyrics of "Tears at the Grand Ole Opry," a song that is equally melancholy and boisterous, with taut ribbons of fiddle shaped around the echo of Wanda Jackson's plaintive holler.

Ask the Grand Ole Opry here in Nashville Tennessee
Everyone will be happy
Everybody but me

When I saw Wanda Jackson play at the Village Underground in New York City in 2002 her crowd was rockabilly, but I was there for the country. Jackson came out and did a bit of both and hammed for the audience with her pink acoustic guitar, which, she said, was custom designed with extra curvature for the female form, and as she said it she traced her hand under her breast to demonstrate. In her autobiography, *Every Night is Saturday Night*, she confesses this was a joke, that her guitar didn't feature a deeper curve. But maybe the guitar itself is simply suited to the female form, or why else is it shaped like that?

She didn't play my favorite song when I saw her live, and it turns out Wanda Jackson never even liked "Tears at the Grand Ole Opry," which I find so sublime and full of depth. It was an early number from her pure country repertoire. She recorded it in 1955, on her first visit to Nashville, when she was seventeen years old. She was making so much noise playing her guitar in the recording booth that the producer asked her to record her vocals alone. (Chet Atkins played the guitar parts on the album.) "Could I just hold mine if I promise not to strum it?" she asked.

Jackson learned guitar at the age of six, when her father got her a cheap Sears Roebuck model and taught her to play it. Her father was a hobbyist fiddle player. They would practice duets together nightly. Jackson's parents were Dust Bowl Okies who had moved out to Los Angeles, *Grapes of Wrath*-style, during the Depression, with a mattress in the back of their coupe. Jackson's father enrolled in barber school on Skid Row. He learned to cut hair by practicing on the area's drunks. Her mother worked for a furniture company, upholstering chairs for chrome and Formica dinette sets.

Her parents loved to dance and would take Jackson, an only child, to ballrooms in Venice and Santa Monica, where they saw Bob Wills and his Texas Playboys and the Maddox Brothers and Rose, who were known as "the most colorful hillbilly band in America." The Maddoxes were the first country act to go full Western glitz, in outfits decorated with rhinestones and piping and bright blooming embroidery. The girl singer, Rose Maddox, was astonishingly liberated and one of a kind. She played stand-up bass and sang with a brash confidence and vocal force, an insistence that Wanda Jackson studied and mimicked. Jackson's mother had Jackson sing in the bath to confirm she wasn't drowning while her mother worked on her sewing machine at the kitchen table. This early function of voice—to project—is audible in Jackson's recordings: the voice is never meek. It doesn't apologize or coo or submit. Rose Maddox sang that way also: flat out, and big, nothing held back and nothing to hide.

Seven-year-old Wanda Jackson would not have known the details of the Maddox family story, but she might have apprehended that the colorful hillbillies up on stage were not of a distant ilk from her own. Like Jackson's family, the Maddox kids were from a family of sharecroppers who rambled West, if from Alabama instead of Oklahoma, and not in their own car, but by hopping freight trains. They camped in cement culvert pipes in Oakland, California, before they found permanent housing in Modesto.

Jackson's family lived, then, in South Los Angeles (formerly South-Central), and Jackson would take an underground pedestrian tunnel by herself to cross a busy roadway to get to school at Vermont Avenue Elementary. The tunnel was scary to Jackson, who held her breath to run through. There are still pedestrian tunnels around Los Angeles, and they are still places where you want to hold your breath. Vermont Avenue Elementary is still there. It's eighty percent Latino, like much of South LA, and I'd like to think some little girl at Jackson's former elementary school will be taken to a dancehall or rodeo and see Lupita Infante up onstage as Jackson encountered Rose Maddox, and this contemporary child might understand that a girl like her, whether from Downey, or South LA, a girl whose parents were forced to come from elsewhere in order to survive, can become a singer in white gabardine with blood-red embroidery, like Lupita Infante.

Wanda Jackson's father wasn't able to find work as a barber in Los Angeles, so they moved to the unincorporated rural outskirts of Bakersfield, where they had relatives who had migrated to the Central Valley, just like thousands of others from Texas and Oklahoma—among them Buck Owens and Merle Haggard, who later put the imprimatur on Bakersfield as a country capital with its own sound. On Saturday nights, Jackson's family would gather around an aunt and uncle's radio for the Grand Ole Opry. "We'd all just sit there and stare at the radio while the show was on," Jackson says in her book. "I wonder now why we thought we had to actually *look* at the radio while we heard the show." Live music had taught them to want something to look at, a stage show, which is what Jackson later learned to deliver.

If Rose Maddox had been the first to sport elaborate Western get-ups, Wanda Jackson was the first to wear tight clothes. Her idol was Marilyn Monroe, and instead of the full crinoline-skirted cowgirl outfits with inlay boots that other female performers were wearing, Jackson shimmied around in a form-fitting slip dress with spaghetti straps, spike heels, and long glittering earrings. Her mother used her professional skills to make Jackson's costumes, employing silk tassels instead of the more common leather or suede ones, because the silk, more lightweight and fluttery, moved as Jackson did.

Her parents both worked full time, but they doted on Jackson and supported her pursuit of music, and by age nine, when they moved back to Oklahoma from Bakersfield, she was singing and playing guitar for her classmates at school. She didn't like academics and considered the schoolroom a prison. You don't have to understand it, her father said of schoolwork, just learn it enough to pass. She loved Hank Williams and taught herself to yodel, having decided that yodeling like Hank Williams was a necessary rite of passage for a performer. She was a class clown, an entertainer, interested in boys and glamour. She stole movie magazines to study the looks of Hollywood. Carried a guitar with her everywhere she went. From the account of her life that she provides in the book, it seems that no one important to her told Wanda Jackson she could not be a star.

She casually recounts various humiliations and setbacks but none seem to deter her. She almost has to repeat fourth grade. After she's hit in the mouth with a ball, bad rural dentistry results in the unnecessary pulling of her four front teeth, and thereafter a bridge—lifelong dentures. Unaware of menstruation, she bleeds all over the seat on the school bus and is convinced she's dying. With almost no models in her dream to become "a girl singer" except that early memory of Rose, she hustles her way into her own local radio show by pounding the pavement around Maud, Oklahoma, at age fourteen. Walks into businesses alone with her guitar, looking for a sponsor. A lumber company signs on. She starts doing live radio shows, writing ad copy for the lumber company and performing it on the air. She'd been singing and playing guitar for more than half her life at this point, but had never heard a recording of her own voice. The radio show was live on Saturday nights and replayed on Sunday mornings, but she wasn't allowed to listen because it conflicted with church. One Sunday her mother tells her she can go out to the church parking lot and listen in the car as long as she completes Sunday school lessons first. Hearing herself on the car radio, Jackson is shattered. She hates the sound of her own voice and decides she will quit. Her parents talk her out of it.

On that same trip to Nashville when Jackson recorded "Tears at the Grand Ole Opry," she was meant to appear on the Opry itself, on Ernest Tubb's segment of the Saturday night show. It was a huge step, a professional anointing. Her mother had made her a dress for the occasion, red, with rhinestones and a "sweetheart" halter neckline. As the story goes, Ernest Tubb came backstage and asked, Are you Wanda Jackson? Yessir. He told her she was next, and she said I'm ready. He looked her up and down and told her she could not perform "dressed like that." Like what? With her shoulders uncovered, which was against Opry rules.

Crestfallen, she threw on the jacket she'd worn to the theater over her beautiful outfit and performed in it. While she played her set, the audience distractedly paid attention not to Wanda but to stage comedian Minnie Pearl and banjo player Stringbean, who were hamming behind Jackson's back. She vowed never to return to the Opry.

A year after this happened, Rose Maddox routed the Opry's decency restrictions on women's bodies by hiding her outfit until the last moment. When it was too late to stop her, she went onstage in a bare midriff. Later, she was invited to be a part of the theater's house act, but after six months, Maddox told the Opry managers to shove it. The Grand Ole Opry was an institution at the top of a hierarchy, and famously snobbish to anyone who didn't submit to its rigid conventions, but what true star would submit? Certainly not Elvis, who was snubbed by the Opry audience in 1954. Elvis vowed never to return, and he didn't.

The summer of 1955, after Wanda Jackson got her taste of Nashville and didn't like it, she toured with Elvis as his opening act. On the first occasion they met in person, at a radio station in Missouri, Elvis was wearing a lemon-yellow blazer. He had arrived to the station in a pink Cadillac, and he wore his hair in a perm. This was before Mary Kay Cosmetics, Jackson points out in her book, as if that would have better explained why a male country star was driving a luxury car custom-painted pink. At a dollar-ticket fundraiser for cerebral palsy, she watched girls fling themselves at the stage in sexual frenzy as Elvis performed. Over the next several months she performed on stage bills with Elvis, Carl Perkins, Ferlin Husky, Buddy Holly, and Johnny Cash. This was a time when women in country music were universally demure in their singing style. Jackson's goal was to be perfectly audible, at any rowdy honkytonk, to the person in the very back of the room. She was learning to belt it out.

Her father quit his job (by that point he'd given up barbering and was a taxi driver) to be Jackson's tour manager and chaperone (she was still seventeen). Her father allowed Elvis and some of his bandmates to ride in their car on occasion, but Wanda was never allowed to ride with the other musicians unmonitored. She and her father sat up front, with Elvis and company in back. Elvis and Jackson were working up a flirtation. One night, riding to the motel after a late, post-show hamburger, Elvis swatted at Jackson's ponytail and asked, "Wanda, don't you ever wash that thing?" The ponytail was a fake one, set on a comb, and she knew Elvis would not have realized. She pulled off the false ponytail and tossed it in the backseat, where it landed in Elvis's lap. "Here, *you* wash it."

As this charged psychoanalytic moment foretells, they began dating shortly after. Elvis played R & B records for Jackson in his bedroom in Tupelo, Mississippi. He coaxed her into rock and roll, and away from traditional country. He told her to pick strings instead of strum. After being chided for playing in too energetic a style in the recording booth in Nashville, she'd tried not to play so heavy. "Elvis wanted me to unlearn," she writes. That year, Jackson became the first girl rocker, with raucous live favorites like "Fujiyama Mama" and "Hardheaded Woman." There were few female models in country. Onstage, according to Jackson, "Kitty Wells barely moved. Same with Jean Shepard." There was, of course, Big Mama Thornton with her electric energy, unmentioned by Jackson in her account of influence, just as so much Black artistry has gone unacknowledged in what white performers borrowed in order to evolve and innovate.

Jackson's version of "Fujiyama Mama" (it had first been performed by a Black singer named Anisteen Allen) didn't chart in the United States but became a huge hit in Japan. Jackson toured there in 1959. Her father went with her. Neither had ever left the United States. Her father shocked their hosts by insisting on pouring milk and sugar over bowls of rice. Wanda learned to back-comb her hair, a technique popular in Japan but new to her.

Eventually her husband, Wendell Goodman, replaced her father as manager. The day after she and Wendell married, they left to tour for two weeks with Johnny Cash; that was their honeymoon. She performed in Las Vegas, which she loved, and in Branson, Missouri, whose staid "family" atmosphere gave her the creeps. She traveled through the South with a Black pianist and gave up gigs when racist club owners barred her pianist's entry. Her life wasn't typical of her time. She had never cooked. She didn't even know how to mix her own martini. When she became pregnant, she started to inch her guitar to the side, to accommodate her growing belly. She toured constantly with Wendell, who had given up his job at IBM to manage her. She was the breadwinner, the single career she and he shared. They had two kids, raised by nannies and by Jackson's mother. In her book she says she wasn't a good mother. Even when she was home she was distracted, busy, unavailable. "My entire family depended on my career," she writes.

The sacrifices she made for her music career cut both ways: because she and Wendell were dependent on extended family to raise their children, she felt they had to remain in Oklahoma, instead of moving to Nashville—which, despite having alienated her, was the center of the music industry, where valuable connections with songwriters and producers were made.

Wanda Jackson was always straddling the line between country and rock and roll, not quite fitting perfectly into either, and her career in the 1960s, as she narrates it in her book, becomes a string of missed opportunities, misrecognitions, and disappointments. At the same time, she took great pride in her identity as a live performer. They were always on the road. The stress of travel, and her husband's constant jealousy, began to harm their marriage. He even threw a fit at the sight of her dancing with her own father. "Everywhere we went, we tried to drink the place dry. We were running." After a two-week set of shows in Alaska ("all I remember is drinking"), back home in Oklahoma for a brief visit, she and Wendell were asked by their own children to please attend church. They went, and both had a conversion.

They found God, and sobriety, and subsequently Jackson reinvented herself as a gospel singer. Her hair got bigger and her skirts hung down to the floor. Certainly she wasn't the first, in country, to go in this direction, but she went all the way: renounced rock and roll, renounced nightclubs, and only recorded with religious labels. For income, she and Wendell lived on good-will offerings from their church ministry, until they embarked on a real-estate venture in Dallas that they felt was God's plan for them. In 1979, they moved with their kids to Texas, where they had no friends, no connections, and where Wanda Jackson was not famous. Clerks asked her for identification when she wrote a personal check at the grocery store: did God's plan really intend to include such indignities? She and Wendell prayed and fasted for direction. They decided to go back to Oklahoma, where they reintegrated into secular life and rock and roll gigs. They sold Amway products for a short-lived spell—"a pyramid scheme." Money troubles are not narrated with any shame in Jackson's account of her life. Nor are they unusual for a country singer. Around this same time that Wendell and Jackson were selling Amway, Rose Maddox, who continued to perform at nightclubs until the end of her life, was selling off her entire (and possibly priceless) collection of Nathan Turk-designed Western wear in order to pay her bills.

In the mid-1980s Wanda Jackson was rediscovered as an original rockabilly queen by younger musicians who had been influenced by her. She was eventually inducted into the Rock and Roll Hall of Fame, after the campaigning of Elvis Costello. She recorded an album with Jack White of the White Stripes. They went on *Saturday Night Live*. In the footage of their performance you can tell that Jackson is having a blast.

After initially feeling displeased with her face on cover of the album she made with Jack White, she decided it was good to be herself, and OK to have wrinkles. She has continued to play live, up into her eighties. "I'd like to show the younger girls who do respect me that it's all right to be old."

Wendell died in 2017. Wanda Jackson is still alive. She wasn't available to be interviewed when I was writing this, because she was busy recording an album with Joan Jett.

What Is Going On in Rap Music, the Music Called "Trap" and "Drill"?

Simone White

What is going on in rap music, the music called trap and drill? This music has for several years been an informative area of ecstatic activity; it resonates with my own rageful, productive, and *unrelenting* unhappiness; more to the point, listening seems to have disorganized the possibilities presently signified by the idea of flight, being fugitive, fugitivity. Listening has changed me and makes demands.

Trap music is stunning. An initiating dilemma is the blankness many listeners report when asked to account for the difference between listening pleasure and disavowal, if not condemnation, of the music's ostensible content.* The music's true content is all that it is as a material thing, all that it is as an imaginary and actual space for gathering practitioners and audiences, and all of the ways it travels in the symbolic realm. Criticism has always struggled with the true matrix of rap music, with academic

---

* Which isn't to say there aren't people who experience nothing but revulsion when they hear this music. Perhaps its sound is also revolting.

criticism tending to resort to methodologies of reading that privilege and isolate sound and swagger from the words rappers write/say/record—the song's "lyrics." Clearly, I do not think this is the right term for the language that contemporary rap music employs, and people have begun to speak of "ad-libs," which at least distinguishes between static written lines, extemporaneously developed narrative statements, and exclamatory and/or nonverbal utterances. The upsetting words are a lot of different things in thousands of songs, but I think what upsets people is precisely what permits trapping to signify in the popular imagination, to transform criminal enterprise into aesthetic enterprise into escapist phantasm.

Trap endlessly generates language and images relating to selling drugs, heavy use of opiates and benzodiazepines, weed and alcohol, and gang warring. Plus misogyny. I commend to your attention Future's outstanding *DS2*, of which almost every recorded word is a magnetic aggregate of menace and misery. (*bitch ima choose this dirty over you / you know i ain't scared to lose you.*) Megan Thee Stallion gets shot by Tory Lanez in a nauseatingly straightforward meeting of the cartoonish woman-bashing that has constituted a big swath of the linguistic tradition of rap for four decades—*bitches ain't shit but hoes / i been known this*—and the inescapable violence from which all rappers ironically/nervously proclaim that they have themselves escaped or become exempt.

In trap music, as in Black life, there is a very thin line between escape and annihilation. A few persons acquire substantial wealth and become celebrities, even icons, in rap music. Jay-Z, P-Diddy, Dr. Dre, and Kanye West are enormously wealthy people who have traded on their status as global rock stars in the late twentieth-century tradition of such figures as Michael Jackson and Mick Jagger to diversify and consolidate corporate power in music, fashion, and other cultural industries. But don't sleep on Drake, Future (*i made forbes every year lil baby*), or Cardi B, stars of their respective moments and masters of the contemporary art of *extending the moment*, all of whom have made truly astonishing amounts of money "off that mumbling shit."* Trap's innovative vocabulary of spending and adornment (and, as patriarchal power cannot separate sexual desire from accumulation, hedonistically fucking an endless parade of desiring admirers) is a center of pure linguistic pleasure. (*drip too hard, drip or drown, Patek water, Skrrrttt skrrrttt.*) Yet baller/rock star culture is inextricable from the killings of rappers, their associates and enemies, the revolving prison door, overdoses.† When I play the music in my work, people say, "I don't hear the lyrics." They giggle over Playboi Carti's anthemic, brutal "R.I.P.";[1] they lower their heads and two-step in their theater seats when Future shouts *WHOOOOOOOO* like he might faint.[2] So much shame and bewilderment and so much potential energy falls into this unspeaking blank, which is the location of this writing's emergence.

---

* Future's words likely refer to Zack O'Malley Greenburg's coverage of the earnings of rappers in Forbes during his tenure at the magazine in "Cash Kings" features and annual lists of the "highest paid hip-hop artists"; *bought a crib for my mama off that mumbling shit*: The "mumbling shit" is "mumble rap," a derisive moniker describing the tendency of contemporary rap and rappers to forego verbal dexterity and speed, wordplay and narrative in favor of a more careless style. Playboi Carti, "R.I.P.," *Die Lit*, 2018 (AWGE/Interscope).

† Taking as an arbitrary moment the time since publication of *Dear Angel of Death* in 2018, XXXtentacion, Pop Smoke, Nipsey Hussle, and King Von have been murdered. Mac Miller and Juice World have died of accidental opioid overdoses. 03 Greedo, Kodak Black, Tekashi 6ix9ine are currently incarcerated. Meek Mill. Lil Wayne was notoriously pardoned by Donald Trump during his last week in office. Bobby Shmurda, whose government name is Ackquille Pollard, was released from prison in February 2021, having served seven years under a RICO plea deal entered into in 2016. See James C. McKinley, Jr., "Rapper Bobby Schmurda Takes 7-Year Plea Deal in Gang Case," *New York Times*, September 9, 2016. The NPR podcast Louder Than a Riot, hosted by Rodney Carmichael and Sidney Madden, provides reporting and nuanced commentary on "the interconnected rise of hip hop and mass incarceration in America," including their multi-part series on Bobby Shmurda's involvement with the unprecedented conspiracy prosecution of "GS9," "The Badder the Better."

Something is in that blank, something that is not content, but the indistinction between form and content. Yet attending to the sonic materiality of the general genre—how it moves through space and gets heard, a profile or print that produces its character (capable of being visualized as wave patterns in common audio/DJ software), a particular relationship between signature vocal innovations and the grammar of race consciousness—doesn't even get me halfway there. How to account for this thing's commonly experienced perceptual effects of intense pleasure and disavowal, effects that we are supposed to understand as *mutually negating*?

This question leads me to contemplate another zone of indistinction, the vortical feelings suggestive of gyrating machine action trap music produces in me, surprising or even paradoxical given the squeezing, potentially numbing sensation one might experience in the presence of its characteristically "strange new forms of low-end."[3] I can't overstate the significance of the fact that this is *a (bass) sound that could not even be made before 1980*, when the Roland TR-808 Rhythm Composer came to market, only to be discontinued two years later after twelve thousand units had been sold because the company ran out of a slightly mutant and unsubstitutable transistor crucial for creating the machine's sounds.[4] Musicians starting to make synthesizer-heavy dance tracks didn't like the TR-808 because it sounded... fake. What could they do with a drum machine that didn't make drum sounds? The sounds we know as "808s" are the result of a sonic accident combined with a typical capitalist reversal wherein a relatively cheap product is repurposed in an unanticipated (black) market to become extremely desirable, in this case a "bedrock" sound of rap music.[5]

The best part is that the aforementioned new forms of low-end, the signature "808" kick, don't typically come from the TR-808. "808s" are not 808s. In 1980, the TR-808 retailed for about a thousand bucks (about $3,240 in 2021 dollars). Today, one of the twelve thousand original machines sells on the secondary market for between four and fourteen thousand dollars. It's an instrument only collectors and high-end recording studios can afford. Ubiquitous beat-making software and plug-ins, like FL Studio (known as "Fruity Loops") and Virtual Studio Technology, produce most of the digitally sampled 808s we hear in trap, close, but not exact, approximations of the bass sine waves produced via analogue synthesis and made beat-ready on the Roland TR-808.[*]

You have to understand, I wasn't listening to Kanye West when *808s & Heartbreak* came out in 2008; there isn't a single song I enjoy on that record. Regardless, it is an undisputed touchstone for understanding how rap and R&B stylistically coalesce in the late 2000s. We can take the 2015 release of Future's DS2 and the Future/Drake collaboration *What a Time to Be Alive* as a demonstration of the point. Drake has a perfect ear; he is simultaneously an early adopter of the music of street rap artists and a pop tastemaker who has indeed pioneered, through carefully curated features (Waka Flocka Flame "Round of Applause," Future's early "Sh!t" remix, Blocboy J, "Look Alive," Trouble "Bring It Back," Lil Baby, "Yes, Indeed"), a kind of power rap/R&B super collab that also reflects or is evidence of how R&B's anodyne erotic palette and vocal melodies have become intertwined with trap's vitriolic, kinkier, more graphic and violent romantic complaint. I have yet to recover from the video for Rihanna's "Bitch Better Have My Money." For some commentators, West's "808s & Heartbreak" blew up the intelligible forms of masculine self-performance in Black

---

[*] Approaching the fortieth anniversary of the 808 (in 2020), versions of its history proliferated, at the same time as interest in the machine as a primary element in trap's globally lucrative soundscape grew. Notable are: 808, Directed by Alexander Dunn, Atlantic Films, 2015; Themba Kriger, "A Brief History: The Roland TR-808 Rhythm Composer," *Redbull*, August 8, 2018; Hanif Aubdurra-qib, "The TR-808 Drum Machine Changed the Sound of Pop Music Forever," *Smithsonian Magazine*, July 2020.

popular music and changed the sonic and verbal texture of the music going forward.[6] In this view, West and his co-writers' use of the (actual) Roland TR-808 repitches Black popular music—gives it both an acoustic and an affective musicological adjustment that counts as a profound innovation.

For me, 808s are a source of technical and acoustic information and more importantly for this essay, they open a rich vein of new words for a poetic and theoretical conversation about how sound means opened up by Katherine McKittrick and Alexander Weheliye in their brilliant "808s & Heartbreak," where they trace a "painful musicological history" through Marvin Gaye, R. Kelly, and Rihanna, among others, to describe how "The thump, the boom, create shivering circuits of pleasure laced with damage, loss, sorrow."[7] My understanding of the 808 sound comes out of rap music and is shaped by lifelong involvement with its worlding. House and techno, EDM, I do not physically connect with. For me, dancing has always had to do with places where only rap music was being played. "Rave" is just a word. In 2008, rap and R&B had not yet thoroughly merged in the manner that allows Future to emerge. By 2010, Lex Luger had made—with FL Studio—"Hard in da Paint" for Waka Flocka Flame's *Flockaveli* and that was it.

Recently I am obsessed with the vocal arpeggios in Chaka Khan's "I Was Made to Love Him," which takes up through a Stevie Wonder cover the problematic sociality of Motown that reverses with heartbreaking intensity in the astonishing *Here, My Dear* (both in 1978), which seems to prefigure the emotional register Marvin Gaye would find with the 808 in "Sexual Healing." It's not the machine.

In his essay on trap bass, Jace Clayton writes, "Sine wave bass is ur-bass, pure and uncut": the single pitch bass sine wave is "non-directional" and its manipulation in trap music deprives us of the ability to "locate things, or ourselves in the world" simply because bass sine waves are too long for the human hearing apparatus to calculate the sound's origin in relation to the ears.[8] Trap bass, Clayton writes "lives in you and on you." My nipples get hard right before the bass drops in "Hot Nigga," "Bodak Yellow" and "Faneto," "Krew/Time Afta Time." Its form is a surround. "What to do," Clayton asks, "with a situation you cannot think yourself out of, whose very conditions mean that while inside it you cannot orient yourself to any outside?"[9]

The first thirty seconds of Keith Cozart's p/k/a Chief Keef's "War" (2014) are supposed to be prefatory to a straight diss track with a quasi-normal lyric intro: "Pussy boy don't WANT WAR." Dactyl and spondee—stressed unstressed unstressed stressed stressed—spitting on the adversary and then whooping on them/striking, then dancing on the prone body. The six-bar prelude culminates in spasmodic coughing and choking (:20) literally mixed, in the sense that Cozart continues to cough out the slant rhyming syllables that make up the words "want war" (wunh wuh), and also mixed insofar as the coughing and choking having been recorded on a separate vocal track and blended so that the song structure can regroup/stabilize and proper dissing can proceed in the first verse, albeit punctuated by an extremity of on-drugs contempt: I am so high I can't even be bothered to say words. When the verbal attack comes—"nigga fuck yo mama / she shoulda wore a condom" (:26), hilarious, scary*—I am so disoriented by the coughing outburst, which has already shifted listening off-center of a certain kind of traditional battle/gangsta rap performance, that hearing the song unfold *as song* might be said to occur in a

---

* Typical yo mama jokes riff on negative qualities ascribed to yo mama—yo mama so fat…yo mama so hairy…lateral/horizontal in terms of intensity so the game can in principle *go on*. Yo mama is a hoe is a horizontal limit. Yo mama is a *stupid* hoe and you shouldn't have been born is a double pincer diss that creates a pulse of palpable tension. There is no game, or the game jumps the horizon of signification.

formal vacuum. Generic reference points having been filed away both sonically and linguistically, a non-space of not-song displaces a formulaic occurrence with miasmic honking, sawing noise. It is repetitive, oppressive. Cozart's voice uncloaks a narcotized super-being, becoming through murder, through *self*-murder:

> i'm high off this Aiki pack
> i'm high off this Tutu pack
> smokin on this Jay Loud
> smokin on this Fat Head
> ...
> i'm high off this Chief Keef, got me feeling superman*

Utterances celebrating the murders of rival children ought to jar out of the music any listener who is not determined fungibly to identify with this being, while the song continues to achieve and communicate hype approaching hysteria and thus to be party music of the dopest kind. I am no killer, no superman; I do not know where I am or what I am listening to or who is being addressed. Pussy boy. Me? "What, What...I'll mutter, swinging my arms around spastically."[10]

---

* Aiki Muhammad, Carlton "Tutu" Archer, and Joshua "JayLoud" Davis were murdered in gang-related attacks in 2011 and 2012. The lyrics refer to smoking their ashes in a blunt. See "Chief Keef Sparks Controversy After Dissing Slain Chicago Teens in War," KollegeKidd, February 10, 2014; see also Deanese Williams-Harris, "Teen Dies 5 Days After Englewood Shooting," *Chicago Tribune* July 21, 2011; "Teen Found Dead in Southside Alley," *Chicago Tribune* November 11, 2011; Peter Nickeas, "Overnight Shootings Leave 1 Dead, 5 Wounded Across Chicago," *Chicago Tribune* December 26, 2012. Forrest Stuart's *Ballad of the Bullet: Gangs, Drill Music and the Power of Online Infamy* (Princeton: Princeton University Press, 2020) and Chapter 3 of Roberto R. Aspholm's *Views from the Streets: The Transformation of Gangs and Violence on Chicago's South Side* (New York: Columbia University Press, 2020) provide detailed accounts of the relationship between drill music and gun violence in Chicago.

What Is Going On in Rap Music, the Music Called "Trap" and "Drill"?

*

It is ever our intention to imagine and consequently to provide language that describes, but beyond that, liturgically extends the circuits along which Black people might continue to reach and carry one another, always in ways that are foreclosed to authorities. Allowing for the possibility that reaching and carrying may be anti-historical modes of association, incapable of being memorialized, suppressed hustle until a nigga can get hfReet, the greatest trap music can have nothing to do with what Foucault calls "little polemical professional activities that are called critique."[11]

Art criticism and literary criticism employ a conceptual apparatus around desire and racial capitalism (time, then, also time) that are the subject of its destructive play and the butt of the music's jokes (*i just fucked yo bitch in some gucci flip flops / i'm in a laaaaamb[horgini] i don't give a damn. fuck. nyooouuuhm*), while sociology would treat trap as an iteration of a bad man tale, as if the life that makes the work possible were a figment of the artist's imagination. The idea is to grasp without violating Black imagination and to bring into focus a passionate relation with an art practice that has, as Benjamin Krusling says, "so many ideas" from which no one on the earth today does not ruthlessly take.*

Criticism will not and cannot fuck with trap. Would not fuck with it if it could. Trap will block thinking in terms of sociogeny; it will block thinking in terms of double consciousness. Black feminism's account of experience, which has interrupted criticism with information about extremities of conjoined pleasure and pain, will

---

* Rodney Carmichael makes a more measured claim, writing of the "trap-rap innovation economy from which Atlanta perpetually feeds" in "Culture Wars: Trap Music Keeps Atlanta on Hip-Hop's Cutting Edge. Why Can't The City Embrace It?," *NPR*, March 15, 2017.

emerge as the North Star. This is not only because Linda Brent, Ida Wells, Nikki Giovanni, Gayl Jones, Audre Lorde, and Imani Perry orient themselves beyond the language of subjectivity, the representational power of our perfect failure, and the ethical event horizon defined by modern political theory to reckon with our screams, our flesh, the ferocity of intent to become *whole*. The circumstances that have extruded our living as being denied are not what we are. It is also because and more than because this thought concerns radiance and the absorption of rays, as prone, as being risen.

*

Here is Jesse McCarthy in his 2018 essay "Notes on Trap":

Q. What is the subject of trap?

A. Money, a.k.a. skrilla, paper, green, gwop, currency, stacks, bands, bundles, racks, currency, fetty (confetti), ends, dead presidents, bankrolls, $100,000 in just two days, fuck-you money, fuck up some commas, money long, run up a check, fuck up a check; a master signifier in falling bills, floating, liquid, pouring down on bitches in the proverbial rain...[12]

McCarthy's question rests on the problem word "subject" in a poetically explosive manner. Does he ask, What is the ontological status of the being who traps? "Money" might be a correct answer. Or, What terrain does the matrix of the songs outline as the genre's territorial borders, so that listeners apprehend and vicariously participate in a distinct zone of activity? The subject would become the activity of worldbuilding on the order of science fiction or video games. And/or, if it is possible to isolate the material (sonic) elements of a given song, accepting that these will be heard together with its grammatical and linguistic properties, from performances and persons, what would it mean for these to "have a subject" anyway? Do rocks have subjects? Does water? Do moods? Can trap confer its sonic subject upon others? How? How does it do that?* Is the conferral an accolade or an assault or what?

"What is the subject of trap?" is a riddle because it is a question that does not work; it does not work if you have come to believe, as I do, that trap is a machine for aboutness itself, a practice of inventing concern, requesting to take part in connection that exists only as potentiality and that this is an operational logic distinct from the "form of soft power" McCarthy recognizes in Note #20. Our friendly disagreement arises out of the institutional and intellectual conditions that make the care and attention McCarthy's extends to the music in "Notes on Trap" so rare that the most exciting thing about the essay is that it exists at all. There is plenty of commentary on trap music—on HotNewHipHop.com, in *Complex*, *XXL* and *Fader*, and in SoundCloud and YouTube comments. I am also grateful for the work of writers like Rodney Carmichael, who McCarthy approvingly cites, who have diligently reported on trap's development beneath the noses and notice of the urban political and financial classes in the cities from which it has emerged—certainly Atlanta, but also Houston, Chicago, and New York.[13] But I want to bear down on the ways in which trap, "the only music that sounds like what living in contemporary America feels like…the soundtrack of the dissocialized subject that neoliberalism made," has developed without and beneath the aesthetic and philosophical notice of a Black studies establishment where afropessimism and declaration of the end of the liberal democratic episteme are widely accepted frameworks for approaching the persistence of racial violence and structural inequality. Doubtless the growth of the Black studies establishment

---

* McKittrick and Weheliye's formulation, "What does the 808 do *to us*?" continues to guide my inquiry in this regard.

is noncoincidental with the increasing intensity and abstraction of its claims about Black nothingness and escape, but that is the subject of the other Part.

The excellence of McCarthy's essay therefore, is an excellence that happens in spite of his impulse to historicize drill's music signature sound as indicative of a "special relationship…to Black marching bands…where they are a sonic backdrop of enormous proximate importance to the producers of trap," thereby situating it in exactly an intellectual history of the people and the music that it spastically, physically protests; the excellence of McCarthy's piece is that it manages to hit upon the onliest-ness of the music's not being heard by those of us supposedly attuned to Black frequencies but unable to listen to what we don't want to hear. Its power and should-be aesthetic instructiveness and opportunity is in its onliest-ness.*

> Imagine a people enthralled, gleefully internalizing the world of pure capital flow, of infinite negative freedom (continuously replenished through frictionless browsing), thrilled at the possibilities (in fact necessity) of self-commodification, the value in the network of one's body, the harvesting of others.[14]

Yes to this. Yes, and no one was looking or asking for or imagining Future's negative ass. He was anyway. Negative as in Nikki Giovanni, as in calculation. Imagine trap's counter-progressive emergence against the drive of known radicalism, an emergence, which, at the time I am writing may already have reached its half-life.

Under one analytical framework, trap music is pop music, and I am a consumer; everything I say will have said in some

---

* This quality is the subject of my essay "Onliest-ness," Whitney biennial catalog 2022, forthcoming.

way contemplated the objection that I am a high bourgeois middle-aged woman with no cognizable politico-economic relation to the people who make this music. A vast divide cuts off creators from consumers; we cannot hear or speak to one another. (I should therefore shut up.) This mode of analysis does not allow for the possibility and fact that the matter in question is made of physical displacement, movement, actual waves. These can be activated and put to search; the signal, the searching and the contact together are how blackness is and must be partially constituted as a mode of communication and consciousness that does not know class, nation, or culture, at least not as they are historically signified. Locating and responding to such signals, I believe, is a response to the call Denise Ferreira da Silva has put to all Black people, a call to "come on in" that is more intimate than Baraka's call and cannot be separated from it.[15]

Under this framework, the contortions of attitude or posture that trap can apparently induce, craning to see myself in the throes of the greedy and deviant pleasure the works occasion, constitutes desire, pleasure, curiosity, and thought; the contortions must themselves be the subject of any serious effort to critically engage these artworks. They demand consideration of *the placement of the self near the thing, changing regard, pauses, reorientation, black speed today* and *attack*. In other words, the music demands that I concern myself with the manner in which I am not cut off from the works or the artists who make it, the fucking obvious fact of my twisted engagement, which isn't supposed to take place. Modalities of interpenetration, irresolute clinging, statements that explore the horrific possibility of being swallowed up as a terminal reality for all new gatherings of force—these interest me poetically, erotically, technologically.

What is taking place and not taking place when I impossibly allow hearing trap music to occur, when I hear it and I am near it?

Let us try to speak of the subject of Chief Keef's "Sosa Chamberlain." If you are interested in the kinds of conversation it is possible to get into with a Black man, which involves passionate interest in Black gender and how gender moves in desire, "Sosa Chamberlain" is an exemplary song in an exemplary cultural development. A period of industrial confusion engulfed Chief Keef after the massive debut single "I Don't Like" came flying out of Chicago in 2012 when he was sixteen years old. The mixtape *Sorry 4 tha Weight* (2015), on which "Sosa Chamberlain" was officially released, bubbled up out of a period of trippy experimentation with a trap/drill vocabulary blurred by samples, heavily autotuned vocal melodies, blip and plink sounds apparently derived from gaming—see for example 2014's (self-produced) "Wait" or "Nobody" featuring Kanye West—that some listeners found off-putting and abnormal. Keef's trouble with the law, being barred from live performance under policing authority, failure to cooperate with media and anti-social behavior during this period is well documented (media buzzed with gossip and speculation about whether or not Cozart has autism) and not the subject of this essay.

The fact is, the post-"I Don't Like" Cozart did not, which is not to say could not, publicly function in the industrial system that pursued him and would have consumed him, a fact deposited most painfully in the internet archive as a four-minute "Back and Forth" interview on Noisey, a music content subsidiary of the Vice media group, with Donald Glover p/k/a Childish Gambino.[16] In 2012, Glover had already achieved entirely mainstream success as an "alternative" rapper (and would go on to create the brilliant and acclaimed television show *Atlanta*). He sits down in front of a graffiti-covered wall with Cozart to conduct said back and forth about Cozart's breakout single, whose lyrics consist almost entirely of a list of shit Keef don't like.

Glover: That shit spoke to people. A fart…that's that shit I don't like…

Cozart: Who said that?

Glover: Huh?

Cozart: Who said that?

Glover: Is that not on there?

Cozart: Hell naw.

Glover: What's that first part? [inaudible, gestures off camera as if to blame someone for providing wrong words]

Cozart: Fuck nigga.

Glover: [casually raps] A fuck nigga that's that shit i don't like / a snitch nigga that's that shit i don't like

Cozart: Uh huh. Bitch…

Glover: A bitch nigga that's that shit i don't like

Cozart: Sneak diss…

Glover: A sneak disser that's that shit i don't like

People said: Glover was trying but it was like he was talking to the wall in the background. Meanwhile I'm thinking to myself, *here is a motherfucker who cannot win smdh they will not let him win.*

Many viewings and years later, the scene, for me, has become one of wild incongruity—Glover's Black hipster ironies and authorized inquisition swim in Cozart's simultaneous star power and structural misalignment. Witness an instant of uncalled for and *successfully deflected* linguistic re-territorialization: the verbally gifted Donald Glover is commanded to speak in terms *he cannot hear* or prefers to understand as a registered form of scatological humor—a fart joke—that Cozart is having none of. One loves the reversing, uncontrolled fart joke, here leading to Glover's shitting of the bed. No, I was not joking, nor am I the object of this interview; or, this is the only acceptable manner in which humor between us can emerge.

"Sosa Chamberlain" is seeded partially in that exchange with Glover. At some point, Cozart taught himself to produce. Like "I Don't Like," "Faneto" (2014), whose production is credited solely to Cozart, seemed to occasion especially frenetic responses in crowds. This notable crowd effect is the subject of some hilarious memes captioned "When 'Faneto' comes on in the club" and seems to have been the cause of two building collapses.* In 2020, it became one of the songs frequently played at Black Lives Matter protests. These songs drive crowds with a nearly distorted bass kick that drops super hard on the one, cemented in verbal repetition of single words (aye, bang, gang) and thick with menace but rhythmically straightforward phrases (*i'm a gorilla in a fucking coupé finna pull up the zoo / your bitch won't do the team bet she won't fight*).† They really do seem to be derived from martial music and importantly define "drill," in addition to showcasing vocal innovations that would go on to be adopted by far more commercially successful rappers including Lil Uzi Vert and 21 Savage, and are now virtually universal in contemporary rap music. "Sosa Chamberlain" presents Keef-ian innovations as a kind of sedimentation—aye, gang, bang—while otherwise departing from the juvenile style.

yo bitch got that wet wet, my gun got that wet wet

"Wet," a word so slippery and ungendered, suspended between sexual arousal and bleeding, that there can be no equivalent or

---

* People jumping and dancing caused floors to collapse at parties in two separate incidents: one in Denton, Texas, in 2017 and another in Greenville, South Carolina, in 2018.
† The crowd-sourced lyrics and annotation site Genius transcribes the line "The bitch want do the team," implying that a woman wants consensual group sex with the whole crew. But then what sense would "she won't fight" make? I have always heard "won't" do the team, which makes the line about the threat of gang rape.

sufficient rhyme pair; so that it extends wackily to embrace the midwestern sound of "that" as "thet" and then to "ear"/er; that is the base rhyme sound for "Sosa Chamberlain," an elongated "eh." Mumbled or garbled phrases that don't fit the time of the bar "water what I drink cat me(ow) all i get." The thing presents as a fait accompli a dramatic and complex compositional shift and a complete character called "Sosa Wilt Chamberlain":

> blunts just flamin
> watch just blangin, phone just rangin
> i'm a no belt rockin, no sock rockin
> pull up show stoppin, you know how 'm rockin
> i came in the game man, and you know i changed it
> Sosa what's your language? bitch i speak them acres[*]
> favorite team the Lakers, favorite team the Bulls
> wanna put up your paper? 'm like okay cool

Happy to take your money, fool. I DO WHAT I WANT is a known register of rock star cool. Baller literalism is a known performative function. The fundamentals, soundwise, had been aesthetically established. What continues to baffle and interest me about "Sosa Chamberlain" is the appearance of two "she"s, one with whom Chief Keef dialogues/bickers in Verse 1 about her having to pee while riding with the gang, and Chief Keef's little daughter, who "calls [him] mad and says she gon eat all [his] chips." If "Sosa Chamberlain" can be a known kind of high-energy superhero theme music whose closest musical relative may be Black Sabbath's "Iron Man," laying down a sonic carpet for a charismatic/freaky constant-return (most beautifully enlivened by Ghostface Killah's *Ironman*), it can also be an unknown kind of sounding that reveals a mundane area within which is it possible to have contact with a person who would not exactly uncloak and cannot.

* Anyone know what this means? [Is this rhetorical?]

A person possibly known as Keith Cozart stages a conversation regarding actual stuff in a totalizing surround otherwise lacking a relational vocabulary for being with such a person; that is, he addresses a social world that lacks a relational vocabulary that is not rooted in the assumption (not ascribed, but worn, as a garment) of social, political, and moral deficiency; a sociality within which the explicit cost of being included in social life is willingness to be that-which-will-be-the-subject-of-freedom.

Further, "Sosa Chamberlain" opens a conversation that has to do, for me, with the permanent, regulatory separation white supremacy—the ghost, the beast—would impose upon Black people who wish to survive and those who would be expendable. Trap and drill therefore insist that we consider what the subject of freedom can do or say together with the one who will not pay the cost and yet thrives in the unsettling light of what he owns and what he makes in some narrow strip in an apolitical outskirt that is on no map, defined only by First Class airfare between Chicago and Los Angeles. I wish to extend myself into the thought world of the person who issues a call to discuss this separation.

---

[1] https://www.youtube.com/watch?v=GRoa6w-wnT4.

[2] https://soundcloud.com/freebandzglobal/future-shit-prod-by-mike-will.

[3] Jace Clayton, 2020. "Invasion of Privacy" in *Black Futures*, eds. Kimberly Drew and Jenna Wortham, pp. 322–325. New York: Penguin.

[4] "The mysterious heart of the Roland TR-808 drum machine," *The Secret Heart of Synthesizers*, 19 May 2018, https://secretlifeofsynthesizers.com/the-strange-heart-of-the-roland-tr-808/, September 23, 2021.

[5] Jayson Greene, "The Coldest Story Ever Told: The Influence of Kanye West's *808s & Heartbreak*," *Pitchfork*, September 22, 2015. www.pitchfork.com/features/overtones/9725-the-coldest-story-ever-told-the-influence-of-kanye-wests-808s-heartbreak/.

[6] See, e.g., Greene.

[7] *Propter Nos* 2:1 (Fall 2017), 15.

[8] Clayton, 323–324.

[9] Clayton, 325.

[10] Eileen Myles, 2016. "Exploding the Spring Mystique," *I Must Be Living Twice*, Ecco/HarperCollins.

[11] Michel Foucault, 2007. "What is Critique?," *The Politics of Truth*, ed. Sylvere Lotringer, trans. Lysa Hochroth, p. 42. Los Angeles: Semiotext(e),

[12] *n*+1, Issue 32, Fall 2018.

[13] "Culture Wars," cited in McCarthy, note 10; see also note 12 infra.

[14] McCarthy, note 19.

[15] Amiri Baraka, 2014. "SOS," SOS: *Poems* 1961–2013, ed. Paul Vangelisti. New York: Grove.

[16] https://www.youtube.com/watch?v=aTH8Fj9S3fA.

Auld Lang Syne in July

Yiyun Li

On New Year's Day fifteen years ago I made a solo trip across west Texas in a rental car. There were not many vehicles on the highway, and once in a while a cluster of tumbleweeds chased one another across the road, blissfully, bleakly, befitting the mood of the American southwest. The landscape was vast, and the pale wintry sky, too. The scenery would be best accompanied by some music about the harmony and the disconnection between men and nature, between the small loneliness within an individual and the boundless loneliness without. But the car radio could only pick up one station: a man was preaching the second coming of Jesus Christ with a maniacal passion. Outside El Paso, just when the highway lost its last sign of urbanity, a man was trekking by the roadside, away from the city, carrying on his back a giant white cross. It must have been heavy, from the way he leaned forward and dragged on slowly, and it would be a long journey for him, wherever his destination lay. A few seconds later he was no more than a dot in my rear-view mirror.

I drove on in the silence that, after some time, was as hypnotic as the static signals from the frequencies other than the Christian station. I had not thought of bringing CDs with me for the CD player. I had only my own singing voice—not a great one—to break the monotony. But what could I sing? I had been living in America for ten years by then, and could only sing in English the nursery rhymes to which I was being exposed for the first time along with my children. What I had in my Chinese repertoire: the propaganda songs I grew up with in China, and the military songs from my year in the People's Liberation Army. Of course there were the pop songs from Hong Kong and Taiwan, which we used to listen to on a Sony Walkman in high school and, in the army camp, on a shortwave radio after lights-out. Though for some reason those songs, when I tried to sing them, about unrequited loves and wounded hearts and withering flowers and changing seasons, were as flat and enervating as the static signals on the radio.

To stay alert, I needed something to keep my mind separate from my immediate surroundings, the rental car with its industrial sterility, the cloudless sky seemingly low, the ever-expanding landscape in the earth tones. What I did not know—I was then a young mother with an infant and a toddler—was that an unaltered landscape, like eventless days, could be a solace, too. My goal was to get from one place to another. I wanted to drive safely, staying in my lane, just under the speed limit; and yet, I was impatient.

For hours I sang to myself, from "Communism is Good" to "The Sky Over the Liberated District," from "My Motherland" to "Warsaw Marching Song," my stringent self-consciousness doing little to constrain myself. What I heard was an unfamiliar voice—I rarely sing, even in the shower, and I had never until then sung solo those songs from the past. In the army I used to only mouth the lyrics without making a sound, a futile gesture of incompliance meaningful only to me. My younger self would never have imagined that one day I would be in America, driving through a landscape known to me from cowboy movies, and singing the songs against which I once rebelled with a youthful purity.

Perhaps it is not farfetched to say that while I was singing in the car, the voice I heard was not quite mine, but the memory of a collective voice: the broadcast that had played throughout my childhood on the loudspeakers in our residential compound. Five hundred children singing together at our school assemblies, and the chorus of my fellow soldiers in the army. I then encountered a problem that I first encountered when I was seventeen, after giving a patriotic speech at a school oratory contest, moving my audience and myself to tears and winning the contest that I had been forced to participate in. I only meant to keep myself occupied and awake while driving, but I was so touched by the propaganda songs that I was in tears. From nostalgia, no doubt; even so I felt a bit ashamed, just as I had felt when I won the oratory contest. Can feelings, induced by mind-numbing and brainwashing propaganda, be called genuine?

When my sister was thirteen, she and her friends taught themselves to sing the Chinese version of "Auld Lang Syne" from a newspaper. It was the golden age of newspaper days—I looked for serialized novels on the last page of every day's paper. My sister had a notebook to collect songs, published in a column under the title "One Song A Week," with their lyrics and music notes printed. They were newer than the propaganda songs from the 1950s and 1960s, which we could all sing in our dreams. Many of them were odes to our happy lives in our motherland, and to our bright futures in a new dawn, but once in a while there would be a song that stood out. I was nine, and did not need anyone to explain to me that they were the rare beauties in our lives. My sister and her teenage friends all recognized the fact, as with some of the songs, they would learn to sing and forget, but others would remain their treasured possession.

I like to imagine that the newspaper editor, harboring some subversive spirit, tallied the songs that fell into different categories: patriotic, positive in attitude, forward-looking, and historical. When the moment felt right, he or she would sneak a beloved song into print. I like to imagine that the editor knew that such an act would make a difference, to all those hungry minds out in the world, and to the months and years to come. "Auld Lang Syne" was one of those songs, appearing inexplicably in print, capturing many young hearts.

There was another incident once, similar to "Auld Lang Syne," with a song entitled "Longing for My Old Home." The lyrics were credited to an unnamed poet; the music, elegiac, was from the second movement of Antonín Dvořák's Symphony Number Nine, "From the New World." The most well-known theme in D-flat major in that movement was unknown to anyone in our world, yet listening to my sister and her friends working out the tune, I instantly memorized it. Years later, when I listened to Dvořák's New World Symphony for the first time—I was in my early twenties, and I was in Iowa City, not far from Spillville, Iowa, where Dvořák spent a summer composing in 1893—I recognized the theme from the song my sister and her friends used to sing. I, too shy to join the big girls then, had only sung it in my heart without making a sound.

The Chinese title of "Auld Lang Syne" is "May Friendship Be as Enduring as Earth and as Long Lasting as Heaven." The lyrics were archaic and poetic, with references to memories that were beyond our experience as the children of the 1970s, growing up in cramped apartment complexes in Beijing: the blue mountains and green valleys where we once left our carefree footprints; the ocean that separated us; the long harsh years of wandering—rootless, roofless—and then, the reunion, where glasses of wine are raised to celebrate our everlasting friendship. Who were the *we* that the song referred to? We who sang the song had no idea. It was not us. And yet they, having lived through joys and pains, must have articulated some mood, some sensitivity, and some yearning for that which we had no words or music in our daily life. Why else would the girls sing the song again and again in the falling dusk, on their balconies, their voices transparent with a melancholy tenderness.

It was 1981, and our family was about to acquire our first television set. My sister and her friends—none of them had heard of the original song—did not know that the very first note of the music was misprinted in the paper, so they were perpetually starting "Auld Lang Syne" out of tune. This I learned a few years later, when a friend gave me sheet music for the song, arranged for an accordion. I learned to play it on my accordion, an instrument less plaintive than a violin or an oboe. Even so, I preferred "Auld Lang Syne" to the other pieces my teacher had me play on the accordion: Soviet wartime music, folk music from Eastern Europe, and, of course, the propaganda songs we'd grown up singing.

The summer I was thirteen, I played "Auld Lang Syne" over and over on my accordion, not knowing that the song is traditionally sung on New Year's Eve, or that the mood of the song may be more festive or less melancholy than I imagined. I was at the age when my sister and her friends had first fallen in love with "Auld Lang Syne." They were older girls now, seemingly ready for that awfully big adventure called life. Thirty-five years later, where are they, who once sang wistfully about a reunion when glasses would be raised for the everlasting friendship? Two of them died, both from cancer, both leaving young children and old parents to mourn. The other five are scattered, living on three continents now.

In September 2017 I was in London to attend William Trevor's memorial service. I did a few other things, including going to Hull to see a Philip Larkin exhibition. I thought of going to the West End to see *Les Misérables*, but decided not to. I took a screenshot of the show's information and sent it to Vincent, my older son, and said that we should plan a trip to London and see the show together some time soon.

Vincent was the one to bring the musical into our family life. When he was in fifth grade he discovered *Les Misérables*, and for the next few years, we watched the movie and then the stage production of the musical every weekend, sometimes as a mere background for what we were doing: parents reading, and the two boys playing on their computers. On holidays—driving in California, in Quebec, in Ireland, in Scotland—Vincent and his little brother would sing the musical from the beginning to the end. My favorite was the duel scene between Jean Valjean and Javert. "Confrontation!" Vincent would say, and that alone was enough to lead to the sung-out accompaniment and then to the duet.

I was twelve when I fell in love with Victor Hugo's work. A friend loaned me *Les Misérables* and *The Hunchback of Notre-Dame*, and for a summer I read them many times. There was always a sense of hunger when I think of my childhood. Food was never abundant, but beyond that, good books and beautiful music were not always available. (I had not been allowed into a library until middle school; books in the shops, even if we could afford them, were of unequal quality, many of them falling into the category of revolutionary literature.) One had to devour anything. There was no waiting for tomorrow, as tomorrow might never come.

I told Vincent that he should read *Les Misérables*—it would be different from just watching the musical, I said, though I did not tell him the circumstances of my reading Hugo. He fell in love with the book, and read it three times the summer before middle school. On a family trip to Paris, right after we checked in at the hotel, we went out to look for the old house of Victor Hugo. To this day, a copy of *Les Misérables* and a small bust of Hugo sit on Vincent's shelf. For a few years the book and the musical were part of the fabric of his life, and of our family life, too.

But we never did go to West End for the musical. Four days after I returned from London, Vincent died. I have not listened to the entire musical since then, but sometimes, when I feel sturdy enough, I would listen to the few bars of an oboe solo, after the final battle and all the young people are killed at the barricade.

For a while, Vincent and I shared an ongoing joke. Once I had a conversation with an older writer at a luncheon. He asked if my children played any instrument. I told him my older son played the oboe. "Oboe, what a beautiful instrument," he exclaimed, his wrinkled face turning expressive.

I agreed that an oboe was a beautiful instrument.

"My first girlfriend was an oboist, and that was—" the man's face turned dreamy in his calculation, "—that was fifty-eight years ago."

A similar conversation occurred, another time, with an older woman, who told me that she had once dated an oboist. "It's a special instrument," she told me. "Ah, how I love the sounds of an oboe."

"An oboe is a beautiful instrument," Vincent used to joke with me. "And an oboist is a perfect ex."

An oboist in the past, who lives on in someone's heart. Perhaps he would still make that joke today.

Years ago, a student of mine, an aspiring writer, gave me an album by her husband, who had taken a year off to write the lyrics, compose the music, and record the songs. The album never gained any notoriety, and he went back to his day job as a lawyer. My student, who had grown up working in her parents' Chinese takeout in an inner-city neighborhood, behind metal bars and bullet-proof glass, spent two years working on her writing, and then admitted to me her frustration of not being able to write as well as she wished. Soon after, she returned to her day job as a real estate agent.

Once I told a friend about the couple—we were having a general conversation about people's career choices. Horrified, my friend called the couple's stories an American tragedy, an example of capitalism engulfing young, aspiring artists, leading them astray from their artistic dreams and into materialism. But is it such a bad thing to be pragmatic, I wondered; is it such a bad thing to have loved their art forms, tried, and acknowledged—wisely, it feels to me—that they can be limited in what they can achieve, despite the love for their arts?

I had listened to the husband's album when I received it, and then placed it on a shelf. A few years later, when Vincent was in middle school, he discovered the album, and fell in love with the songs. He played the album often, and was disappointed to know that the singer/songwriter did not make a name for himself. There was only one clip of the singer playing the title song on YouTube, Vincent informed me, and even that was recorded from afar, with the man's face vague in the semidarkness.

For some time I thought of introducing Vincent to the creator of his most favorite album. Would it make the man sad, or happy, that his album, though unknown to the larger world, had become a treasured possession for one boy? Would it be a solace to the artist that his songs had made a different in one person's life? It was one of those plans that one has intended to carry out but never done.

And in the end, one supposes, that is where life takes a different stand from music. All those songs, musicals, albums, played or sung at the right time or the wrong time, for the right reason or the wrong reason, in the right mood or the wrong mood—what are they but placeholders of life? Memories of my childhood and youth were partially preserved in the communist propagandas. "Auld Lang Syne," played in a sultry July, had more meaning to me than a chorus of "Auld Lang Syne" heralding a new year. An album, forgettable to the world, was a daily presence in the life of a boy for as long as that boy was alive. Music, in its absolute right to exist, perhaps is not unlike mood, or landscape—external or internal. No mood can be the wrong mood, no landscape can be the wrong landscape, as no music can be the wrong music. Often, we have the context in our minds when we call something wrong: its timing, its consequence, its relationship with others.

The aspiring artists who are now a lawyer and a realtor—if there is some loss in their decisions, the loss should be put into a perspective. Arts are only placeholders for life. Some are masterful placeholders, some, less so; but all the same it is the life held by those holders that has to be lived through. One does not wrestle with life's placeholders, but with life itself.

After the couple's first child was born I visited them in their sunny house in Oakland, California. I remembered thinking, when I looked at the infant, that here's a child who will grow up with plenty of books and music, and who will not be working behind metal bars and bullet-proof glass at seven. What more can parents do for their children, but keep their bodies and minds nourished? The lives they go on making are theirs, leaving, as always, some placeholder in their parents' memory: a book, a musical, an album, a joke, and an oboe that has to go on living its own version of a life story.

Hearing Voices

Zakia Sewell

I don't remember the first time I heard it, but I've listened to it a hundred times before: the crackle of tape hiss, like some old ethnographic recording, the jangly guitar intro that sounds like it's being played at the other end of the room, the clattering of cymbals, and then, her voice…Ethereal and soulful, familiar and strange. She sounds remote at first, like she's singing off-mic, and then there she is, in full beam. The bass and the drums and the flute and the keys are all much louder, and yet, to me, barely audible—I can only hear her voice.

She sounds so high-pitched and young; like a different person almost. Her voice is much lower now; it sounds like it emanates from the deepest parts of her, or deeper still, from the very center of the Earth. Back then—so delicate, sinuous, soaring high above the rest of the band, striving for something just beyond her reach—she sounds happy, but there's something telling in her vibrato, in the way it swells and quakes. My mother: a ghost, immortalized on tape.

I think it was recorded at a rehearsal. The quality isn't so great but I like the feeling that I'm there in the room with them all, somewhere amid the cables and the instruments and the half-smoked spliffs. Perhaps I was there, in some form—the promise in a loving glance exchanged between her and my dad. It was definitely recorded before I was born, though. Everything had been filled with hope before that. They were about to sign with a record label, and were gigging all over the country; legend has it that she performed until she was eight months pregnant. Perhaps if I tried hard enough, I'd be able to remember what it felt like, bouncing around on stage in her belly, hearing the hum of her voice through all the fluid and flesh.

The tape resurfaced recently when my dad was clearing out the attic, sifting through dusty boxes full of records and flyers and mini-disks from the old days; a repository of memories, some happier than others. The band was called Fat Caspar, after him. I don't think he was actually fat, but he certainly didn't like the name very much. He played the bass, accompanied by Mark on guitar, Paul on drums, Elliott on keys, Simon on flute, and, my mom, Amey, on vocals. They were part of the Acid Jazz generation, brushing shoulders with bands like Jamiroquai and D'Influence and the Brand New Heavies. Some say the genre hasn't aged very well but it'll always have a special place in my heart; I like hearing my mom in that sound-world: jazzy chords, Latin rhythms, and her sweet, hopeful voice, preserved in eternal sunshine.

Music was the foundation of my parents' love-affair. My mom had fled her chaotic family home to go to drama school in London, where she met my uncle, a dashingly handsome actor, wearing eyeliner and a feather in his ear. He was keen to start a band, and introduced her to my dad—a dashingly handsome musician (without the makeup) who wore oversized tweed suits and was a dab hand on the guitar and bass. They used to go busking together on the tube, singing Martha and the Vandellas' "Heat Wave" in three-part harmonies through the carriages, before spending their hard-earned cash down at the pub.

In many ways they were an unlikely match. My dad was brought up on the outskirts of London by my grandmother—a six-foot-tall bohemian with jet black hair, who wore Indian sarongs, sunbathed topless in public (a habit she's only recently given up), and who'd turn up at the school gates in bare feet, much to the horror of my dad and uncle. She experimented with alternative parenting methods and made "exotic" dishes like moussaka and hummus and rocket salad, while my dad longed for fish fingers, baked beans, and discipline. His dad was an Australian animator, a legend of old Soho, who claimed he could change the weather, and yet despite his fluency in magic, failed to conjure up the cash when it came to his kids. He died at a transcendental meditation retreat when my dad was just eleven.

My mom's family were from a different world. They came to England in the sixties, from a tiny island in the Caribbean called Carriacou, settling down on a terraced street in sunny Bedford. The family home had all the trappings of a typical West Indian household: the glass cabinet filled with tacky ceramics; plastic coverings on the sofas; fake flowers; net curtains; garish wallpaper; and the sounds of the country and western star, Jim Reeves (an unlikely hit with the Windrush generation), emanating from the radiogram. My grandma worked as a cleaner in the hospital, while my grandad did shifts down at the local crayon factory, and after long, hard days at work, they'd invite friends over for rum, records and, sometimes, fist fights. My mom and her three brothers were exiled to their bedrooms during such events, but would have Jamaican-style sound clashes with their neighbors while their parents were at work, blasting Dillinger and Big Youth at earth-shattering volumes to vanquish the rival sound-system across the road.

Despite hailing from opposite ends of the globe, these two families had one thing in common: dysfunction. My mom sometimes wished that she had nice, middle-class English parents like her friends from grammar school, parents who would cuddle and kiss her and buy her gifts and call her "darling." While my dad—who spent a large proportion of his childhood sitting outside pubs while his parents got drunk with their artist friends—simply

245

wished for a mom and dad that were "normal." For both of them, music was a refuge, a balm. My dad found fatherly wisdom in Elvis Presley and the Beatles, while my mom, just down the M1, sought solace in the voices of Syreeta, Carol Kenyan, and Grace Jones. Both had grown up feeling other, feeling misunderstood, and music offered them a way to find meaning.

I like to think that I'm woven from the same fabric as the songs they wrote together; that from a very young age, the music emanating from amplifiers and home stereos somehow played its part in making me, *me*. I spent a lot of my childhood at rehearsals and parties (and, in the family tradition, pubs), sleeping on sofas late into the night, soothed by the music and chatter all around me. I was taken to gigs, made to sing on family recordings, and would spend evenings after school sitting in the living room, listening to my dad practice Wes Montgomery standards on his Gretsch guitar—I still have the opening bars to "Four on Six" permanently inscribed in my memory. I was enveloped by music, folded in by it. We all were. But its healing powers could only extend so far.

*

I was three months old the first time it happened. My mom had had a string of sleepless nights (not uncommon for a new mother, of course) but this time it wasn't me who was keeping her up; it was the muffled sounds of conversation, floating up from the flat below. We used to live in a poky little council block on a main road, where the traffic and the airplanes and the sirens and the sound of the neighbors' television made up a kind of comforting drone, an inner-city lullaby. That night it had the opposite effect.

My mom has told me this story several times now. She says she sat in bed for hours, with my dad fast asleep next to her, listening to what she thought was the neighbor's conversation. She tossed and turned, straining to make out what they were saying, until it became apparent that they were talking about her, saying all kinds of horrible, malicious things. She says their voices became clearer and clearer, coming up first through the floor, then through the walls; from opposite sides of the room, and then whispering in her ear; growing louder and louder and more insulting, until she could no longer bear it.

She decided to go downstairs and confront the neighbor face-to-face. But the innocent neighbor, rudely disturbed from her sleep by my wide-eyed mother, had no idea what she was talking about; she looked my mom up and down, and told her, plainly, to "go to church," before closing the door and getting back into bed.

In my mind's eye the scene is crystal clear: I can see the yellow glow of the streetlights outside, casting sinister shadows across the room; I can see my mom, sat bolt upright in bed, listening to a patter of voices only she can hear, and I can see the neighbor, bleary-eyed and bemused, looking at my mom and instantly recognizing the whispering force at work.

My mom didn't go to church, she went to the doctor. And after that, everything changed.

*

When I listen to that tape of my mom singing, I hear the voice of somebody I lost a very long time ago, before I could understand what I had lost. That night, a part of her went away, and was never to return.

All throughout my childhood I heard stories about who she was before she got ill—about her creativity, her power, her humor, and her wit. The song was like a time capsule; it gave me access to the parts of her that had been lost. I ransacked the tape, desperate to learn everything I possibly could about her. Was she self-assured, or lacking confidence? How did she move? Was she lithe and elegant, or heavy-footed? Was she funny? Were her eyes dull or did they sparkle? What about her laugh, did it sound the same? I was desperate to recognize myself in the person I heard in the recording, because I couldn't in the mother I had in front of me: a mother who was loving, but absent; lost in a daydream, battling with hidden hurts.

I was six years old when she was finally diagnosed with paranoid schizophrenia, and for a long time, she remained a peripheral figure. Being disconnected from her meant being disconnected from half of my heritage. It was via my white, English father that I discovered the wonders of Caribbean food, devouring Trinidadian rotis with plenty of pepper sauce while parked in his work van; he was the one that took me to Notting Hill Carnival, carrying me on his shoulders, high above the parade; and it was through him that I first heard reggae and dub, the music that had swept up and held my mom's teenage brothers as they navigated a hostile country. I had a sense that this culture was connected to me, but much of it felt distant and remote. Just like my mom. As I grew older, and began searching for answers about my identity, it was music that helped me to find the missing links.

As a teenager I developed a voracious appetite for collecting music. It started with CDs bought with Virgin Megastore vouchers given to me as birthday gifts by my grandparents; 3-disk R&B bumper sets with hits by Amerie, Mis-Teeq, Destiny's Child, Outkast, and Kelis. Then it was grime tracks shared with friends on Bluetooth phones in the school playground and their sketchy music videos that played on Channel U. I remember "Free Yard" by Aggro being a favorite, although its sentiment, looking back, is rather questionable. Next came an obsession with hip-hop; De La Soul, A Tribe Called Quest, MF Doom, Mos Def, Pete Rock, Wu Tang Clan...I'd study blog posts about samples used by producers like J Dilla and DJ Premier, spending nights trawling YouTube uploads of rare groove tracks, straining my ears to find the sections they had excavated. In my late teens I became an initiate of spiritual jazz—a genre that my dad had introduced me to when I was younger, but which sounded far better when I "discovered" it for myself—free, transcendent, and revolutionary music by the likes of Pharaoh Sanders and Don Cherry and Max Roach and John and Alice Coltrane, who fused mysticism with radical politics. This music stirred unanswered questions within me, about who I was and where I came from; it taught me about Black power and the fight against racism and inequality, filling in the gaps that my mother's absence had left.

My obsession with music landed me a job at a record shop called Honest Jon's on the Portobello Road in West London—a site of pilgrimage for reggae heads, techno-nuts, and jazz freaks from across the land. Compared to these lifelong collectors—a large proportion of whom were gray-haired men in their fifties and sixties—I was a humble novice, and was more than happy to play the role of the student. I'd spend quiet days in the shop making my way through the CD and record racks, listening to dub experiments by King Tubby, Indonesian gamelan, musique concrète, Bollywood disco, and everything in between. One day, I came across a collection of CDs by Alan Lomax, an American ethnomusicologist who had traveled the world, archiving folk traditions on the precipice of extinction. I started with recordings he made in the deep South in the thirties and forties—early gospel and blues, negro spirituals and field hollers; hissy recordings of the long-dead, singing the stories of their struggles. After some searching online, I found out that he'd made recordings in Carriacou, in the early sixties, just after my grandparents had left; I visited once as a baby, but the island and its music were largely alien to me. I ordered a CD called *Carriacou Callaloo*, for the cover, if nothing else: it was a photograph of four older ladies (one with several missing teeth) mid-song, with their arms in the air and smiles on their faces. To me, they looked like angels, black and beaming, their brightly colored dresses vivid against a cloudless sky.

*

Lomax's recordings uncovered a history hitherto obscured from my view. I listened to the "Big Drum" ritual, a tradition passed down since the days of slavery: pounding drums and group chants, animated by dancers who step and whirl to the rhythms of their ancestors. The drum patterns carry the names of West African ethnic groups brought as slaves to the island—Igbo, Temne, Kromanti, Bongo, Chamba—and who are still honored by their descendants today. I listened to the Quadrilles—screeching Scottish fiddle tunes interlaced with African polyrhythms, which tell of the interwoven fates of planters and their slaves. And I listened to crackly recordings of elderly ladies singing hymns in their lilting accents, listening out for familiar voices, and wondering if my blood ran through the veins of any singers in the crowd.

I listened and I listened, dreaming of a long line of mothers and daughters, fathers and sons, who had sung, danced, and drummed on this distant island, under the sun; people who I longed to know. I listened and heard the whispers of unknown relations, asking why I hadn't come. I listened, thinking of my mother, with the songs, stories, and sorrows of ages washing over me. And I grieved for all that I had missed.

*

We went back to Carriacou seven years ago, my mom, my grandma and me; three generations who hadn't spent very much time together at all—and it showed. My mom and I got on fine, but the unspoken wounds between her and her own mother—wounds that had lain dormant for years—began to surface. There were beautiful moments, but on the whole, despite the backdrop of sunshine, sea, and golden sand, the trip was tense and difficult.

I found my escape in the music. One night, I followed the patter of drums down to the beach, where a circle of dreadlocked drummers were beating out rhythms under the full moon. I remember looking out to sea, watching silvery trails of light dance on the water's surface, like sound waves; thinking of the people who were brought to this island as slaves, held captive against their will, and forced to work under the hot sun. Stood alone on this beach, with drums pounding in the distance, I felt the blood of these people, of my ancestors, running in mine, for the first time. And I felt eternally grateful to the drummers, dancers, singers, and storytellers of this remote island, for keeping their memory alive.

For my mom, the pain of remembering was too much. She became distant, reverting to the mother I had known as a child—paranoid that the locals were talking about her behind her back, and conferring, privately, with an unseen world. I could tell that something was up, but she didn't tell me that she'd been hearing voices until we got back to London. She said she could hear the voices of slaves on the wind, and that she could feel their bones crushing underfoot as she walked through the sand. For her, the pain of centuries past had erupted into the present, and she was desperate to get back home.

Thankfully, after a few weeks back in London amid the familiar traffic and sirens and streetlights, she was herself again. But something within me had changed. I began to see my mom in a different light. For most of my life I had been frustrated with her, for not being like the other mums; for being "there" but not there. But after our trip to Carriacou, I understood that the voices she'd been hearing were the echoes of ancient traumas, reverberating through the family line. Her great sacrifice meant that I didn't have to bear the burden of the past, and that the troubled spirits of our ancestors could be put to rest. When she got ill, a door closed within her, and although I'd always wished I could know what was beyond it, now I see that that closing it protected me.

It's still bittersweet, though, when I listen to the tape. I love my mom and the person she is today; I love her dark humor, her earth-shattering laugh, and her booming, bassy voice. But I will always be curious about the high-pitched, carefree young woman, who left just as I arrived.

I will never know that version of my mom. Nor will I ever know my distant ancestors, whose rhythms were immortalized in Lomax's crackly recordings. But I can commune with her, and with them, through the music that they left behind.

Notes on Contributors

Fatima Bhutto was born in Kabul, Afghanistan, and grew up between Syria and Pakistan. She is the author of several books of fiction and non-fiction, most recently the novel, *The Runaways* (Penguin) and the non-fiction reportage about the changing world of global pop culture, *New Kings of the World* (Columbia Global Reports).

Anne Enright is the Booker Prize-winning writer of seven novels and two books of short stories. Her fiction and essays can be read in the *New Yorker*, the *London Review of Books*, the *New York Review of Books*, and the *Guardian*. She was born in Dublin, where she still lives, and was Ireland's first Laureate for Fiction in 2015. Her most recent novel is *Actress*.

Sinéad Gleeson is a former music journalist and now author. Her debut essay collection *Constellations: Reflections from Life* (Picador) won Non-Fiction Book of the Year at the 2019 Irish Book Awards and the Dalkey Literary Award for Emerging Writer. It was shortlisted for the Rathbones Folio Prize, the Michel Déon Prize, and the James Tait Black Memorial Prize. Her short stories have featured in various anthologies, including *Being Various: New Irish Short Stories* (Faber) and *Repeal the 8th*. She has edited several award-winning anthologies of Irish short stories. She is currently working on a novel.

Kim Gordon is a visual artist, writer, producer, actor, and a founding member of the post-punk experimental rock band Sonic Youth. Founded in the early 80s, Sonic Youth was one of the most iconic and influential alternative rock groups. In 2012 Gordon formed Body/Head with Bill Nace, releasing their debut album *Coming Apart* in 2013. She subsequently formed Glitterbust with Alex Knost, releasing a self-titled debut album in 2016. Body/Head released their second studio album, *The Switch*, in 2018. She released her first solo album, *No Home Record*, in 2019. Gordon is author of the bestselling memoir, *Girl in a Band*.

Juliana Huxtable is an artist, writer, and DJ/musician based in New York City.

Leslie Jamison is the *New York Times* bestselling author of four books: *The Empathy Exams, The Recovering: Intoxication and its Aftermath, Make it Scream, Make it Burn*, and a novel, *The Gin Closet*. She is a contributing writer for the *New York Times Magazine* and teaches at Columbia University. She lives in Brooklyn with her daughter.

Megan Jasper has worked at Sub Pop for most of her adult life. She started as an intern and receptionist in 1989 and currently works as the label's CEO. Through her years at the label she has worked with numerous artists including Mudhoney, Nirvana, Soundgarden, The Shins, Band of Horses, Shabazz Palaces, Fleet Foxes, Sleater-Kinney, Clipping, Beach House, and so many more. When she isn't listening to music, she's probably swearing, training for a triathlon, or gardening. Megan currently resides in Seattle, WA, with her husband and dogs.

Margo Jefferson, a Pulitzer Prize-winning critic, is the author of *On Michael Jackson* and *Negroland*. *Negroland* won the 2015 National Book Critics Circle Award for Autobiography, the International

Bridge Prize and the Heartland Prize. It was also shortlisted for the Baillie Gifford Prize. She has been a staff writer for the *New York Times,* and her reviews and essays have been widely published and anthologized. She lives in New York and teaches in the writing program at Columbia University.

Rachel Kushner's first two novels, *The Flamethrowers* (2013) and *Telex from Cuba* (2008) were both *New York Times* bestsellers and finalists for the National Book Award for Fiction. Her novel *The Mars Room* was a finalist for the Booker Prize, the National Book Critics Circle Award in Fiction, and winner of the 2018 Prix Médicis Etranger. *The Hard Crowd: Essays 2000–2020* was published in spring 2021. Her books have been translated into twenty-six languages. She is a recipient of fellowships from the Guggenheim Foundation and the American Academy of Arts and Letters, and lives in Los Angeles.

Yiyun Li is the author of eight books, including *Where Reasons End*, which received the PEN/Jean Stein Book Award; the essay collection *Dear Friend, from My Life I Write to You in Your Life*; and her most recent, *Tolstoy Together, 85 Days of War and Peace with Yiyun Li*. She is the recipient of a MacArthur Fellowship, Guggenheim Fellowship, and Windham-Campbell Prize, among other honors. She teaches at Princeton University.

Ottessa Moshfegh is a fiction writer and screenwriter from Massachusetts. She is the author of six books, including the novels *My Year of Rest and Relaxation* and *Lapvona*. She lives in southern California.

Maggie Nelson is the author of several acclaimed books of poetry and prose. Her non-fiction titles include the national bestseller *On Freedom: Four Songs of Care and Constraint* (2021), *The Argonauts* (2015; winner, the National Book Critics Circle Award in Criticism),

The Art of Cruelty: A Reckoning (2011), *Bluets* (2009; named by *Book-forum* as one of the top 10 best books of the past 20 years), *The Red Parts* (2007), and *Women, the New York School, and Other True Abstractions* (2007). Her poetry titles include *Something Bright, Then Holes* (2007) and *Jane: A Murder* (2005). She writes frequently about art, including catalog essays for Carolee Schneemann, Matthew Barney, Sarah Lucas, Nayland Blake, Tala Madani, and Rachel Harrison. In 2016 she was awarded a MacArthur "genius" Fellowship. Currently she teaches at the University of Southern California and lives in Los Angeles.

Jenn Pelly is a contributing editor at Pitchfork and author of *The Raincoats*. Her writing has appeared in the *New York Times*, the *Los Angeles Times*, the *Guardian*, the *Wire* and others. She lives in New York.

Liz Pelly is a writer in New York covering music, culture, and media. She is a contributing editor at the *Baffler*.

Zakia Sewell is a broadcaster, writer, and DJ from London. She has presented and produced podcasts and radio documentaries on arts, history, and culture for the likes of BBC Radio 3 and 4, Tate, Resident Adviser, and Boiler Room. She also hosts a weekly Saturday morning show on NTS Radio, playing spiritual jazz, folk, dub, and other eclectic sounds from across the globe, and DJs regularly in London and abroad.

Simone White is a New York-based poet and critic. She is the author of *or, on being the other woman*, *Dear Angel of Death*, *Of Being Dispersed*, and *House Envy of All the World*, as well as the chapbooks *Unrest* and *Dolly*. She teaches at University of Pennsylvania where she is Stephen M. Gorn Family Assistant Professor of English.

Acknowledgments

Sinead: Thank you to the writers for their kaleidoscopic stories, the rhythms and glitter of their language, and to their agents and publishers for helping with the whole process.

We're so grateful to Lee Brackstone for his vision in commissioning this book and his enthusiasm throughout. Huge thanks to Ellie Freedman for support, legwork, and advice and to Rosie Pearce for her excellent, beady-eyed copy-edits and legal clearances.

And to Kim—a hero and friend—who made this a joy to work on.

Thank you always, Stephen Shannon.

Kim: I'd like to thank Yoshimi Yokota for agreeing to be interviewed, Hashim Bharoocha for his translation and Junko Futagawa for helping to facilitate it.